The Collector's Book of Detective Fiction

BY THE SAME AUTHOR

Ballantyne the Brave, 1967
The Ruin of Sir Walter Scott, 1968
R. M. Ballantyne: A Bibliography of First Editions, 1968
The Collector's Book of Books, 1971
The Collector's Book of Children's Books, 1971

A wood-engraving by Fritz Eichenberg for the Heritage Press, New York, 1938, edition of *Crime and Punishment* by Fyodor Dostoevsky.

THE COLLECTOR'S BOOK OF DETECTIVE FICTION

Eric Quayle

Photographs by Gabriel Monro

Studio Vista

Produced by November Books Limited, 23–9 Emerald Street, London WC1N 3QL

Published by Studio Vista Publishers, Blue Star House, Highgate Hill, London N19

Typesetting by Trade Linotype Limited, Nechells, Birmingham B7 5NG

Printed by Compton Printing Limited, Pembroke Road, Stocklake, Aylesbury, Bucks.

Colour printing by C. J. Mason & Sons Limited, Cater Road, Bishopsworth, Bristol BS13 7TP

Bound by Dorstel Press Limited, West Road, Templefields, Harlow, Essex

© Eric Quayle and November Books Limited 1972

Printed in Great Britain

ISBN 0 289 70263 1

House editor: Frances Kennett.
Designed by Linda Hanley.
Typographical preparation: John Leath.

TO

Quinton Quayle

IN APPRECIATION OF THE HELP HE HAS GIVEN ME

Contents

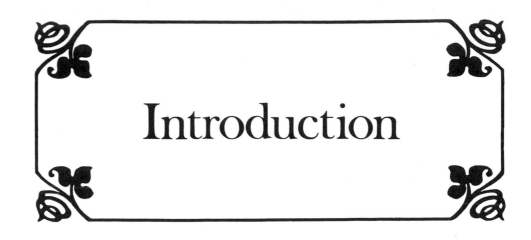

Introduction

'I think I may go so far as to say, Watson, that I have not lived wholly in vain.' These were almost the last words he spoke to his friend. A few hours later, on the afternoon of 4 May 1891, Sherlock Holmes, the greatest and most brilliant of detectives, plunged over the edge of the precipitous ravine at the Reichenbach Falls, while locked in a death-grapple with his supreme enemy and ruthless opponent, Professor Moriarty.

Today, some eighty years after that melancholy event, Holmes and Watson enjoy an immortality accorded only a select handful of fictional characters in literary works known all over the world. Every year, hundreds of letters reach London from all parts of the world intended for two men who never actually lived, posted hopefully to an address in Baker Street that has never existed. Their fame spreads far beyond the English-speaking world. Their names, and the exploits and adventures woven with such skill by their creator, Sir Arthur Conan Doyle, are spelled out in over a hundred different languages in as many foreign lands. The eccentricities and mannerisms of Sherlock Holmes, with his dressing-gown and hypodermic syringe, his deer-stalker cap and Inverness cape, and the stubborn, head-shaking obedience of his devoted friend and colleague Dr Watson, set a style in characterisation, and created a fashion for the modern detective story.

Although we tend to forget the names of authors other than Conan Doyle, we remember their book titles, and the stories written by both the most famous

The first appearance of the Inverness cape and famous deer-stalker cap. Holmes and Watson drawn by Sidney Paget for the story, *The Adventure of Silver Blaze*, in the December 1892 issue of *The Strand Magazine*.

Special note
All prices quoted with US equivalents are given at the current UK/USA exchange rates prevalent at the time of writing.

If the date given after the title of any work quoted here is enclosed in parentheses, this bibliographical device indicates that it was published in that year but appeared without a date of issue on its title-page or elsewhere in the book.

jacke
quiet
street
" C
Step
It
room
upon
phon
wall.
down
" V
Mr. F
" I
garm
who
conce
ance
of Le
" Y
and
inqui
" S
him h
" Ir
" Is

S P

THE DEATH OF SHERLOCK HOLMES.

writer and his contemporaries continue to defy the dating hand of time and the fickle reading public. They exude an atmosphere that instantly translates us back to a far more leisurely world, and to a way of life we picture nostalgically, with a deepening envy as time passes. Instead of the whine of jets and the roar of motor traffic, we hear the clop and jingle of the hansom cab. The flare of the street gas-lamps is shrouded by a pea-soup London fog. The bull's-eye lantern of a helmeted and caped London policeman sways in rhythm to his measured tread as he patrols his beat. For a moment we imagine we have glimpsed the slim figure of Holmes leaving the cab as it pauses before a darkened portico. Then the fog closes in and we are left with the fleeting image of a pale, thin-featured man with a lithe, cat-like walk, before the vision fades and he is swallowed in the darkness. When tonight's business is satisfactorily concluded there will be the tranquility of his waking in those famous rooms, donning the silk dressing-gown and slippers for a leisurely breakfast with Watson, and a glance through the morning's supply of five or six newspapers. Then, the housekeeper will announce the arrival of the day's first anxious client with the bizarre details of a mystery that has so far defied solution by lesser men.

Above left
Sidney Paget (1860–1908) captured the personality of Conan Doyle's master detective in a manner unequalled by any other artist before or since. This illustration appeared in *The Strand Magazine* in December 1892.

Above right
The frontispiece of the first edition of *The Memoirs of Sherlock Holmes*, 1894, by Conan Doyle. The author was forced to resurrect his hero.

Size of engraved surface: 19 cm × 12.5 cm.

This is not the beginning of the story. To trace the history of detective fiction and define its origins we must go back at least another forty years before. We enter a period of which the classics of the *genre*, those earliest titles treasured and secure in glass-fronted cases, are now priced as first editions in the four-figure bracket. The present-day collector of moderate means can only look and sigh at these rare volumes. It is a measure of the upsurge of interest amongst collectors and literary historians in the field of early detective fiction during the last few decades. This interest will undoubtedly increase in vigour – and in the financial value of the books concerned – during the coming years.

In the 1930s, the number of bibliophiles in Britain and the USA who were prepared to sacrifice valuable shelf-space to house first editions of even the best-known titles of detective fiction could have been counted on the fingers of both hands. The only works which found their way into a collector's shelves were the finest examples of the *genre* in unblemished condition, whose writers are now household names. Even in those days Sherlock Holmes in pristine state was a welcome guest, usually represented by shining examples of his *Adventures* and *Memoirs*, which are still the corner-stones of any self-respecting collection of detective fiction. A place would be found for *The Moonstone*, 3 vols. 1868, by Wilkie Collins, providing it was respectably dressed in clean and unfaded condition in its original sand-grain cloth. Edgar Allan Poe always occupied an honoured place in collections of those fortunate enough to find early copies of his works. All his first editions, detective fiction or otherwise, were avidly sought by American collectors, for he is one of the most prominent figures of their literary history.

The fate of most of the rest of the talent was to lie undisturbed at the bottom of the sixpenny boxes which appeared each fine day outside the windows of antiquarian and second-hand booksellers' premises. But by the mid-1930s the first discernible bibliographical stirrings of conscience could be observed in the most forward-thinking book-collectors. Detective fiction was recognised by astute bibliophiles as a comparatively unexplored field in the years immediately preceding the outbreak of World War II. First editions of books of genuine literary worth, and the works of authors with something entirely new to say, could be purchased in fine condition for very little money. Whole shelves could be filled with almost mint copies of late Victorian and Edwardian detective fiction titles, and it was only when the works of authors who had established a reputation in other fields of literary endeavour were sought that one was sometimes asked to pay pounds rather than a few shillings.

Those halcyon days are a fast-fading memory. Early detective fiction is now a quarry hunted with open cheque-books on both sides of the Atlantic Ocean. Titles that could once have been bought by the boxful for less than the price of a modern novel now command figures that have promoted them to full-page rating in the catalogues of booksellers and auctioneers as individual items. Yet it should be emphasised that there is still plenty of scope for the collector of average means to have the satisfaction of filling his shelves with desirable copies of first editions of detective stories. Some of the books still to be discovered on the shelves or in the lists of the smaller and less exalted booksellers will certainly excite the admiration and envy of other collectors in the same field, now, and in the future.

Collecting first and other important editions of detective fiction need not be only a rich man's diversion, or a lucrative investment for those with many thousands to spare. Everyone, no matter what his or her income, can have at least a shelf or two of personal favourites in the style of binding in which their original writers would have handled them. Often, they will cost the collector less than a modern reprint of the same title, yet within a year or two from now, these second-hand acquisitions could more than treble in value. It would be difficult to find a sounder financial investment than copies of some of the works I shall describe in the following pages.

Except for the few acknowledged sources, I have deliberately used as illustrations only books from my own collection. My purpose in so doing is to point the way to the titles and first editions that are still available to resourceful present-day collectors of moderate means who may have the inclination to tread a similar path.

Good books are pleasurable things to own, whatever they may cost, but the intrinsic value of any collection entirely depends on the taste and skill of the person who compiled it. The appreciation and understanding of what is, and what is not, important in the particular field of literature which you collect, together with the specialised knowledge that comes from the intelligent use of works of reference and bibliographies, are both augmented by reading books for the pleasure they bring. This observation applies with special force to works of detective fiction, and those collectors whose libraries appreciate most quickly in value over the years will owe much of their good fortune to their own knowledge and skill. Any collector who wishes to be accorded the respect of his like-minded fellows in the world of books must be able not only to recognise almost immediately, in catalogues and on the shelves, the editions he is seeking for his library (and this, as I have said elsewhere, pre-supposes a degree of bibliographical know-how) but also to assess their approximate market value. The condition of the volume he wishes to add to his collection is an all important factor in arriving at its financial value, both as regards its binding and in its internal make-up. I shall be discussing these points more fully in this book, and also how the uninitiated can decide whether or not a particular edition is the first to be published.

I started collecting detective fiction titles some twenty years ago, when I began consciously to seek out first editions rather than be content with later versions of the texts. I am constantly adding to this section of my library, despite the fact that I now live in a remote country area. Occasionally, I weed out part of the collection, discarding and selling works of which I have obtained better copies. Unless one has unlimited space and a pocket to match there is the necessity of keeping one's hobby within the bounds of shelf-space. The pleasure is in the collecting, and this observation applies to every aspect of the art. Once you have an author complete (and how rarely this happens) the thrills of the chase are gone and the time has come to perhaps permit others to use this section of your library for scholarship and research. To pass on part of your collection to an institution where it will be preserved intact means that your hobby can be made self-supporting financially. This is a comforting thought : while you continue to indulge your passion for books which are of a quality that make them desirable possessions for others, there is never any difficulty, if the need arises, in translating them back into cash. In the entire field of literature, I know of no section that has appreciated more quickly in value during the last two decades, than works of detective fiction. Any student of the laws of supply and demand would prophesy with complete confidence that this upward trend in prices will continue far into the forseeable future.

I have purposely extended the range of this book to include a periphery series of works of a similar quality. The purist will be able to assert quite rightly that a number of the titles illustrated in this volume can make no valid claim to be classified as works of detective fiction. I have attempted to define exactly what constitutes an authentic detective story in the chapter which immediately follows, but a rigid interpretation of this rule would, I feel, exclude so many titles that have long since established themselves as firm favourites with readers of the detective novel, that I have applied a more liberal formula. No apology is needed for considering these near relations, especially as their authors are well-known for their classic contributions to the field of detective fiction itself. The gradual evolution of the *roman policier* had led to a series of works, nearly all of which contain some ingredients of detective fiction without being detective novels in the strict sense of the term. It is also apparent that those making author collections require dated descriptions of every work created by their particular writer. Well-known names in the world of detective fiction have frequently been known to turn their hands to poetry, biography, historical novels, and even theological works of the most serious import. For the sake of completeness, titles are sometimes quoted that stray far from Baker Street and the annals of crime.

An illustration of the difficulty experienced in keeping to a straight and narrow path can be given with the works of Anthony Berkeley Cox, an author who wrote some excellent detective stories under the name of Anthony Berkeley. He also contributed two masterly crime novels, using the pseudonym Francis Iles. In these works, *Malice Afore-thought* and *Before the Fact*, the reader knows from the first chapter the crime being planned and the identity of the criminal, yet the suspense and tension of the story is maintained throughout the book, and he remains completely absorbed in the plot until the final pages. To exclude such titles from *The Collector's Book of Detective Fiction* on the grounds that there is little or no mystery for the reader to solve, and no discernible detective activity on the part of any amateur or professional, would deprive this present work of a number of well-known titles that are eagerly sought by specialist collectors all over the world.

By the same indulgence, I have included a number of other related books, culminating in the computer-activated counter-espionage dramas played out by James Bond and his eager band of imitators. I dare not go any further than this without taking the risk of being translated into the fourth-dimensional world of science-fiction. All of which seems a very long way from the eccentric and impoverished Chevalier Dupin and *The Murders in the Rue Morgue*.

The
Historical
Background

One of the graphic woodcut illustrations by Fritz Eichenberg for the Heritage Press, New York, edition of 1938, of Fyodor Dostoevsky's classic *Crime and Punishment*. Size of engraved surface: 19.3 cm × 12.5 cm.

One of the many forms into which the novel has evolved is that of the detective story. Originally, the word novel meant a new or freshly told tale, thus distinguishing it from the legends, fables and fairy stories of tradition. With all its present day variations, the detective novel has come to appeal to an enormous public, and in some of its extreme forms reaches a wider variety of social and intellectual classes than any other style of writing. It is a formulae which embraces Rabelais in the 16th century and Agatha Christie in the 20th. Even today, with all the competition from other media, the novel still shows little sign of flagging. Would-be novelists and writers of detective fiction (the latter, it has to be admitted, to a far lesser extent in recent years) still jostle for recognition, and the manuscripts of the hopeful lie piled in ever-renewing heaps on the desks of publishers in many parts of the world.

An author's inscription usually enhances the value of a work; but few are as dramatic in content as the one shown here. Four days after writing this inscription, the 21-years-old author was taken from the Iron Room, Edinburgh Jail, and hanged. *The Life of David Haggart*, 1821, is one of the best accounts we have of the activities of the Scottish criminal classes in the late Georgian era, and has since been used as background material for several novels of crime and detection set in that period.

Size of page of text:
16.7 cm × 9.5 cm.

Below
The final scene in *The Hound of the Baskervilles*, 1902, as depicted by Sidney Paget.
Size of plate: 18.5 cm × 12 cm.

The novel is a far earlier literary form than is commonly imagined. John Bunyan's *Pilgrim's Progress*, first published nearly three hundred years ago in 1678, earns the title of novel in some respects, but the first 'true' novel in English, in a style recognisable today, is generally considered by literary historians to be *Pamela; or, Virtue Rewarded*, 4 vols. 1741–42. It was written by Samuel Richardson (1689–1761), one of the printers to the House of Commons. At the prompting of two of his fellow printers he prepared 'a little volume of letters, in a common style, on such subjects as might be of use to country readers who are unable to indite for themselves'. This appeared in 1741 and provided, in addition, directions 'on how to think and act justly and prudently in the common Concerns of Human Life'. Out of these dissertations appeared Richardson's first novel, *Pamela*, to be followed by *Clarissa; or, the History of a Young Lady*, 7 vols. 1748, later known as *Clarissa Harlowe*. This tale far surpassed the success of his first novel and brought Richardson international fame. *The History of Sir Charles Grandison*, 7 vols. 1754, completed a trio of works which had a marked influence on subsequent writers of prose fiction, both in England and abroad. Although the novel as a form of literary expression was well-established by this time, there was little evidence of mystery, and none of crime detection in any work published until well into the latter half of the 18th century. It is only with the advent of the 'Gothic novels' as they came to be called, a class of fiction centred around spine-chilling aspects of the supernatural, that a definite, imitable style for later writers of detective fiction can be clearly discerned.

Readers of the works of Jane Austen (1775–1817) will remember the list of

"HOLMES EMPTIED FIVE BARRELS OF HIS REVOLVER INTO THE CREATURE'S SIDE."

'horrid mystery novels' described with relish by Isabella Thorpe to Catherine Morland and satirised so effectively by the author in *Northanger Abbey and Persuasion*, 4 vols. 1818. These tales transported their readers to mysterious ruined castles haunted by the spectres of murdered noblemen or walled-up nuns, and the bloodstained plots usually consisted of a series of horrific episodes in which torture chambers, mass murder and a variety of unspeakable terrors riveted the attention of those brave enough to continue the story to its inevitable gory ending. Their immense popularity with all classes of the literate population dated from the appearance of *The Castle of Otranto*, 1765, by Horace Walpole, fourth Earl of Orford (1717–97). The story takes place in the 12th and 13th centuries, and concerns Manfred, the villainous prince of Otranto, who poisoned the rightful heir Alfonso. His ghost now haunts the castle. A series of murders and uncanny goings on finally culminates in the overthrow of Manfred and a happy ending in true novel style. Walpole, like some later writers, called his book 'A Gothic story' (on the title-page of the second edition, also dated 1765), and thus coined a name for a series of similar tales that followed from other hands. The work was described by Sir Walter Scott as 'remarkable, not only for the wild interest of the story, but as the first modern attempt to found a tale of amusing fiction upon the basis of the ancient romances of chivalry'. The Gothic tales that came after, took an even more bloodthirsty and horrific path and their influence on Poe and other writers of detective fiction is manifest. It is as easily apparent in *Frankenstein; or, the modern Prometheus*, 3 vols. 1818, by Mary Wollstonecraft Shelley (1797–1851), as it is at the other end of the time scale in *Dracula*, 1897, or *The Lair of the White Worm*, 1911, by Bram Stoker (1847–1912).

The three principal contributors to the genre of the Gothic novel who are remembered today well deserve a mention for the influence they had on the writers of crime and mystery novels who followed during the 19th and early 20th centuries. Ann Radcliffe (1764–1823), was much admired by Scott and suggested to Byron at least one of his heroes. *The Romance of the Forest*, 3 vols. 1791, was followed by her most famous work, *The Mysteries of Udolpho*, 4 vols. 1794, and by *The Italian; or, the Confessional of the Black Penitents*, 3 vols. 1797. These three works set the seal on her career as a novelist of suspense and mystery, and also, of long-drawn-out, but easily predictable, happy endings. It was after the publication of *The Mysteries of Udolpho* that the increasing popularity of such works, due largely to their element of the supernatural, led to the close identification of 'Gothic' with haunted castles, black magic, moonlit ruins, eerie landscapes, and any supernatural happenings that appeared to transcend the 'powers above' or the ordinary course of natural events. Some of

Tales of Terror, 1801, issued under a Dublin imprint, was apparently a satire on M. G. Lewis's *Tales of Wonder*, 1801. The work contains four full-page hand-coloured plates (including the engraved title-page), and was published when the popularity of the Gothic novel was at its height.

Size of title-page: 20.5 cm × 12.5 cm.

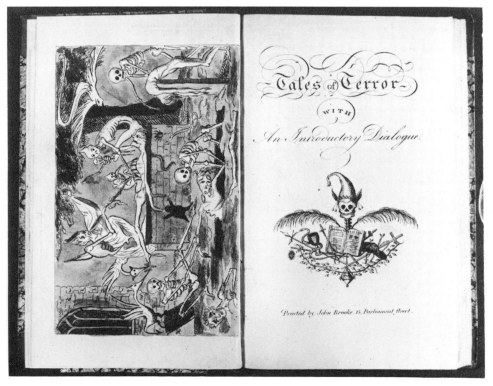

the elements used in conjuring up a frightening atmosphere have been traced to other and earlier genres, such as Jacobean tragedy and 18th-century graveyard poetry. Mrs Radcliffe added to these a few samples of the tricks still used in more modern forms by up-to-date fictional criminals – sliding panels, secret passages, coded messages, kidnappings, and dark suggestions of dealings with the Evil One. From all these vicissitudes, dear Emily, the heroine of *Udolpho*, finally escapes to the sanctuary of her lover's arms, while Montoni, the robber baron, suffers the extreme penalty for his wicked crimes. The author concludes the final 1797 pages of her novel with a homily addressed to her readers:

> O! useful may it be to have shewn, that, though the vicious can sometimes pour affliction upon the good, their power is transient and their punishment certain; and that innocence, though oppressed by injustice, shall, supported by patience, finally triumph over misfortune!
> And, if the weak hand that has recorded this tale, has, by its scenes, beguiled the mourner of one hour of sorrow, or, by its moral, taught him to sustain it – the effort, however humble, has not been vain, nor is the writer un-rewarded.

These sentiments were no doubt applauded by her well-satisfied readers, who eagerly awaited the next title to appear from her pen. Some two years later they were delighted by the appearance of the goriest and most sought-after of all the Gothic romances, but from a widely different source. Matthew Gregory Lewis (1775–1818), always known as 'Monk' Lewis, was a writer of strongly sadistic tendencies. Unlike his predecessors in the same field, he deliberately denied his readers the consolation of a good night's sleep when they finally reached the concluding passages of one of his tales of blood by the bucketful and horror piled on horror. His story *The Monk*, 3 vols. 1796, was a streaming mess of natural, unnatural and supernatural depravity, in which murder, rape, torture, indecency and *diablerie* all played their part. Even Byron confessed himself revolted by some of the passages contained in this book. The ending of Lewis's work, in which the Devil finally claims his victim, the monk Ambrosio, was deemed so horrific that the outcry from readers and critics alike caused the publisher, John Bell, to insist that cuts be made in the text and that the ending be suppressed totally. It is therefore only in the first (1796) edition that the full unexpurgated text is found. The first issue of the first edition, with some leaves watermarked '1794', now fetches will over £200 at auction, if it is in a binding contemporary with the period in which the book was written. A set in the original boards with uncut leaf-edges might well command up to three times this figure. Part of the ending, not found in later editions, reveals the author's uncompromising style. The monk, having sold his soul to the Devil, attempts to escape the bargain by raising his hands towards heaven for forgiveness:

> The fiend read his intentions, and prevented it – 'What?' he cried, darting at him a look of fury: 'Dare you still implore the Eternal's mercy? Would you feign penitence, and again act the hypocrite's part? Villain, resign your hopes of pardon. Thus I secure my prey!'
> As he said this, darting his talons into the monk's shaven crown, he sprang with him from the rock. The caves and mountains rang with Ambrosio's shrieks. The demon continued to soar aloft, till reaching a dreadful height, he released the sufferer. Headlong fell the monk, through the airy waste; the sharp point of a rock received him; and he rolled from precipice to precipice, till, bruised and mangled, he rested on the river's banks. Life still existed in his miserable frame: he attempted in vain to raise himself; his broken and dislocated limbs refused to perform their office, nor was he able to quit the spot where he had first fallen. The sun now rose above the horizon; its scorching beams darted full upon the head of the expiring sinner. Myriads of insects were called forth by the warmth; they drank the blood which trickled from Ambrosio's wounds; for he had no power to drive them from him, and they fastened upon his sores, darting their stings into his body, covered him with their multitudes, and inflicted on him tortures the most exquisite and insupportable. The eagles of the rock tore his flesh piecemeal, and dug out his eye-balls with their crooked beaks. A burning thirst tormented him; he heard the river's murmur as it rolled besides him, but strove in vain to drag

The Return of Sherlock Holmes, 1905, is much the rarest of the three first editions shown here. Fine copies now command as much as £100.

A cross-section of part of the author's library of detective fiction novels.

The Secret
of Scotland
Yard

A·ERIC BAYLY

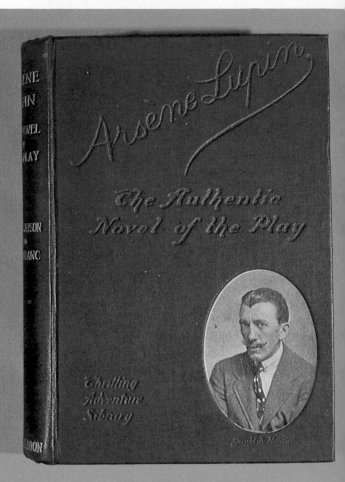

Arsène Lupin

The Authentic
Novel of the Play

Thrilling
Adventure
Library

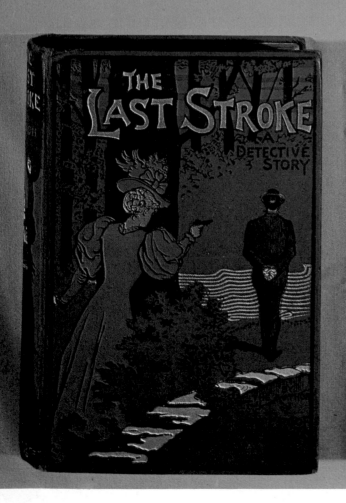

THE
LAST STROKE

A
DETECTIVE
STORY

THE BEETLE
A MYSTERY

RICHARD MARSH

First editions of three novels that form part of the historical background to the continuing saga of detective fiction.

Height of *Caleb Williams*: 17.8 cm.

himself towards the sound. Blind, maimed, helpless, and despairing, venting his rage in blasphemy and curses, execrating his existence, yet dreading the arrival of death destined to yield him up to greater torments, six miserable days did the villain languish.

On the seventh a violent storm arose: the winds in fury rent up rocks and forests: the sky was now black with clouds, now sheeted with fire: the rain fell in torrents; it swelled the stream; the waves overflowed their banks; they reached the spot where Ambrosio lay, and, when they abated, carried with them into the river the corpse of the despairing monk.

Within a few weeks of the publication of *The Monk* its author found himself famous. The outcry against the work stimulated sales to a degree that demanded five editions in the space of less than two years.

The third figure of the later Georgian era whose shade hung darkly over '*le roman noir*', as the increasingly popular 'Tales of Terror' had come to be known in European translations, was Charles Robert Maturin (1782–1824). A Dublin clergyman of French extraction, he published *The Fatal Revenge; or, The Family of Montorio*, 3 vols. 1807, under the pseudonym of 'Dennis Jasper Murphy'. But his masterpiece was *Melmoth the Wanderer*, 4 vols. 1820, first published under an Edinburgh imprint, and later reprinted as a three-volume work in 1892. Its central theme was once again the bargain with the Devil for the sale of a human soul, but the plot was refreshed by the author's dramatic revelation to his readers that the contract was transferable – always providing the victim could persuade another gambler to take the risk of having to pay the ultimate price. This idea, first used by Maturin, has been praised by writers as far apart in outlook as Balzac and Rossetti. Oscar Wilde encouraged the publication of a second edition in 1892, and some six years later himself adopted the name of 'Sebastian Melmoth', the first part being suggested by the broad arrows on his prison uniform and the saint's martyrdom.

The Gothic novelists to some extent relied for their background material on details of famous crimes, usually murders of one sort or another, set out in *The Annals of Newgate; or, Malefactor's Register*, 4 vols. 1776, by Revd. John Villette, Ordinary of Newgate Prison, London. Early in the 18th century a prison chaplain was included in the official staff of Newgate, being given the title of 'The Ordinary Chaplain', soon shortened to 'The Ordinary'. One of his most lucrative perquisites was the publication of confessions, last dying speeches, and potted biographies of the more infamous of the prisoners in the gaol. These were usually first published as broadsheets and circulated amongst the crowds that congregated for the frequent public executions taking place at Tyburn. First printed in book form in the four volume work quoted above, and with 37 full-page copperplate engravings of distinguished members of the 18th-century convicted fraternity – usually in the act of perpetrating their more heinous crimes – the collection is of great interest to historians and students of criminology alike. It is also important in this present context, for it relates several cases in which the art of detection is used to bring the guilty to justice. The vast majority of several hundred trials and convictions cited, however, relate that the accused had either been caught red-handed or had been informed upon by his confederates or so-called friends. The final apprehension of the notorious Dick Turpin, at that time using the alias 'John Palmer', is given in the third volume. An amateur in the art of detection, a Mr James Smith, of Hampstead, Essex, was solely responsible for unmasking the true identity of the supposed horse-thief who was being detained in the Castle Prison, York. Turpin, using the name of Palmer, had been living quietly in York for several months, making frequent trips to Lincolnshire, and returning, under the guise of a horse-dealer, with at least three or four valuable horses which he then sold or exchanged for others in York. He lived well, spending his leisure hunting and shooting, a pastime at which he was an acknowledged expert; and it was his propensity for showing off to all and sundry his skill with the pistol that led to his ultimate undoing. To quote from the passage in the *Annals of Newgate*:

On his return from shooting in the beginning of October 1738, seeing one of his landlord's cocks in the street he wantonly shot at it, and killed it; which one Hall, a neighbour of his, taking notice of, said – 'You have done wrong in shooting your neighbour's cock.' Palmer [i.e. Turpin] replied, 'If he would only stay while he charged his piece he would shoot him too.'

Four much-sought-after titles, all of which are discussed in the text.

As one can well imagine, Mr Hall was incensed by this remark and immediately reported the so-called Palmer to the magistrates for threatening his life. Next day Turpin was arrested 'and carried before the bench of justices then sitting at their quarter sessions at Beverley'. He was examined and cautioned about his future behaviour, but the magistrates, before agreeing to release him, demanded assurances and securities for his future good conduct from reliable persons in his own home town. These Turpin resolutely refused to give, knowing full well his true identity would be immediately discovered. He was later committed in custody and spent four months in York Prison while enquiries were being made about his past life. There was still no thought in the minds of the authorities that the man they knew as John Palmer was anything more than perhaps a common horse-thief and they allowed him to write to his brother-in-law for sufficient money to buy his way out of difficulty. This letter was duly delivered in Essex to Turpin's relation, who, however, refused to pay the postage demanded and it was returned, unopened, to the post office. Here it lay in a pigeon-hole for several days, until James Smith, a local schoolmaster, going into the office to post a letter, examined those awaiting claimants in the hope that there might be mail for himself. Noticing the unopened Turpin letter, stamped with a York postmark, he had an instinctive feeling that he had seen the hand-writing before. That night he rummaged through the old exercise books of his former pupils until he opened one filled with the early efforts of a local butcher's son. Taking this with him to the post office next day he compared the hand with that found on the sealed unopened letter that lay in the rack before him. Gathering up the evidence he hastened through the town to the house of a magistrate who finally agreed to break the seal and read the contents. The letter was signed 'John Palmer', but Smith had no doubt by this time that Palmer and Richard Turpin were one and the same man. An identification parade held at York Castle proved the schoolmaster to be correct in his analysis, and Turpin was instantly clapped in the heaviest irons. Notices were posted throughout the town that the notorious highwayman had at long last been captured. Smith gave evidence at the subsequent trial and conviction of Turpin, who was hanged at York on Saturday 7 April 1739.

This is one of the earliest examples we have in print of the logical analysis of hidden clues leading to the identification and conviction of a criminal. *The Annals of Newgate* contain more than one instance of similar methods, and for several decades the work was the most popular text-book on the lives and exploits of British criminals. Its immediate literary influence resulted in the appearance of what came to be called the 'Newgate Novel', a distant relation of the later detective novel. A late example, again featuring the career of Dick Turpin, but in a largely fictional, highly-romanticised manner, was *Rookwood*, 3 vols, 1834, published anonymously by William Harrison Ainsworth (1805–82); which was followed by *Jack Sheppard*, 3 vols. 1839, illustrated by George Cruickshank. Both were based on the facts imparted in *The Annals of Newgate*.

We can, however, go back in time a good deal earlier than this, to the closing years of the 18th century, in order to find the first hint of a detective at work amongst the pages of prose fiction. This was the age that witnessed the publication of what was not only a very early example of the propagandist novel, that most effective awakener of consciences and stimulator of public opinion, but also one of the first clear-cut examples of a fictional prose romance. Its plot concerned the perpetration of a crime in mysterious circumstances, and the ultimate exposure of the criminal by an investigator who deduced the identity of the guilty party from a series of clues set out by the author. In other words, this was a book in which we had at least some elements of the essential ingredients vital in any work which can be classed as detective fiction, although it still failed to qualify in the modern sense of the term.

It was in 1794, some fifteen years before the birth of Edgar Allan Poe, that an enterprising London publisher, Benjamin Crosby (1768–1815), who had premises in Stationers' Court, just off Ludgate Street, published a three-volume novel from the pen of that controversial atheist and philosopher William Godwin (1756–1836). Educated at Hoxton Academy, London, Godwin was at first a dissenting Minister, but later came to believe that men acted according to reason, and that it was impossible to be rationally persuaded and not take action accordingly. Reason must of itself teach benevolence, and therefore human beings, as rational creatures, should be able to live in harmony without the discipline of laws and repressive institutions. (He married Mary Wollstonecraft, whose *Vindication of the Rights of Women*, 1792 (Vol. I only published) was a courageous attack on the conventions of the day. She died in 1797, after the birth of her daughter, the future wife of the poet Shelley.) Godwin, having written several biographies and works of a political and philosophical nature, including the influential work, *An Enquiry concerning the Principles of Political Justice*, 2 vols. 1793, turned his attention to a work which would show, as he put it, 'the tyranny and perfidiousness exercised by the powerful members of the community against those who are less privileged than themselves'. The result was the appearance of his most famous novel, first published in 1794 under the title of *Things as they Are; or, The Adventures of Caleb Williams*. It was issued in three volumes (a two-volume piracy appearing under a Dublin imprint the following year, dated 1795) with the second (authorised) three-volume edition bearing the date 1796. The title of this edition was changed to the more familiar *Adventures of Caleb Williams*. The present market price of a copy of the first edition, if in the original boards, with uncut leaf edges, and complete with its half-titles, (very often missing) would be in the region of £500.

From the viewpoint of this present work, *Caleb Williams* is an important text, although it must be realised that in so considering it, the political import of the book, which was the author's main aim in writing, has to be set aside. The originality of the plot makes the book of fascinating interest even today. Godwin introduced several unorthodox features not present in the contemporary Gothic novels, or, as far as the present writer is aware, in any literary work published up to that date. The hero of the story, Caleb Williams, is also the narrator of the tale, stating within the first paragraph : 'I am incited to the penning of these memoirs, only by a desire to divert my mind from the deplorableness of my situation, and a faint idea that posterity may by their means be induced to render me a justice which my contemporaries refuse.' It is a plea that has been used with good effect in many a modern novel. He starts by reviewing his life : 'I was born of humble parents in a remote county of England. Their occupations were such as usually fall to the lot of peasants . . .', and tells us how, as a studious and sober-minded youth, he entered the service of a rich young landowner, Ferdinando Falkland. A quarrel takes place between Falkland and a neighbouring country squire, Tyrrel, a man of irascible and tyrannical character, who has succeeded in ruining a tenant on his estate, Hawkins, for refusing to yield to one of the squire's whims. In the dramatic circumstances so enjoyed by readers at that time, Tyrrel drives to the grave his innocent niece, Miss Melville, who has resolutely refused to marry the husband he has chosen for her. Falkland, a man of high-minded and benevolent disposition, is felled to the ground during a quarrel with Tyrrel. Shortly afterwards, the latter is discovered murdered. Falkland is suspected, accused, but acquitted, but the unfortunate Hawkins and his son later are condemned and executed for the crime, on the strength of certain circumstantial evidence.

It is at this point that Caleb Williams commences his detective work. He first begins to suspect his master when he notices his gloomy moods and fits of depression. As Falkland's secretary, he has easy access to his personal papers and is also able to follow him at will. He works out a series of seemingly haphazard questions to put to his master, but these are phrased in such a way that they unwittingly inflict the maximum possible psychological distress. Finally, Falkland catches him in the act of searching a secret chest of papers, and at this point Falkland confesses to being the murderer of Tyrrel. But to discredit Williams, in case he should ever be tempted to talk, the squire has him imprisoned on a charge of theft. Caleb Williams escapes, and the remainder of the book is taken up with his unrelenting persecution by Falkland, in spite of his devotion to his erstwhile employer, and his refusal to betray the secret. Falkland's agents track him from hideout to hideout, until, driven to desperation, he lays a charge of murder against his persecutor and is confronted with him before the magistrates. The final scene, in which the murderer acknowledges his defeat, has been re-echoed in countless stories of detective fiction ever since :

'Williams,' said he, 'you have conquered! I see too late the greatness and elevation of your mind. I adore the qualities that you now display, though to these qualities I owe my ruin. I could have resisted any plan of malicious accusation you might have brought against me. But I see that the artless and manly story you have told, has carried conviction to every hearer. All

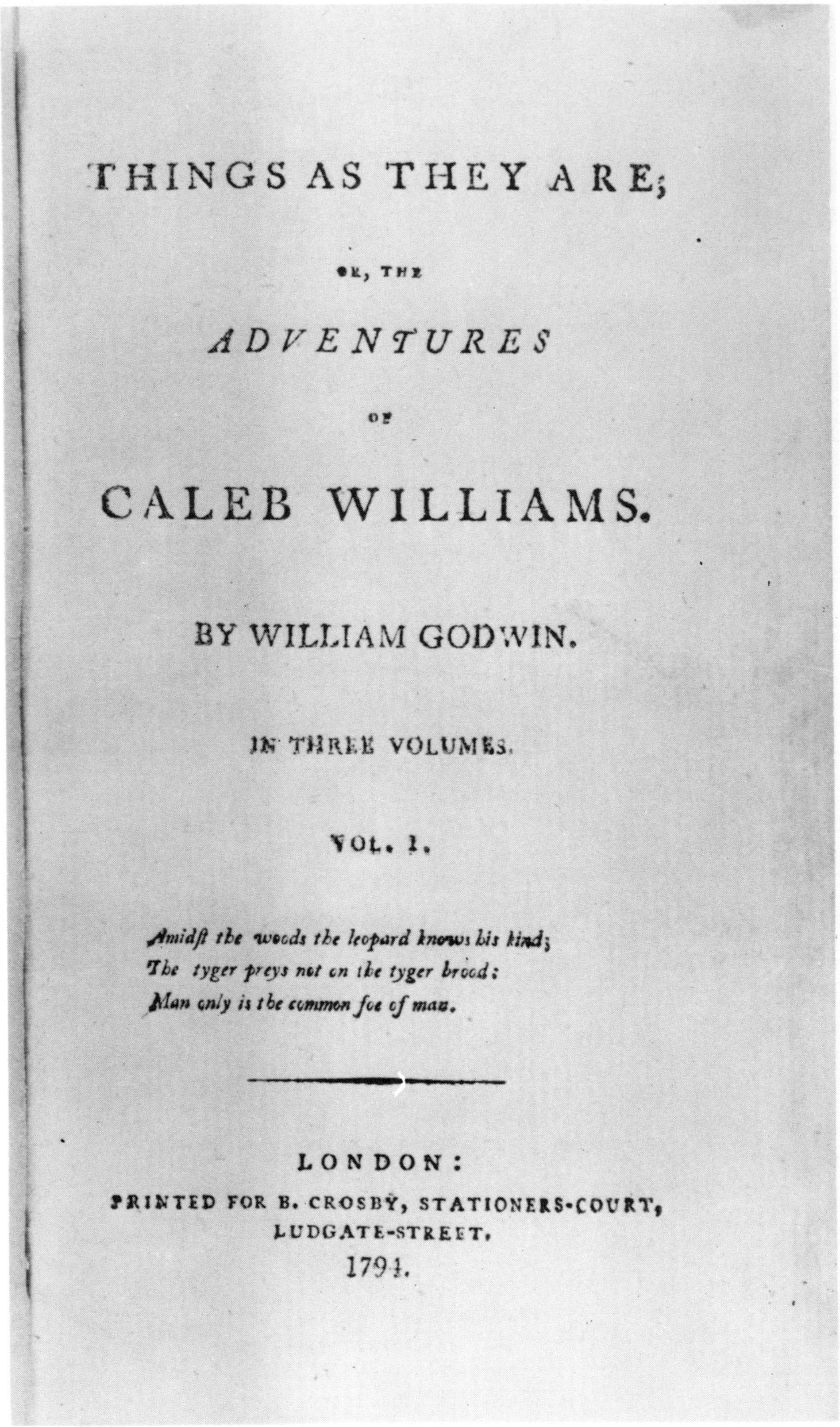

THINGS AS THEY ARE;

OR, THE

ADVENTURES

OF

CALEB WILLIAMS.

BY WILLIAM GODWIN.

IN THREE VOLUMES.

VOL. I.

Amidst the woods the leopard knows his kind;
The tyger preys not on the tyger brood:
Man only is the common foe of man.

LONDON:

PRINTED FOR B. CROSBY, STATIONERS-COURT,
LUDGATE-STREET,
1794.

The title-page of the first edition of a work made famous under the later title of *The Adventures of Caleb Williams*. In this three-volume novel, Godwin came nearer to creating a detective story than any of his predecessors in the world of fiction.

Size of title-page:
17.2 cm × 10 cm.

my prospects are concluded. All that I most ardently desired is for ever frustrated . . .'

The story ends with the cornered Falkland dying of shame, while unhappy Caleb Williams, overcome with remorse at thus exposing a man whose basic good qualities he had come to admire, slinks off to write the narrative of the course of events, and to ask the reader's forgiveness for a consuming curiosity that led him to expose the one guilty secret of his master.

In his preface to *Fleetwood; or, The New Man of Feeling*, 3 vols. 1805, William Godwin set down in detail the methods he employed in writing what was soon to become his most successful novel. He first spent several months engaged in research into criminal practices, as detailed in *The Annals of Newgate* and elsewhere. Having obtained his background information, he set to work and wrote the final volume first, planning the rest of the book as he went along and working backwards to the chapter which opened the tale. He is probably the first novelist to employ this sophisticated technique, a plan of construction which has often been used by writers of the detective story to the present day. In his essay on *The Philosophy of Composition*, a similar strategy was advocated by no less a master than Edgar Allan Poe, although the characters in a well-told story sometimes exhibit a vitality which takes control of the narrative and moulds the plot to their own designs.

Godwin had succeeded in producing a refreshing new style of literary fiction, and unwittingly came nearer to creating a detective story than any of his predecessors. Despite its affinities, the *Adventures of Caleb Williams* cannot be placed in the category of detective fiction by any of the usual criteria. Much of the plot is concerned with the pursuit of the investigator by the criminal, and the logical deduction as to the identity of the murderer which was employed by Williams was more a case of satisfying an appetite whetted by curiosity rather than any overweaning desire to bring the criminal to justice. The work quickly passed through several editions, and in March 1796, the playwright George Colman the Younger (1762–1836), produced *The Iron Chest*, a tragedy based on Godwin's novel, at Drury Lane Theatre, with the great J. P. Kemble in the leading role. The play was often revived during the first half of the 19th century, and made its final appearance in September 1879, at the Lyceum Theatre, with Henry Irving playing the principal part.

It is only with difficulty that we are able to define exactly what constitutes an authentic detective story, despite the fact that literary historians and most book-collectors who seek out titles in this limited field are only too eager, when asked, to set out their own terms of reference. Obviously the story must be largely occupied with the solution of a mystery surrounding a crime (usually, but not essentially, a murder or murders), and this task must be the concern of an amateur or professional detective. How he or she fares is of little consequences. In the story he may bungle the job and fail ignominiously; he may triumph and live to see his erstwhile adversary standing handcuffed in the dock; or, with honours even, he may topple over the edge of the precipitous Reichenbach Falls, locked in a death-grapple with the infamous Professor Moriarty. Win or lose, the detective, male or female – for lady detectives have been quick to assert their rights in the pages of detective fiction – must have spent a considerable portion of his or her time in the story detecting crime and/or thwarting the designs of the criminally minded. Occasionally he is himself the victim and presents the reader with the solution from the prison cell or the grave. But only very occasionally, for the writer sees to it that his creation is mentally a little too quick on the draw for even a master-mind.

There were already elements in the fiction of the late 18th century that were to be combined with other ingredients to form the earliest 'modern' detective stories. These in time led to the masterpieces of crime detection in the form that we know today. One fact had been proved – even the most genteel of readers seemed to enjoy stories of crime, and tales of the dark doings of the criminal fraternity. Horace Walpole, Mrs Radcliffe, 'Monk' Lewis, and Charles Maturin, were first to supply fictional blood-and-thunder, with the murderer in full view a room or two ahead. There was little or no mystery and no call for deduction on the part of the reader, who was kept fully informed of the identity of the criminal. William Godwin was the first to advance from this base. He created an amateur crime-investigator in an age when the professional real-life detective was still unknown.

The turn of the century saw the stage set for the dramas of fictional prose romances that followed in increasing numbers. By 1814, Scott had published the first of his historical novels, and *Waverley* was being enjoyed by thousands. Within a few years, the rapidly increasing readership of middle- and working-class people was demanding books that projected exciting new vistas, of a world spiced with romance and danger. The detective story still awaited the appearance of the first of the detectives, and the first of the uniformed police had yet to pace the darkened streets of the world's capital cities.

The Father of the Detective Story

By the very nature of events there could not be writers of classic detective fiction until the 19th century was well advanced. Until there were real-life detectives there could be no detective stories. And before there could be detectives in any professional sense there had to be a properly organised and regulated police force to support a plain clothes branch.

18th-century England knew only the tithingmen, or parish peace officers. These had become the police constables, usually unpaid in this capacity, of each town and community throughout the land. But as the century advanced and the Industrial Revolution increased its effect with a proliferation of townships and rapid growth of urban population, these officials became quite unable to cope with its consequences. By the early part of the 19th century the attenuated forces of law and order had become so impotent that, at times, riots and mob violence went uncontrolled and a wave of crime swept practically unchecked through London and the larger cities of Great Britain.

Something had to be done, and done quickly, or civilised society might well be in danger of breaking down. The turning point came with a revolutionary change in the methods of law enforcement. In June 1814 Sir Robert Peel (1788–1850), established a body of men in Dublin which was later consolidated into the Royal Irish Constabulary. Immortalised as the 'Peelers' or 'Bobbies' after their founder, this team now stepped into the breach. Peel established, by means of the Metropolitan Police Act of 1829, London's new police force. On 29 September of that year the first thousand of Peel's policemen, resplendent in blue tailcoats and shining top hats, began a daily and nightly patrol of the streets and by-ways of the capital.

The first Commissioners of Police were two exceptionally able men : Colonel Charles Rowan, a veteran soldier, and Richard Mayne, a brilliant young barrister who had conceived and planned the structure and administration of the whole organisation. It was not until some thirteen years later, in June 1842, that the two made a concerted approach to the Home Office with a suggestion that a department wholly devoted to the detection of crime should be formed as a specialist branch attached to the uniformed police. It was to be composed of eight men – two inspectors and six sergeants.

The first public notice that the new force of trusted men were officially engaged in crime detection appeared in print in 1843. An unknown correspondent reporting news from London in *Chamber's Edinburgh Journal*, a periodical at that time enjoying a national circulation, informed his readers that : 'Intelligent men have recently been selected to form a body called the "detective police" '. He further confided he had been reliably informed that : 'At times the detective policeman attires himself in the dress of ordinary individuals'. The first burly figures were already self-consciously buttoning civilian overcoats over their dark-blue police trousers and highly polished regulation boots, before attempting to mingle in this disguise with the jostling crowds in the streets of London. The forefathers of New Scotland Yard had begun to prowl.

In Paris, the Sûreté had been formed. As early as 1829 the lurid memoirs of François-Eugène Vidocq (1775–1857), a notorious French criminal, were on sale on the book stalls. In later life he became a bastion of law and order, with his appointment as the highly-paid head of the criminal investigation branch of the French police. His *Life and Extraordinary Adventures*, 1840, appeared in London in an English translation with woodcut illustrations by Pierce Egan, Jnr.

At any time from 1840 onwards, despite the fact that paid professional full-time detectives would not be acknowledged in print for two or three years, it was on the cards that some writer would conceive the idea of a fictional crime story in which the criminal would be tracked down and finally unmasked by a process of detection. It was well against the odds that the first avowedly fictional detective story should be written by an American author. The explanation almost certainly rests in Edgar Allan Poe's lifelong interest in the French way of life, and the fact that he was obviously familiar with Vidocq's *Mémoires*. (Indeed, this work served Emile Gaboriau equally faithfully a quarter of a century later, as Howard Haycraft has already pointed out in his valuable and well-researched *Murder for Pleasure*, 1942.) Edgar Allan Poe (1809–49), was born in Boston, Massachusetts, to David and Elizabeth (Arnold) Poe, who were both actors. His father came from a well-known Baltimore family, and his mother was English. Both died when he was still an infant. The young orphan, and his brother and sister, were

The Father of the Detective Story. This photograph of Edgar Allan Poe is taken from the Whitman daguerreotype.
Reproduced by permission of Brown University Library, Providence, Rhode Island, USA.

parcelled out among foster-parents, and Edgar was taken into the family of John Allan, a prosperous tobacco merchant of Richmond, Virginia. Although Poe added the name of Allan to his own, he was never legally adopted.

In 1815, he sailed for Europe with his foster-parents, for John Allan hoped to establish branches of his firm in Great Britain. For a short period the boy attended a school in Irving, Scotland, and was later sent to the boarding school of the Misses Dubourg in Chelsea, London, followed by a period at the Manor House School, Stoke Newington. Allan had no success with his business ventures in England and the family returned to Richmond, Virginia, in 1820, where young Poe attended a local school. But in 1824 he discovered that his step-father was having a love affair with another woman. Up to this point he had done well at school and had read widely in contemporary literature, but from then onwards things began to go wrong. Relations between John Allan and Poe became extremely strained, and in 1826, when the young man entered the University of Virginia, his guardian refused to pay the charges and Poe was forced to leave after only one term.

As he had only a pittance to maintain himself, Poe tried to increase his financial resources by gambling – with the disastrous results expected of such an aim. He lost heavily, and turned to drink to drown his sorrows whenever he had the chance. It was plain, even at this early stage, as more than one of his biographers have pointed out, that the first drink led to a protracted bout of all-night (and all-day) drinking which gradually amounted to dipsomania. His irresponsible behaviour enraged his guardian, who resolutely refused to pay his gambling debts for him. Despite this, he gave him a place in his own office. Poe hated every moment of it, despising business life, and finally left for Boston to try and support himself by writing.

He arrived in April 1827, and within the year, succeeded in publishing his first volume, *Tamerlane and Other Poems*, which he issued under a pseudonym. The work went unnoticed, and Poe became destitute. He enlisted in the US Army under an assumed name, but was bought out next year by the relenting Mr Allan, and appointed to a cadetship in the Military Academy at West Point. His second volume of poetry, *Al Aaraaf, Tamerlane, and Minor Poems*, was published in Baltimore in December 1829. His military career was brought to an abrupt conclusion by a court martial, caused by his deliberate neglect of duties, and Poe found himself once more a civilian, free to pursue a literary career.

I have set out the details of Poe's early life at some length deliberately, as they are of considerable importance. They reflect on the tenor and quality of his literary work. From 1831, he earned his living only as a writer. That year saw the appearance of his third volume, *Poems by Edgar A. Poe*, a work which contained some of his most famous lyrics, including *To Helen, Israfel*, and *The Doomed City*. In March, he went to live in Baltimore, where he remained until the summer of 1835. At last his work was beginning to attract some attention from the critics, notably *A MS. found in a Bottle*, which appeared in the *Baltimore Saturday Visitor* in October 1833. Three years later while acting as editor of the *Southern Literary Messenger*, he married his thirteen-year-old cousin, Virginia Clemm. His brilliant editing and critical writing soon increased the magazine's circulation more than sevenfold, but his continued bouts of heavy drinking were the cause of constant trouble to the owners. The whole of his journalistic career was plagued with the same trouble. His position as literary editor of *Graham's Lady's and Gentleman's Magazine* came to an end in May 1842, because of Poe's general ill-health caused by excessive drinking. *Tales of the Grotesque and Arabesque*, 1839, brought him to the notice of a wider public, but it was not until the appearance of *The Raven*, first printed in the *New York Evening Mirror* on 29 January 1845, and published in book form as *The Raven and Other Poems*, that his fame was assured and the author's name became a household word.

In the meantime, Poe wrote the short story that ultimately earned for him the title that heads this chapter. *The Murders in the Rue Morgue* (entitled, in the original draft of the manuscript, *The Murders in the Rue Trianon Bas*), first appeared in print in the April 1841 issue of *Graham's Magazine*, mentioned above. At that time Poe was the salaried editor, and it is extremely doubtful if he ever received any extra remuneration for printing his own works in this periodical. During his lifetime, he received little or nothing in royalties from most of the stories he wrote. In one of his letters to a publishing company, dated 13 August 1841, he said: 'I should be glad to accept the terms you allowed me before – that is – you receive all the profits, and allow me twenty copies, for distribution to friends.' This was his only payment for a volume of stories (including the recently published *Murders in the Rue Morgue*), which on a

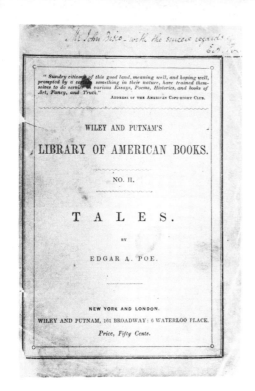

An inscribed copy by Edgar Allan Poe of the first edition of the first book to contain all three Dupin stories. This is probably the rarest, and most-sought-after, title in the history of detective fiction.
Reproduced through the courtesy of the Berg Collection, New York Public Library.

present-day royalty basis would have netted the author and his estate something in the region of a million dollars! The story made three separate appearances in print during the author's lifetime (not including foreign translations): firstly, in *Graham's Magazine*; then as the only number in an unsuccessful paperback series published in 1843, entitled *The Prose Romances of Edgar A. Poe*; and finally, in *Tales*, 1845, edited by Evert A. Duyckinck. It also appeared in the first collected edition of his *Works*, 3 vols. 1850, New York, containing a portrait frontispiece, and edited by N. P. Willis and others.

Poe was the first writer to give a definition of the short story, and certainly one of the first to practise the art. With *The Murders in the Rue Morgue*, and the introduction of the eccentric and impecunious Auguste Dupin, we have the first fictional detective story and the first fictional detective. We even have an anonymous friend and chronicler of events, a Dr Watson of sorts, who accompanies Dupin during his investigation and is constantly astonished at his powers of deduction. The plot Poe used has proved to be the archetype of thousands of variations on the same theme which have followed. There is a preliminary account of the crime; Dupin's visit to the scene; his musing satisfaction after inspecting the clues; his anonymous companion's Watson-like head-shaking in complete mystification; the bungling efforts of the police; and, finally, the logical and highly satisfying solution to the mystery as recounted by the detective-investigator.

Edgar Allan Poe stands as a writer whose influence on the short story may be compared with that of Turgenev or Dickens on the novel. He was a writer of genius who was deeply interested in crime, especially violent death, in cryptograms, and the whole process of logical deduction. Given these interests, it should not be a matter of wonder that he originated the detective story, and the Chevalier C. Auguste Dupin – the first detective of fiction.

Poe's second venture into the genre was *The Mystery of Marie Rogêt*, in which he deliberately set out to expose the bungling inefficiency of the New York police. Once again he set the scene in Paris, and it was to Dupin that he entrusted the solution of a thinly-disguised real-life crime: the murder in New York in July 1841, of a beautiful young girl named Mary Cecilia Rogers. In later years, the characters and scenes in the story were printed with footnotes which identified the author's fictional actors with their actual names. The real crime was never solved, despite many claims to the contrary, so it will never be known with certainty if Poe's solution was correct. *The Mystery of Marie Rogêt* first appeared in print in the magazine *Snowden's Ladies' Companion*, in the issues for November and December, 1842, and February, 1843. It appeared in book form in *Tales*, 1845, and in the posthumous *Works*, 1850.

The third, and much the best, of Poe's detective tales was *The Purloined Letter*, in which the author cunningly introduces the solution of the mystery almost at the beginning of the story. The Prefect of the Paris police approaches Dupin and explains the problem of a vitally important stolen letter, a problem which, on the face of it, is extremely simple to solve, but, as he explains to the detective, proves to be extraordinarily baffling:

> 'Perhaps it is the very simplicity of the thing which puts you at fault', said my friend.
> 'What nonsense you *do* talk!' replied the Prefect, laughing heartily.
> 'Perhaps the mystery is a little *too* plain', said Dupin.

The police are quite certain that the letter is hidden in one particular house. They spend hours probing chairs and cushions with fine needles, unscrewing table legs, measuring the thickness of book-covers, prising up floor-boards, and probing into every secret crack and cranny. But they overlook the obvious. The missing letter, torn almost in two, has been carelessly slipped into a 'trumpery filgree card-rack'. Dupin assesses the daring and intelligence of the man responsible and discovers it almost immediately.

The tale first appeared in a periodical, an American annual of the type which had been published in England from 1823 onwards, such as *The Keepsake*, *The Forget Me Not*, and *The Amulet*. The popularity of the annuals extended into the mid-1850s. Their miscellanies of prose and verse by well-known literary figures of the day were embellished with steel-engraved illustrations of a very high quality. Poe's story, *The Purloined Letter*, was printed in *The Gift*, 1845, which dated its title-page forward. It was on sale in September 1844, in the

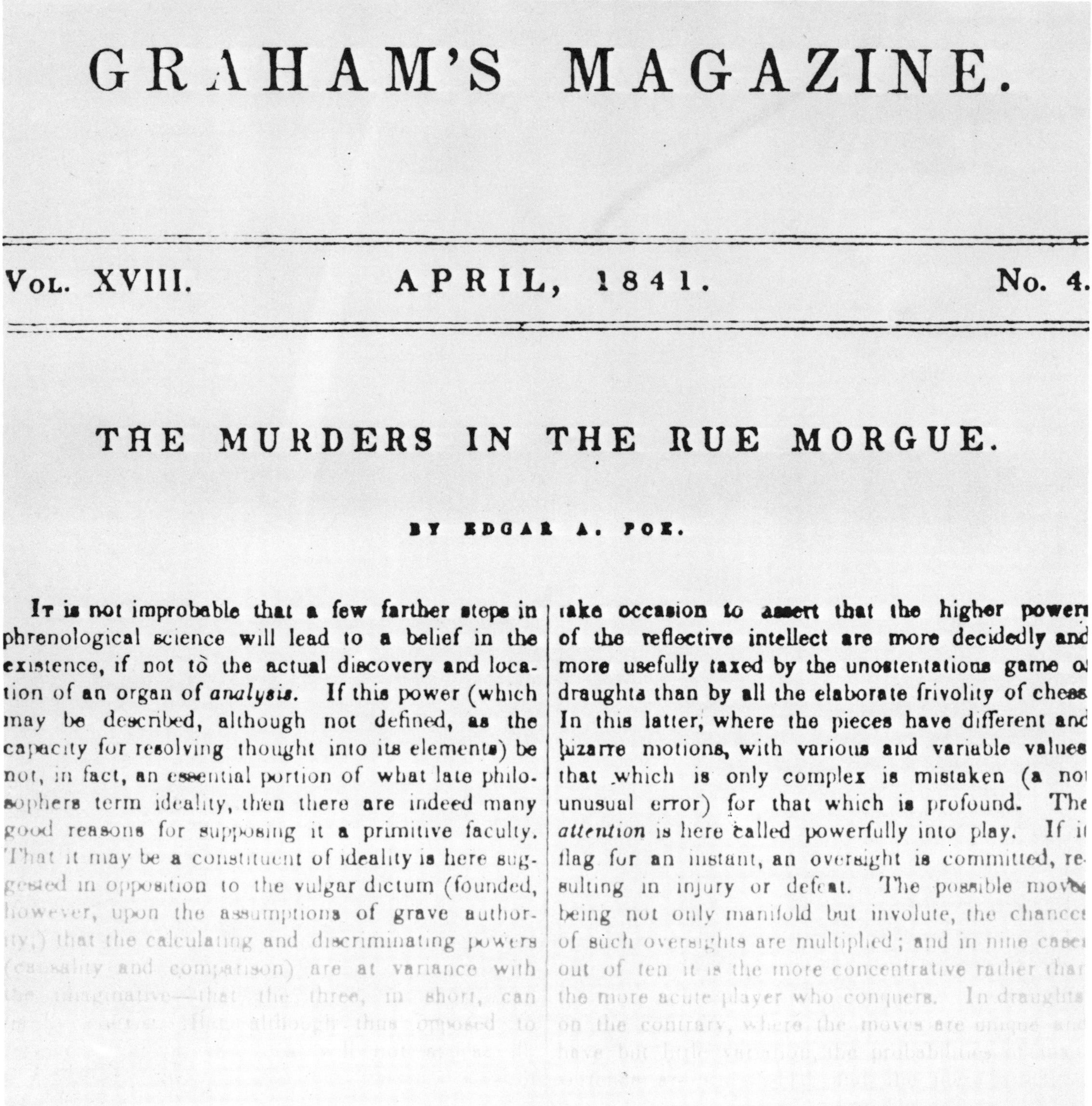

GRAHAM'S MAGAZINE.

VOL. XVIII.　　　APRIL, 1841.　　　No. 4.

THE MURDERS IN THE RUE MORGUE.

BY EDGAR A. POE.

It is not improbable that a few farther steps in phrenological science will lead to a belief in the existence, if not to the actual discovery and location of an organ of *analysis*. If this power (which may be described, although not defined, as the capacity for resolving thought into its elements) be not, in fact, an essential portion of what late philosophers term ideality, then there are indeed many good reasons for supposing it a primitive faculty. That it may be a constituent of ideality is here suggested in opposition to the vulgar dictum (founded, however, upon the assumptions of grave authority,) that the calculating and discriminating powers (causality and comparison) are at variance with the imaginative—that the three, in short, can ...

... take occasion to assert that the higher powers of the reflective intellect are more decidedly and more usefully taxed by the unostentatious game of draughts than by all the elaborate frivolity of chess. In this latter, where the pieces have different and bizarre motions, with various and variable values that which is only complex is mistaken (a not unusual error) for that which is profound. The *attention* is here called powerfully into play. If it flag for an instant, an oversight is committed, resulting in injury or defeat. The possible moves being not only manifold but involute, the chances of such oversights are multiplied; and in nine cases out of ten it is the more concentrative rather than the more acute player who conquers. In draughts, on the contrary, where the moves are unique and have but little variation, the probabilities of ...

usual manner of such publications. They were intended as Christmas and New Year presents, and by dating forward to the coming year, prevented themselves from being left on the shelf as old stock. The story made its second appearance, but in an abridged form, in *Chamber's Edinburgh Journal*, in the issue for 30 November 1844.

This third title in the series was Poe's last detective story in the strict sense of the term, but in addition to these three famous tales, Poe wrote two others that contain many elements of detective interest. *The Gold Bug* centres around the solution of a mystery concerning the whereabouts of a hoard of treasure buried by the legendary Captain Kidd. Poe's hero is once again a Frenchman, a Monsigeur Legrand, who discovers a scrap of parchment bearing a cipher written in invisible ink. He finally decodes the cryptogram, recovers the treasure, and then explains to his mystified readers the process of logical deduction that enabled him to break the code. *The Gold Bug* was first printed in *The Dollar Magazine* in 1843, and was included in *Tales*, 1845.

The author's other mystery story, *Thou Art the Man*, did not find a place in

The first appearance in print of the first detective story. Edgar Allan Poe's epoch-making short-story that marks the start of detective fiction as we know it today is shown here as it first appeared in a long-forgotten American magazine.

Tales. It first appeared in *Godey's Lady's Book,* in the November 1844 issue, published in Philadelphia; and in book form in Vol. II of *The Works of the late Edgar Allan Poe,* 1850 (J. S. Redfield, New York). It tells the story of the murder of a wealthy citizen of a small American country town. His young nephew is accused and sentenced to death, but before the sentence can be carried out the narrator of the story decides to investigate the clues used to secure the lad's conviction. He proves them false, and arranges a terrifying hoax that tricks the murderer into making a public confession. The tale gives us the first use of the stylistic device where false clues are scattered by the real criminal; and, as Haycraft has pointed out, the first complete if awkwardly contrived use of the 'least-likely-person' theme. The fact that the reader is not allowed to assess the importance of a vital piece of evidence, and therefore has no chance of solving the mystery of the identity of the murderer himself, means that Poe's work does not conform to the now established rules of detective fiction, and most authorities refuse it a place in the genre for this reason.

An edition of *Tales of mystery, imagination, and humour; and poems,* 1852, appeared under the London imprint of Simms and McIntyre, as Vol. I in their series called *The Parlour Bookcase.* Under the title, *Tales of Mystery and Imagination,* it was reprinted in re-edited form on numerous occasions and proved one of the most popular forms in which his short stories were read in the 19th century.

Much of Poe's work was relatively unappreciated either at home or abroad during his lifetime, but there is good reason for believing that his detective stories were more popular with the general public than any of his fantasies or his poetry. He often used this fact as a lever when concluding bargains for future literary work with his various publishers, yet he wrote no more of them during the remaining five years of his life. The reasons for this may be found possibly in the increasingly distressing circumstances surrounding his own private life. Although Poe was famous now, he relinquished the editorship of the *Broadway Journal* in January 1846, and in the spring of that year moved his family to Fordham, where he wrote a series of journalistic articles known as *The Literati of New York City.* His child-wife Virginia was critically ill with tuberculosis, and only the efforts of her mother, who was living with them, kept the family together. Virginia Poe died in January 1847, during a winter in which they all plumbed the depths of misery. The head of the family was seldom if ever completely sober. Despite this he managed to compose some of his best known lyrics, such as *The Bells, Annabel Lee,* and *El Dorado.*

Poe's final months of life were punctuated by vicious bouts of drinking and wandering trips to various neighbouring cities and towns. He arrived in Richmond in July 1849, in a moribund condition, and was persuaded to join a lodge of teetotallers. Here he began to court an old flame, Sarah Royster, but with the marriage day set, he disappeared without trace, and was eventually discovered, hopelessly drunk, in a bar-room in Baltimore. Four days later, on 7 October 1849, he died.

A life marked by so much misery, from the time in childhood when he lost both his parents, and the poverty he had to endure for so many years, was reflected in the bitterness which so much of his work contained. The world of literature has produced few poets with his exceptional range, for his verse, though small in total output, exhibits an extraordinary variety of technique and a deep understanding of the subleties of rhythm. Into his tales and poems he was able to weave an uncanny atmosphere of fantasy, which translated his readers into an exotic world. Yet, had he written nothing but his three Dupin tales, his position in the halls of literary fame would have been secure, and his title as Father of the Detective Story a just acknowledgement of his inventive genius.

To the book-collector he presents many problems, and all his first editions are extremely difficult and expensive to acquire. Copies of his early works seldom appear in the market, and as long ago as 1967, a rebound copy of *Al Aaraaf, Tamerlane, and Minor Poems,* 1829, made $10,000 (£4,000) at auction. His detective stories were first printed in such an ephemeral form that it is little wonder that so few copies have survived. An issue of the paper-wrappered *Prose Romances of Edgar A. Poe* (1843), or the even earlier number of *Graham's Lady's and Gentleman's Magazine,* dated April 1841, containing the first appearances of *The Murders in the Rue Morgue,* would now fetch immense sums if offered for sale.

For the collector of only moderate means, a copy of the first collected editions contained in *Tales*, 1845, published by Wiley & Putnam, New York, in which *The Murders in the Rue Morgue*, *The Mystery of Marie Rogêt*; and *The Purloined Letter*, all appear, may well be all he can aspire to own. Even this will probably cost him well in excess of £300 ($750) if complete with its half-title and advertisement leaves in its original cloth binding. The first London edition of the same book, dated 1845 (not 1846 as stated in some bibliographies) consists of the original sheets of the first (New York) edition, with a cancel title-page bearing a London imprint. A copy in good condition in the original publisher's cloth binding would now be catalogued at about £50 ($175).

The Evolution of the 'Roman Policier'

After the Edgar Allan Poe stories, the next significant phase in the evolution of detective fiction took place in France. In the early 1800s, a division of the police, solely concerned with criminal investigation, had been formed under the name Sûreté Générale. Its activities captured the public imagination in the same way that Scotland Yard and its detectives did in a later period in England. The exploits of the publicity-conscious Vidocq, a criminal gang-leader turned prince of thief-takers, focused attention on the newly-formed detective police force and gave novelists an exciting series of fresh ideas. In 1827, Vidocq retired, at the age of fifty-two, intent of exploiting his notoriety and newly-acquired fame. Two years later he published his four volumes of *Mémoires*, packed with as least as much dramatic fiction as dramatic fact, and crowded with several times as much incident and adventure as any one individual could possibly have experienced in a single lifetime. If Vidocq himself wrote all the stories the work contained, then perhaps he, rather than Poe, as Howard Haycraft has previously asserted, was the actual inventor of the detective story.

The fact that he played such a colourful part in the history of criminal investigation stimulated the writers of novels and romances on both sides of the Atlantic Ocean. As Frank W. Chandler commented in his book, *The Literature of Roguery*, 1907, it was 'necessary that a Vidocq should issue his *Mémoires* for the literary transition from rogue to detective to be definitely effected'. Nowhere was this influence so discernible as in the works of his fellow compatriots.

One of the earliest to experiment with the new medium was Paul Féval (1817–87), who included detective episodes in *Les Mystères de Londres*, 1844. In an endeavour to suggest to his readers that the author was an Englishman, he concealed his true identity under the surprising pseudonym of 'Sir Francis Trolopp'. It was after the appearance of his *Le Club des Phoques*, 1841, that Féval accepted a commission to write *Mysteries of London*, in an endeavour to compete with the continuing popularity of similar works from the active pen of Eugène Sue (1804–57). The latter's *Les Mystères de Paris*, 4 vols. 1842–43, later issued in London as an English translation in a series of 90 paper-wrappered parts, during 1844–46, and then in a three volume cloth-bound set, enjoyed an enormous success. In this, and in his *Le Juif Errant*, 10 vols. 1844–45, Sue championed socialism and anti-clericalism with his startling accounts of the underworld of Paris. Féval attempted to do much the same in his *Les Mystères de Londres*, and with Balzac and Dumas *père* he contributed to the development of the detective novel by translating the backswoods pathfinding methods of Fenimore Cooper's dauntless Mohicans, into an urban setting.

As yet, no French writer had made a detective the hero of his tale. Pierre Alexis de Ponsón, known as Ponson du Terrail (1829–71), introduced his readers to a cheeky, twelve-year-old street urchin nicknamed Rocambole. Du Terrail became a prolific writer of adventure stories, but did not achieve his first success until the publication of his *Les Coulisses du Monde*, 1853. He is remembered today for the series of titles that brought him immediate fame, and coined a new word still in use today – *Rocambolesque*, descriptive of sensationalism as applied to the novel. Little Rocambole was at first a minor figure, but eventually commanded the leading rôle in an extremely long sequence of sensational novels in which crime and detection played a considerable part. The fourth title in the series, *Les Exploits de Rocambole*, 1859, with which he achieved his greatest success, was followed, amongst many others, by *Les Drames de Paris*, 1865; *La resurrection de Rocambole*, 1866; *Le dernier mot de Rocambole*, 1866; and *La vérité sur Rocambole*, 1867. After writing 22 of these tales, the author obviously became bored with his creation, and to rid himself of Rocambole, arranged a death-scene, where the boy was scarred and deeply burned with vitriol. An indignant public absolutely refused to allow this betrayal, and as the later titles above show, du Terrail was forced to resurrect his battered hero. His scars faded chapter by chapter, and Rocambole was soon his old self. He quickly repented his various crimes and decided to follow Vidocq's example by helping to apprehend his former associates and evil-doers. Within a few chapters, he became a fully-fledged amateur detective, patronised by leading members of the French aristocracy and waxing fat on his fees. As A. E. Murch has already observed, it is not without significance that Rocambole's metamorphosis from criminal to detective took place in exactly the same year (1866), as that in which one of the greatest fictional detectives made his bow, and immediately captured the enthusiastic interest of the reading public, first in his native France, and later throughout almost the whole of Europe and America.

Monsieur Lecoq, detective *par excellence*, was the creation of Emile Gaboriau, born 9 November 1835, at Saujon, in the Charente-Inferieure, France. Gaboriau was the son of a local notary, and to escape being forced to study the law, he enlisted in the cavalry. In seven years, he rose to the rank of regimental sergeant-major. With no hope of obtaining a commission, he left the army at the expiration of his term of service and managed to find a job as a clerk in a haulier and delivery merchant's business. He supplemented his meagre income by writing mottos and verses for commemoratory cards – even confectioners' cakes – and doggerel songs for street singers and the like. A change in his fortunes occurred when Paul Féval, the popular feuilletonist mentioned earlier, whose articles and stories filled columns in the Paris newspapers of the time, was flattered by some effusive verses which Gaboriau had addressed to him. Within a few weeks, the near-penniless clerk had become Féval's personal secretary, acting as a literary hack by filling in the details and characters in the plots devised by his employer.

The feuilleton – meaning the part of the page in a newspaper (usually at the bottom) appropriated to light literature in the form of serials, verse and humerous criticism – had been promoted to separate entity in the more progressive papers as an inserted leaflet, rather in the manner of present-day newspaper supplements. Some of the sensational serials which Féval turned out with such regularity were now 'ghosted' by Gaboriau, and appeared under Féval's name in the newspaper pamphlets. When he was not writing, he was used for research in the Paris libraries, and for haunting the local police courts in search of background material for his master, whose luridly drawn criminal romances delighted his readers. Before many months had passed, Gaboriau had branched out on his own, and from 1859 onwards he was busy turning out a constant stream of serials for the daily newspapers. Each episode had to end with the hero or heroine suspended, like the story, in mid-air, facing imminent death. Only thus, his editors argued, could their readers' interest be sustained to the following day, and circulation figures maintained. Several thousand words came from his pen every working day, and in the following thirteen years he produced twenty-one full-length novels.

A total of seven novels of military and fashionable life, none of which was in any way concerned with criminal detection, had been written and published by 1863, as well as biographies, lengthy reports of various *causes célèbres*, and reams of journalistic and other literary work. That same year, his first detective story, *L'Affaire Lerouge*, began to appear as a serial in an all but bankrupt journal issued under the now forgotten name of *Le Pays*. It ceased publication before Gaboriau's story had attracted much attention; but several episodes had been noticed with interest by Polydore Millaud, the owner of *Le Soleil* and its even

This work heralded the dawn of a new era in crime detection. Sir Francis Galton (1822–1911), a cousin of Charles Darwin, was one of the first men to realise that our finger-prints remain constant from childhood to death. But it was 1901 before a Finger-print Bureau was established by Scotland Yard.

Size of title-page: 22.5 cm high × 14 cm.

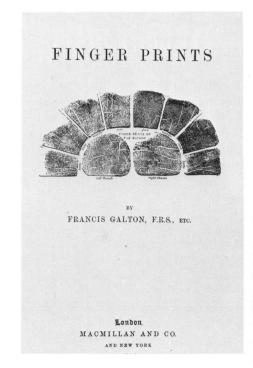

FINGER PRINTS

BY

FRANCIS GALTON, F.R.S., ETC.

London
MACMILLAN AND CO.
AND NEW YORK

more widely-read contemporary, *Le Petit Journal*. Two years later *Le Soleil* started printing instalments of *L'Affaire Lerouge*. The story was an immediate success, circulation increased, and the tale became so popular that it was issued as a novel in volume form, dated 1866. Polydore Millaud was naturally delighted, and Gaboriau was commissioned to contribute to *Le Petit Journal* itself, at a considerably higher financial rate than he had ever previously achieved. *Le Crime d'Orcival* and *Le Dossier No. 113*, appeared in its pages during 1867; *Les Esclaves de Paris* in 1868; and *Monsieur Lecoq* in 1869. All were detective novels within the strict meaning of the words; all were immensely popular; and all were translated within a short space of time, appearing under English titles in both Britain and the USA.

In these tales, typical of the *roman policier* of the period, Gaboriau adhered to a set pattern which embraced both plot and characters. He concentrated his readers' attention on the logical powers of deduction, and the skill in assessing any given situation, which his detective possessed. This character was always a French police detective or an enthusiastic amateur, surrounded by a cast of players with personalities which never allowed them to up-stage the principal. The crime around which the novel centred was usually violently sensational, the victim a beautiful woman, killed to prevent her revealing family secrets. The criminal hunted with ruthless determination by the hero of the story was most often a young and handsome nobleman of illegitimate birth. The family background, with dark secrets bolted and padlocked in chests secured in dingy cellars, formed the basis of most of Gaboriau's novels. Often the reader was aware of the guilty party before the book was halfway through, and the unmasking of the murderer might well take place with six or more chapters as yet unread. Despite all these manifest faults, as they would appear to the purist, Emile Gaboriau had a distinct and enduring influence on the development of detective fiction in his own country and the English-speaking world.

In *L'Affaire Lerouge*, he made the chief detective Pere Tabaret, sometimes nicknamed 'Tir-au-Clair', a wealthy pawnbroker and book-collector who finds much of his inspiration in the memoirs of police informers. Reference is made in the early chapters of the book to a minor police official called Lecoq, whose name, and the fact that he is supposed to have had a criminal background, immediately suggests the influence of Vidocq. Lecoq vanishes from the pages after a few chapters, but reappears to replace Tabaret as the chief detective of four subsequent novels. Gaboriau endowed Monsieur Lecoq with intellectual powers of detection previously unknown. He was the first detective to use logical deduction in evaluating clues left behind by the criminal, and was the first to bring scientific analysis to his aid in solving crimes. He concerned himself with such mundane matters as whether or not a bed had been slept in; could work out from the chimes of a fallen clock the time a murder had been committed; used plaster to preserve a record of footprints; and drew careful sketches (later incorporated in the text of the story) of the scene where the crime had been committed. One glance at the snow-covered ground outside an inn, and he is able to describe in detail the man who has walked across it an hour ago:

'He is middle-aged and very tall, wearing a soft cap and a chestnut-coloured overcoat with a fleecy surface. He is very probably married.'

And in *The Mystery of Orcival*, he is able to deduce almost every action of the murderer after an examination of the house in which the crime took place. He relates to his astonished friends, one of whom is a doctor, exactly what happened, a reconstruction which must be quoted in full:

M. Lecoq was intent on following the thread of his deductions.

'This is one of those trivial details,' pursued he, 'whose very insignificance makes them terrible, when they are attended by certain circumstances. Now imagine the Count de Tremorel, pale, covered with his wife's blood, shaving himself before his glass, rubbing the soap over his face, in that room all topsy-turvy, while three steps off lies the still warm body! It was an act of terrible courage, believe me, to look at himself in the glass after a murder – one of which few criminals are capable. The count's hands, however, trembled so violently that he could scarcely hold his razor, and his face must have been cut several times.'

'What!' said Dr Gendron, 'do you imagine that the count spared the time to shave?'

'I am positively sure of it, pos-i-tive-ly. A towel on which I found one of those marks which a razor leaves when it is wiped – and one only – has put me on the track of this fact. I looked about, and found a box of razors, one of which had recently been used, for it was still moist; and I have carefully preserved both the towel and the box. And if these proofs are not enough, I will send to Paris for two of my men, who will find, somewhere in the house or garden, both the count's beard and the cloth with which he wiped his razor. As to the fact which surprises you, doctor, it seems to me very natural; more, it is the necessary result of the plan he adopted. Monsieur de Tremorel has always worn his full beard: he cuts it off, and his appearance is so entirely altered that, if he met anyone in his flight, he would not be recognised.'

The doctor was apparently convinced, for he cried: 'It's clear – it's evident.'

'Once thus disguised, the count hastens to carry out the rest of his plan, to arrange everything to throw the law off the scent, and to make it appear that he, as well as his wife, has been murdered. He hunts up Guespin's vest, tears it out at the pocket, and puts a piece of it in the countess's hand. Then taking the body in his arms, crosswise, he goes downstairs. The wounds bleed frightfully – hence the numerous stains discovered all along his path. Reaching the foot of the staircase, he is obliged to put the countess down, in order to open the garden-door. This explains the large stain in the vestibule. The count, having opened the door, returns for the body and carries it in his arms as far as the edge of the lawn; there he stops carrying it, and drags it by the shoulders, walking backwards, trying thus to create the impression that his own body has been dragged across and thrown into the Seine. But the wretch forgot two things which betray him. He did not realise that the countess's skirts, in being dragged along the grass, pressing it down and breaking it for a considerable space, spoiled his scheme. Nor did he think that her elegant and well-curved feet, encased in small high-heeled boots, would mould themselves in the damp earth of the lawn, and thus leave against him a proof clearer than day.'

'Well, you are revenged,' remarked the doctor, smiling.

'On the other side of the lawn,' continued M. Lecoq, 'the count again took up the countess's body. But forgetting the effect of water when it spurts, or – who knows? – disliking to soil himself, instead of throwing her violently in the river, he put her down carefully, with great caution. That's not all. He wished it to appear that there had been a terrible struggle. What does he do? Stirs up the sand with the end of his foot. And he thinks that will deceive the police!'

'Yes, yes,' muttered Plantat, 'exactly so – I saw it.'

'Having got rid of the body, the count returns to the house. Time presses, but he is still anxious to find the paper. He hastens to take the last measures to assure his safety. He smears his slippers and handkerchief with blood. He throws his handkerchief and one of his slippers on the sward, and the other slipper into the river. His haste explains the incomplete execution of his manoeuvres. He hurries – and commits blunder after blunder. He does not reflect that his butler will explain about the empty bottles which he puts on the table. He thinks he is turning wine into the five glasses – it is vinegar, which will prove that no one has drunk out of them. He goes upstairs, puts forward the hands of the clock, but forgets to put the hands and the striking bell in harmony. He rumples the bed, but he does it awkwardly – and it is impossible to reconcile these three facts, the bed crumpled, the clock showing twenty minutes past three, and the countess dressed as if it were mid-day. He adds as much as he can to the disorder of the room. He smears a sheet with blood; also the bed-curtains and the furniture. Then he marks the door with the imprint of a bloody hand, too distinct and precise not to be done designedly. Is there so far a circumstance or detail of the crime which does not explain the count's guilt?'

'There's the hatchet,' answered M. Plantat, 'found on the second storey, the position of which seemed so strange to you.'

'I am coming to that. We know that Madame de Tremorel possessed and concealed a paper or letter, known to her husband, which he wanted, and which she obstinately refused to give up in spite of all his entreaties. We will not be rash, then, in supposing that the importance of this paper was immense. It must have been, somehow, very damaging to one or the other. To whom? To both, or only the count? Here I am reduced to conjectures. Madame de Tremorel

Published in hard-covers, and with pictorial dust-jackets, the long series of titles issued under *The Readers Library* imprint sold for only sixpence a copy. The series included a number of first editions by Edgar Wallace and other writers of detective fiction.

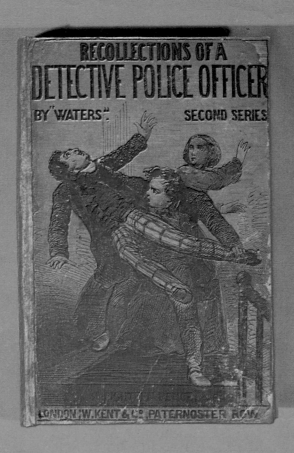

RECOLLECTIONS OF A
DETECTIVE POLICE OFFICER
BY "WATERS"   SECOND SERIES

LONDON W. KENT & C° PATERNOSTER ROW

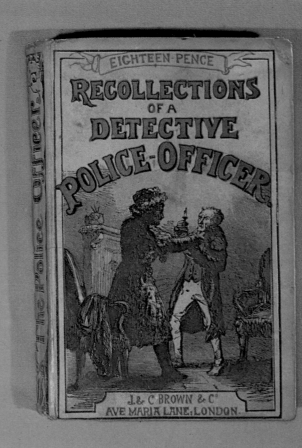

EIGHTEEN PENCE
RECOLLECTIONS
OF A
DETECTIVE
POLICE-OFFICER

J. & C. BROWN & C°
AVE MARIA LANE. LONDON.

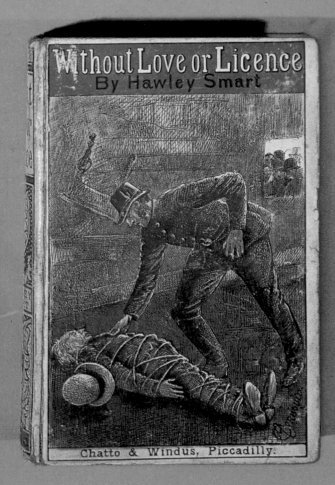

Without Love or Licence
By Hawley Smart

Chatto & Windus, Piccadilly.

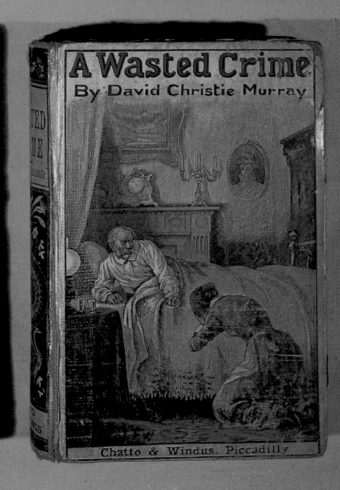

A Wasted Crime
By David Christie Murray

Chatto & Windus, Piccadilly

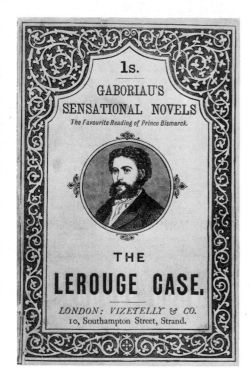

The creator of Monsieur Lecoq, pictured in the first of a twelve-volume series of paper-wrapped novels, the earliest to appear in England. They were published during 1881–5.
Reproduced by courtesy of The Bodleian Library, Oxford.

Four titles in the long series of 'yellow backs'. The two shown at the top, both first editions, are particularly difficult to find, having been issued in the 1850s.

surely regarded this paper either as a security or as a terrible arm which put her husband at her mercy. It was surely to deliver himself from this perpetual menace that the count killed his wife.'

The logic was so clear, the last words brought the evidence out so lucidly and forcibly, that his hearers were struck with admiration. They both cried:
'Excellent!'

Nearly a quarter of a century later Sherlock Holmes was able to stagger his faithful watchdog Dr Watson by similar reasoning.

In *Le Crime D'Orcival*, Gaboriau approaches nearest to our present-day conception of the detective novel. It is much his best work, both from a purely literary viewpoint and from that of a connoisseur of detective fiction. He fathered a host of imitators, and, until well after the end of the 19th century, writers in Europe, as well as their rivals in America, continued to produce faithful copies of his style and plots. Translations quickly appeared under London imprints. A 12 volume set of *Gaboriau's Sensational Novels*, issued in pictorial paper wrappers at a shilling a copy, was published during 1881–85 by Vizetelly & Co. Prospective purchasers were informed that these were 'the favourite reading of Prince Bismarck'. *Monsieur Lecoq*, 2 vols. 1887; *The Widow Lerouge*, 1887; *File No. 113*, 1887; *In Deadly Peril* (1888); *Marie de Brinvilliers*, 1888; *Other People's Money*, 1888; *The Count's Secret*, 1888; *The Slaves of Paris*, 2 vols. 1889; *The Honor of the Name*, 1901; and *The Mystery of Orcival*, 1901; are amongst the earliest London editions that I have been able to trace. In the USA the translations appeared under different names as newspaper serials. *L'Affaire Lerouge* appeared as *The Crimson Circle*; *Le Crime d'Orcival* as *Dark Deeds*; *Les Esclaves de Paris* was changed by perverted reasoning to *Manhattan Unmasked*; and *Le Dossier No. 113* was presented as *The Steel Safe*. Many of the first English translations in book form appeared in the USA under the Boston imprint of Estes & Lauriat, in 1875. All are now extremely rare. At the age of 38, Gabonau died, on 28 September 1873, just when his work was beginning to be recognised, and he was within an ace of achieving the financial security that had eluded him throughout his life. Perhaps not surprisingly, the cause of death was attributed to 'physical and mental exhaustion'.

Of the many French writers who followed in Gaboriau's footsteps, easily the most famous in popular terms was Fortuné du Boisgobey (1824–91). He employed no intellectual reasoning machine such as Lecoq, but he peopled his tales with believeable figures culled from the back-streets of Paris – the market-porters, students, shop-girls, artists, and horse-drawn omnibus drivers, who crowded the stage as the plot unfolded and the guilty were brought to justice. His tales first appeared in England as Vizetelly *Shilling Editions*, uniform with the paper-wrapped series devoted to the works of Gaboriou. 32 titles were published during 1885–88, several of which were in two volumes. Typical of these were *The Severed Hand*, 1885; *The Crime of the Opera House*, 2 vols. 1886; *The Thumb Stroke*, 1886; *The Convict Colonel*, 1887; *Thieving Fingers*, 1887; *The Detective's Eye*, 1887; and *The Mysteries of New Paris*, 2 vols. 1888.

Le Coup de Pouce, 1875, which appeared in English as *The Thumb Stroke*, is possibly the best of his stories, with his detective Julien de la Chanterie ably assisted by M. Jean, a kindly old *curé* whom we first meet jogging along in a horse-drawn omnibus. Unlike G. K. Chesterton's Father Brown, he leaves the actual investigation of the crime to the young advocate Chanterie, but in the end it is M. Jean who proves that the murderer had established a false alibi by changing the position of the hands of the village clock. In his *Le Vieillesse de Monsieur Lecoq*, 1878, first translated into English under an American imprint as *The Old Age of Lecoq*, and issued undated in 1880, du Boisgobey appropriated his late rival-in-trade's central character, with no apology to Gaboriau. In the story, Monsieur Lecoq comes out of retirement in order to clear his son's name of an accusation of murder, but the author lacked Gaboriau's intimate knowledge of police methods in murder investigations and this particular plot seemed unconvincing. It was first published in England as *The Old Age of Lecoq, The Detective*, 1885, in a two-volume work under a Vizetelly imprint, the second volume containing the story of *An Omnibus Mystery*.

These two French exponents of the *roman-policier* influenced the future course of the detective novel in a manner unequalled by any of their contemporaries : Gaboriau, with his rather wooden characters and over melodramatic plots, compensated by the finely-drawn and fascinating personality of his Monsieur Lecoq; and du Boisgobey, bald-headed, his *pince-nez* clamped firmly in place, setting his smoothly interlocking plots into realistically constructed backgrounds.

First English editions of Du Boisgobey's detective novels.

Size of title-pages: 17.2 cm × 11 cm.

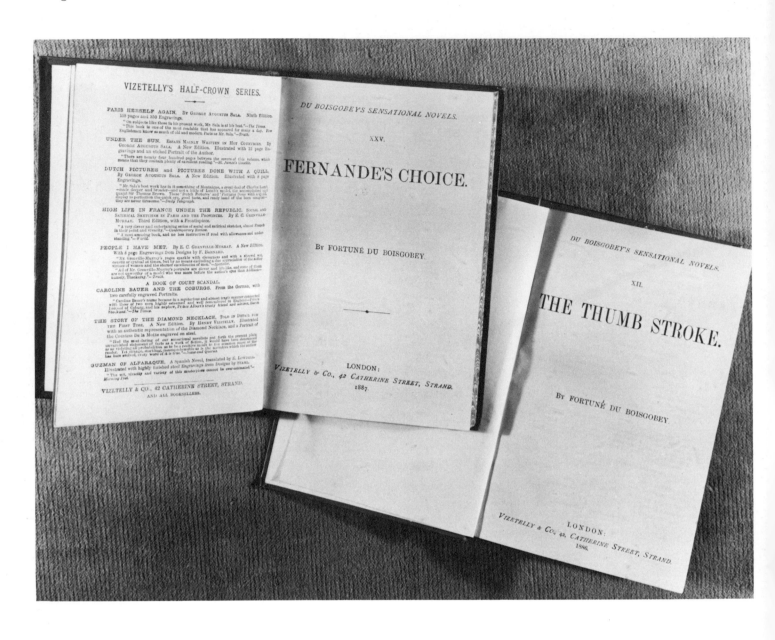

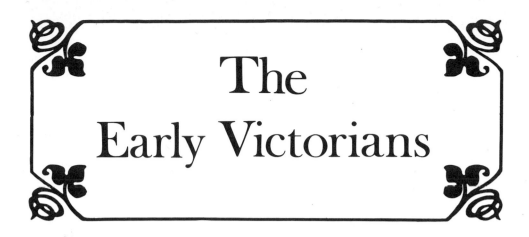

The Early Victorians

The tales written by Poe could be classed only as short stories, and the distinction of having written the first full-length 'modern' crime story in which detection plays an important role must go to a Scotsman. Angus Bethune Reach (1821–56), was born at Inverness, Scotland, the son of a local solicitor. Educated at Inverness Royal Academy, he later attended Edinburgh University where he edited the student's magazine, wrote poetry, and contributed articles on a variety of topics to the local papers.

In 1842, the family moved to London, and it was here that Reach received his first introduction to the journalistic career which he pursued until his untimely death (due to tuberculosis) at the age of 35. He obtained a post with the *Morning Chronicle*, and within a few months had been promoted to crime reporter at the Central Criminal Court, of Old Bailey, London, a building which now occupies almost the whole site of what was once Newgate Prison. He quickly became intimately acquainted with many of the leading members of the newly-formed detective police force, and also with the methods used by the criminal fraternity.

Later, he was able to put to good use the stories he transmitted to his newspaper, and the copious notes he kept of the trials he attended. In 1845, he attended the exhibition opened by the famous French investigator, Vidocq, in a Regent Street warehouse. Surrounded by a variety of gruesome relics brought over from France, the ex-criminal, turned detective, lectured on his exploits to the fee-paying visitors, usually reappearing at the end of each session in a carefully contrived disguise before suddenly unmasking with a cry of 'I am Vidocq!' The crime reporter Reach, and the crime investigator Vidocq, became friends of a like profession, exchanging stories and information far into the night, while the drink flowed.

At that time, the first of a long series of melodramas in which crime and detection played a leading part had been revived at Sadler's Wells Theatre, with Samuel Phelps in the principal role. *The Iron Chest*, a tragedy which George Colman had based on the novel *Caleb Williams* (discussed in the chapter on the historical background), was playing to capacity houses after a successful first night on 7 April 1845. It seems probable that Angus Reach visited Sadler's Wells during the play's run for there are certain similarities between the plot of his book and incidents in the drama. It was not until the summer of 1848 that he completed the manuscript of a work which ensures him a place in the history of detective fiction, even if the finished product fails in some respects to satisfy the strict criteria later devised.

In 1848–49, he published in six, monthly, paper-wrapped parts, a tale of vendetta, murder, racehorse doping, slow poisoning and abduction, among other dark and dastardly deeds, under the title of *Clement Lorimer; or, The Book with the Iron Clasps*. George Cruickshank helped to ensure the work's success by contributing twelve, spirited, full-page illustrations, and the publishers, David Bogue, of Fleet Street, London, later issued the work in book-form from the sheets of the monthly parts, in a binding of heavily gilt and blind-stamped maroon cloth. The volume was dated 1849, and copies of this first edition exhibit the stab-holes in their inside margins used when stitching the original paper covers to the parts issue. The first part was issued in October 1848, and the last of the six appeared in March the following year. The finely-executed copperplate illustrations by Cruikshank rank amongst the best of his work, and copies of the parts issue, and

One of the twelve full-page engraved plates by George Cruikshank for *Clement Lorimer; or, The Book With the Iron Clasps*, 1849, by Angus B. Reach.

Size of engraved surface: 15 cm × 10 cm.

the first edition of the book, have been sought by collectors of his engravings since the latter half of the 19th century. A set in the original parts is now catalogued at about £60 ($150); in the original cloth binding, less than half of this amount.

Clement Lorimer was by no means Reach's first literary work to appear in volume form. At least six lighthearted satires on the 'bores, humbugs, tufthunters and toadies' of his day had been published during the previous two or three years, most of which had originally been printed in magazines. But this was his first and only mystery story, with the unravelling of the tangled skein of clues left only partly in the hands of the protagonist of the title. The terms he had heard used at the Old Bailey, and by Vidocq and others in the profession, make their first appearance in print, including several now in general use. On page 130, detectives are described for the first time as 'sleuth-hounds', a fact that apparently escaped the notice of the compilers of the Oxford English Dictionary, who date the earliest printed use of the phrase as 1856. It is here that Lorimer turns on his adversaries:

> 'Invoke the law, indeed! There is an awful mystery which the sleuth hounds of the law may trace – a mystery of suspicion, perhaps a mystery of crime . . . Tell your employers what I have said. Tell them, that if they can burrow I can dig – if they can plot, I can unravel; and tell them, too that not a peaceable night, not a tranquil day, shall I enjoy, until I have unkennelled them, one and all!'

THE BOOK WITH THE IRON CLASPS.

Cruikshank's spirited engraving for the first part of *Clement Lorimer*, later used as the frontispiece for the cloth-bound volume issued the same year.

Size of engraved surface: 17 cm × 11 cm.

The critics of his day accorded the work an enthusiastic reception: '. . . startling in its interest' said the *Morning Chronicle*; 'Mr Reach excels in what we must call, for lack of a home comparative, the Dumas style of writing . . .' said the reviewer in *The Atlas*; while the *Weekly Dispatch* informed its readers that: 'The plot is excellent – the language terse and vigorous – and the succession of incidents unflagging'. Several editions of the work appeared, with the last published during the author's lifetime, dated 1856.

One of the most prized copies of detective fiction in my collection is a specimen of the first issue of the first edition, *Recollections of a Detective Police-Officer*, by 'Waters', the pseudonym of William Russell. This ephemeral little 'yellow-back' is dated 1856. yet it is still in much the same condition as when J. & C. Brown & Company, Ave Maria Lane, London, issued it nearly 120 years ago. Bright and resplendent in its original pictorially-printed paper-covered boards, it has survived so well because it was enclosed in a wrapping of brown cloth, almost since the day of issue. What prompted the original mid-19th-century owner to cosset and care for a volume he could have replaced brand-new for a tiny sum I shall never know. It was sold to me through a catalogue as a re-bound copy; but when I unpacked the parcel containing it and other bibliographical treasures, I noticed that it still retained its original end-papers. Close to the date of its first publication, a Victorian collector had damped the pasted-down end-papers at the front and end of the book, carefully lifted their edges, and then expertly clothed the volume in a protective suit of cloth specially cut to size. The overlapping margins were placed beneath the end-papers, which were then re-glued into place. But no glue was allowed to mar the printed paper-covered binding. When I realised that the cloth was only a loosely-fitting protective cover, I moistened the edges of the end-papers, removed the margins of cloth, and the whole peeled neatly off the book, revealing the original 'yellow-back' format in almost pristine state. This was a piece of bibliographical good fortune which I am unlikely to repeat, a highlight of a book-collector's career that helped to compensate for a three-volume *Oliver Twist* 1838, that lacked a page of text – discovered too late to stop the cheque – and a prized copy of *Vanity Fair*, 1848, missing its final full-page plate. Book-collecting, like all acquisitive arts, has its ups and downs.

Recollections of a Detective Police-Officer, 1856, forms another cornerstone in any serious-minded collection of detective fiction. The few copies that have survived in their original bindings are also esteemed as early examples of the railway literature of the period, the earliest of which date from 1853. Colour-printed illustrations on paper-covered boards, which had been a feature of children's books since the early 1840s, became common when a cheap form of binding was needed to supply the needs of railway passengers setting out on journeys long enough to need the solace of a book. Sold on station bookstalls and elsewhere, these rapidly became the normal and accepted form of binding for cheaply-priced fiction. The little volumes cost anything from sixpence to two shillings a copy. The rapidly growing popularity of detective fiction was reflected in the number of titles that appeared in 'yellow-back' form, a term derived from the second title in the series. In December 1852, Ingram, Cooke & Co., issued Horace Mayhew's *Letters left at the Pastrycook's* (dated 1853), followed in April, 1853, by *Money: How to Get, How to Keep, and How to Use It*. These two books started the 'yellow-back' era. *Money*, printed predominately in yellow probably gave the name to the series. The first issues were in paper wrappers, later to appear in the familiar paper-covered boards which almost immediately became the format for all 'yellow-backs'. Most titles in this format, other than early detective fiction, were re-issues of well-known and successful novels. A set of detective stories in the pictorial paper covers of the period 1855 to 1900 (the earlier the better), whether they are first editions or not are an enviable possession, as eye-catching as they are rare. Condition plays an important part in assessing their financial value : 'Yellow-backs' in good condition are a delight to behold, epitomising the age in which they were read. The majority of the survivors offered for sale today have been read to death by a succession of unmindful owners, and find a use only as texts.

Angus Reach managed to secure a place in *The Dictionary of National Biography* (which informs us that his name was pronounced Re-ach, a di-syllable). About William Russell, little or nothing is known except the titles of the books he left behind. He was a minor novelist of the Victorian era, who failed to secure a niche in any contemporary or subsequent work of reference, much less the hallowed pages of the *DNB*. Having written his stint, he disappears without trace, in the manner of more than one of the murder victims in his tales, leaving behind a reputation based solely on his contributions to the railway literature of the period. The three-volume novel and a place in Mudie's list of available titles was not for him, and, at the period in which he wrote, such a distinction was essential for financial success as an author. Russell confined himself almost solely to novels set against the three diverse backgrounds of ships and the sea (for which he used the pseudonym of 'Lieutenant Warneford, RN'); the law and litigation; or criminal activities and police investigation (these last two fields under the pen-name of 'Waters'). His tales made their first, often their only appearance as 'yellow-backs', priced at eighteen pence, or two shillings. The bindings were designed and printed by Edmund Evans, whose famous colour-printing establishment was at Racquet Court, Fleet Street. Most titles were also advertised as obtainable in publisher's cloth bindings, blocked in gilt, at 2s. 6d. a copy.

As a pioneer in the art of detective fiction, Russell has earned a place in a bibliography devoted to the craft. As most bibliophiles prefer to seek out every title written by the authors they collect, I have detailed all his known works.

Cruise of the Blue Jacket, 1862

Detective Officer, and other Tales (1878). A reissue of both series of
    Recollections

Experiences of a Barrister, 1856 (published anonymously)

Experiences of a French Detective-Officer (1861). This title was 'taken from the French of Theodore Duhamel'

Experiences of a Real Detective, 1862

Extraordinary Men, 1855

Extraordinary Women, 1855

Game of Life, The (1857). Reissued in 1862 as *Leonard Harlowe; or, The Game of Life*

Heir-at-Law, The (1862)

Kirke Webbe: The Privateer Captain (1860)

Leaves from the Diary of a Law-Clerk (1857)

Leonard Harlowe; or, The Game of Life (1862), See above.

Marriage Settlement, The, 1856. (One of the only books with his correct name on the title-page)

Mutiny of the Saturn (1869)

Phantom Cruiser, The, 1865

Recollections of a Detective Police-Officer, 1856

Recollections of a Detective Police-Officer (Second Series), 1859

Recollections of a Sheriff's Officer (1860)

Romance of Common Life (1861)

Romance of Military Life (1863)

Romance of the Seas (1862)

Serf Girl of Moscow, 1858

Skeleton in Every House (1860)

Tales of the Coast Guard, 1856

Traditions of London: Historical and Legendary, 1859

Two Love Stories, 1861

Undiscovered Crimes, 1862

Valazy Family (1870)

Valerie Duclos, 1854

Russell was writing his novels during a period of about fifteen years, but with the advent of the 1870s the titles cease abruptly. Many of them made their first appearance in *Chamber's Edinburgh Journal*, the year previous to publication in book form. *Recollections of a Detective Police-Officer* was the first and the best of his series of detective tales, and in the preface he informed his readers:

> I make no apology for placing these rough sketches of police-experience before the reader. They describe incidents more or less interesting and instructive of the domestic warfare constantly waging between the agents and breakers of the law, in which the stratagems and disguises resorted to, by detective officers, are in my opinion, and in the opinions of thousands of others, as legitimate, ay, and *quite* as honourable *ruses de guerre*, notwithstanding the lofty rebuke lately administered by a dignified judge to the late Inspector Field, for presuming to speak of his 'honour'; as a military ambuscade, or the cautious creeping of an undistinguishable rifleman within easy shooting distance of an unsuspecting enemy.

Russell had plenty of rivals even at this early stage of the development of the detective novel, and nearly all these minor novelists saw their work published in the cheap but handy format of a single-volume 'yellow-back' binding of paper-covered boards. A cross-section of titles of the period appearing as first editions in this style of railway binding includes:

Autobiography of a French Detective, 1862, by M. Canler

Curiosities of Crime in Edinburgh (1867), by James M'Levy

Curiosities of Detection, 1862, by Robert Curtis

Dark Deeds (1869), by Erskine Neale

Detective's Note-Book, 1860, by Charles Martel

Diary of an Ex-Detective, 1860, by Charles Martel

Female Detective, The, 1864, by Andrew Forrester

Irish Police Officer, 1861, by Robert Curtis

New York Detective Police Officer, The, 1865, by J. B. Williams

Revelations of a Private Detective, 1863, by Andrew Forrester

Secret Service; or, Recollections of a City Detective, 1864, by Andrew Forrester

It would be difficult today, if not impossible, to make a worthwhile collection of 'yellow-back' first editions of detective fiction published before the early 1870s. Copies in good condition were common enough in the 1930s. Even after World War II, at least until the mid-1950s, I was able to add to my collection several titles priced at only a few shillings, or, occasionally, a pound or two. Now they are avidly hunted by collector's of publisher's binding styles as well as those seeking early 'firsts' of detective fiction. In many ways, as the late Michael Sadleir has pointed out in his *XIX Century Fiction*, they constitute the most important and interesting class of 'yellow-back' literature published. They appeared during the best (and now much the rarest) phase of 'yellow-back' production, between the late-1850s and the mid-1870s, although titles continued to be published in this format until the start of World War I. In the earliest stage, they were quite well printed, in a good readable type-face, and were issued in individually designed covers. Many titles, known through the medium of advertisements in other volumes, seem to have completely disappeared. During the first 50 or so years of their existence they were despised by book-collectors and dealers alike. The fate of most that survived the first few years was to be pulped in salvage drives for waste-paper during World War I. The rest nearly disappeared between the wars, and few even found a place in the booksellers' sixpenny box. Another war and another salvage drive, and the species was almost extinct. Nevertheless, copies in acceptable condition still occasionally make brief appearances in the catalogues of antiquarian booksellers, but the collector has to be quick off the mark to secure so elusive a prize.

This chapter would not be complete without mention of one other mid-19th-century writer whose reputation was largely made in other fields of literature, but whose contribution to early detective fiction also had some significance. Joseph Sheridan le Fanu (1814–73), the Irish novelist and journalist, was educated at Trinity College, Dublin, and it was in that city that his earliest literary work appeared. *The Cock and the Anchor*, 3 vols. 1845, was published anonymously, and was the first of a series of novels and poems that culminated in *Willing to Die*, 3 vols. 1873, the year of the author's death. *The Watcher and other Weird Stories* (1894), and *The Evil Guest* (1895), were both published posthumously and contained tales that had appeared in other works during Le Fanu's lifetime. Today his fame rests principally upon these and his other ghost stories. *The House in the Church-Yard*, 3 vols. 1863, was published by Tinsley in a binding of royal blue bead-grain cloth, after the book had been printed and bound in Dublin at the author's expense. It was an eerie tale of supernatural horror, and was followed by *Uncle Silas: A Tale of Bartram-Haugh*, 3 vols. 1864, published by Bentley, London, an equally far-fetched and sensational work. This second plot centres on criminal, not ghostly, activities and holds a deal of detective interest, but it is with *Checkmate*, 3 vols. 1871, which Hurst & Blackett issued in a·binding of apple-green cloth, blocked in black and gold, that we come to a detective novel proper, containing several features new to the art. One innovation is that the criminal's facial appearance has been altered by plastic surgery, making the detective's task much more difficult. (*Finger Prints*, 1892, by Francis Galton (1822–1911), was not published for another 20 years, a work that heralded the dawn of a new era in crime detection. It was however, not until 1901 that a Finger-print Bureau was established by Scotland Yard.) So when *Checkmate* appeared, it was a criminal's features that betrayed him and if these were convincingly altered his chance of escape was high. David Arden, who acts the part of detective and avenger of his murdered brother at last tracks down the surgeon who performed the operation on the infamous Yelland Mace. The criminal is now passing himself off as a respectable city magnate. By using plaster casts and dental records (the first time these devices had been employed in a detective story) Arden finally unmasks the murderer. For this cunning new plot alone, Le Fanu is ensured remembrance as a contributor to the field of detective fiction.

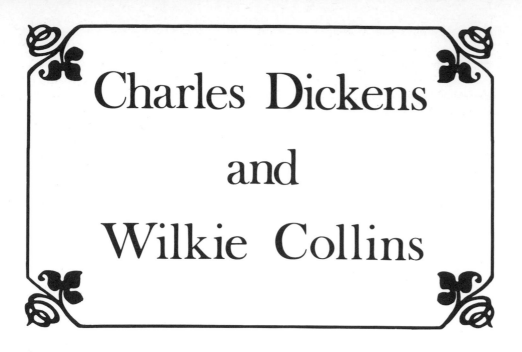

Charles Dickens
and
Wilkie Collins

In the years that followed the formation of the first detective police force in London, an immense popularity was achieved by those writers who specialised in detective fiction novels and works devoted to criminal investigation. This interest was greatly stimulated by the publication in the magazine *Household Words* of articles by Charles Dickens (1812–70), during July to September 1850, describing the activities of the detective branch of the police.

He was the first novelist to portray the British police in a sympathetic light, and had been fascinated by their exploits even before he became acquainted with many of the leading members of the force. They appear in many of his novels – *Great Expectations*, *Our Mutual Friend*, and *Bleak House* in particular – and he studied their organisation and the methods of crime investigation they employed with an attention beyond that of a novelist. As a young man in the 1830s, he had met members of the Bow Street Runners, the first mobile police force, who were used by the magistrates of the day for pursuing and apprehending those for whom warrants of arrest had been issued. Dickens mentions his personal recollections of this ruffian crew in a letter to his friend Walter Thornbury, a contributor to his magazine *All the Year Round*. It was dated 18 April 1862.

> My Dear Thornbury,
>   The Bow Street Runners ceased out of the land soon after the introduction of the new police. I remember them very well standing about the door of the office in Bow Street. They had no other uniform than a blue dress-coat, brass buttons (I am not even now sure that was necessary), and a bright red waistcoat. The waistcoat was indispensable, and the slang name for them was 'redbreasts' in consequence.
>   They kept company with thieves and the like, much more than the detective police do. I don't know what their pay was, but I have no doubt their principal complements were got under the rose. It was a very slack institution, and its headquarters were the Brown Bear, in Bow Street, a public house of more than doubtful reputation opposite the police office . . .

In *Oliver Twist; or, The Parish Boy's Progress*, 3 vols. 1838, Dickens revealed his consuming interest in the underworld, introducing his readers to thieves and murderers. In 1850, he founded *Household Words*, a weekly periodical from which politics were ostensibly excluded and which was aimed at having a more popular appeal than its rivals, such as *Blackwood's*. During the next five years he wrote a series of articles centred on the activities of the London police, and he became a personal friend of several officers, including the Inspector Field mentioned by William Russell. His story, *Three Detective Anecdotes*, includes an account of 'Sergeant Witchem's' success in tracking down and arresting a murderer, in capturing a burglar, and in tricking another thief into handing over a stolen diamond. This was a thinly concealed alias for one of the best-known Scotland Yard detectives, Inspector Wicher, whom Wilkie

Collins later used as a model for Sergeant Cuff in *The Moonstone*.

Dickens devoted part of the plot of *Barnaby Rudge*, 1841, to the solution of a mysterious crime; a fact that intrigued Edgar Allan Poe sufficiently for him to devise his own climax to the story. The work was originally issued in 88 paper-wrapped weekly-parts – or 20 monthly numbers – commencing 4 April 1840. Poe's forecast, after reading the first few chapters, proved to be so accurate that Dickens was amazed at his perspicacity. *Barnaby Rudge*, which formed the third volume of *Master Humphrey's Clock* (the first two volumes were *The Old Curiosity Shop*), told the story of the Gordon anti-popery riots of 1780, and had a sub-plot concerning the unmasking of the murderer of a country gentleman and landowner, Reuben Haredale. Poe criticised the ending of *Barnaby Rudge*, and went on to give his own idea of how the murder plot should have developed. He would have concentrated on making it a detective story, rather than using the *dénouement* which Dickens devised.

Bleak House, 1853, first appeared in 20 monthly parts, commencing in March 1852. The last number of the series is 19, as the conclusion came out in a double issue. Here, the author went to considerable trouble to construct an important part of the plot in the form of a detective story. The first police detective to be cast in the part of a hero in the pages of fiction makes his bow in this book. The story tells how Sir Leicester Dedlock, a pompous old baronet, dotes on his beautiful wife, Lady Dedlock. Before her marriage, she had taken a lover, Captain Hawdon, and later became the mother of his child, whom she now believes to be dead. In fact, the disowned daughter lives on in the person of ·Esther Summerson, and Hawdon in that of a penniless scrivener. It is when a rascally lawyer, Tulkinghorn, discovers Lady Dedlock's secret and is later found murdered, that the reader is introduced to the well disguised and apparently benign Inspector Bucket:

The first printed picture of a fictional police-detective. This Halbot K. Browne illustration of Inspector Bucket appeared in the first edition of *Bleak House*, 1853, by Charles Dickens.

Size across page: 22.2 cm.

Friendly behaviour of Mr Bucket.

He is a sharp-eyed man – a quick keen man – and he takes in everybody's look at him, all at once, individually and collectively, in a manner that stamps him a remarkable man.

After arresting and handcuffing an innocent suspect, Bucket disappears, red-faced, to continue his investigations in secret. The reader only occasionally catches a glimpse of him and is told little or nothing about the clues he unearths or his methods of work. But at the appointed moment, with his reiterated challenge to friend and foe : "I am Inspector Bucket of the Detective, I am!", the first fictional detective to claim the genuine sympathy of his readers makes his arrest of the murderer of Tullinghorn. It is Mlle Hortense, Lady Dedlock's former French maid. In a dramatic ending, the despairing Lady Dedlock, learning that her husband knows her dark secret, flies from the house in an anguish of self-pity, and is subsequently found dead near the grave of her lover. Part of the evidence reaches Bucket through the agency of his wife, who in disingenuous fashion secures much of the vital information he needs to uncover the identity of the murderer.

Bleak House has also earned a place among works of detective fiction because it is the first novel to include an explanatory chapter in the form of a retrospective inquest, in which Inspector Bucket self-confidently recounts the steps he has taken to bring about the imminent arrest. In the circle of his listening audience is the murderer. In thus giving a résumé of his detective's investigation before the inevitable confrontation, Dickens originated a literary device of anticipation which has been used frequently by subsequent writers of detective fiction.

First editions of the novels of Charles Dickens can still be purchased for sums which seem quite moderate, considering his eminence as a writer. Although this can partly be explained by the large size of the initial printing of most of his works (the same observation applies with even greater force to the later three-volume novels of Sir Walter Scott), I still consider them underpriced when viewed from the standpoint of the collector interested in first editions of literary importance. Most were first issued in paper-wrappered parts, the covers being pictorially-printed. All later appeared in volume form, in bindings of publisher's cloth, lettered in gilt on the spine. Contemporary purchasers of the original parts issue usually had the complete sets bound up at the end of the serial : these are now found in contemporary half-calf or half-morocco bindings, in many cases still exhibiting the stab-holes in their inner margins once used for stitching on their paper covers. A copy of *Bleak House*, 1853, in its original binding of blind-stamped green cloth, and with the full-page illustrations by Halbot K. Browne (1815–82) in clean and unfoxed condition, would now cost a collector about £30 ($75). Browne often used the pseudonym 'Phiz' as a complement to the author's 'Boz'.

In 1859, the *New York Ledger* printed Dicken's story *Hunted Down* in serial form. It later appeared in England in *All the Year Round*. Dickens based this tale of murder and slow poisoning on the criminal career of a well-known London journalist, Thomas Griffiths Wainewright. The gentleman had insured the life of his sister-in-law for £18,000, and the lady died in considerable distress, in the same year, from strychnine poisoning. Charles Dickens visited Wainewright in Newgate Prison, where he had been confined after being charged with several murders, but he escaped execution and was transported to Australia. He died in 1852, seven years before Dickens wrote the story of his crimes. In this story, the author had made the detective theme of prime importance, but the tale itself falls considerably below his usual standard and takes a lowly place in his canon of work. Nevertheless, Robert Bonner, owner of the *New York Ledger*, paid Dickens £1,000 for the tale, which appeared in the columns of his magazine during August and September 1859, complete with seven luridly-drawn woodcut illustrations. The work first appeared in book form in the USA in 1861, and was titled *The Lamplighter's Story*; *Hunted Down*; *The Detective Police*; *and Other Nouvellettes*, complete with frontispiece and pictorial title-page. The first English edition was published by John Camden Hotten in a binding of paper wrappers, dated 1870.

Dickens began to give public readings from his works in 1858, and continued them during his second visit to the USA in 1867–68. It was after his return to England that he commenced work on what proved to be his final book, *The*

Frontispiece and engraved title-page of Charles Dickens' unfinished detective story, published in 1870.

Size of title-page:
22 cm × 14 cm.

Mystery of Edwin Drood, 1870. This tale of murder had been planned as a detective story and was to consist of 12 monthly parts issued in the usual format of pictorial paper wrappers. The author began work on the book in August 1869, and publication of the parts issue began in April 1870. Dickens' sudden death on 9 June 1870, resulted in the manuscript ending abruptly at what would have been the half-way mark. Three of the monthly parts had already been issued, and a further three were published after the author's death; but a tantalising situation had arisen with his readers left poised in mid-story. Had Edwin Drood really been murdered? And who was Dick Datchery, the heavily disguised figure who settled in Cloisterham after the hero's disappearance and began ferreting information about the opium-smoking John Jasper? No one will ever know for sure; but there was no lack of volunteers in the years immediately after the author's death, and at frequent intervals ever since, who attempted to supply a solution to the unsolved mysteries, and a logical ending to the book. It remains only as a *potential* detective novel, for Dickens had completed only 23 chapters, and a detective had yet to be introduced. But his possible desire to outshine the recently published best-seller of his friend Wilkie Collins, whose serialisation of *The Moonstone* had caused crowds of enthusiastic readers to collect in the streets while awaiting the appearance of the next instalment, may well have decided the course of the plot and the introduction of a fictional detective whose intellectual powers would surpass those possessed even by the ubiquitous Sergeant Cuff. Before his death, Charles Dickens had been told that, of the first monthly part, over 50,000 copies had already been sold, a tribute to a writer who had delighted countless thousands of readers for over 34 years.

The cover design for the paper-wrappered parts, six in number, of *The Mystery of Edwin Drood*, was by Charles Alston Collins, brother of Wilkie Collins, and the husband of Kate Dickens, the novelist's daughter. The woodcut illustrations were by Luke Fildes. In volume form, the work appeared in a binding of green cloth, blocked in black and gold. The earlier issues have a 32-page catalogue of publications of Chapman & Hall tipped in at the end, and bearing the date 'Aug. 31, 1870'. A set of the parts issue would now be catalogued at about £40 ($100), and the cloth-bound volume about £15 ($38).

In considering the contribution of William Wilkie Collins (1824–89), to the field of detective fiction, we are presented with another cornerstone for our gradually growing collection of first editions. Born the eldest son of the artist William Collins (1788–1847), he took his first name from his father (but seldom, if ever, used the name William on the title-pages of his books), and was otherwise named after his father's intimate friend and brother Academician, Sir David Wilkie. He spent three years with his parents in Italy before being articled to a tea firm in the City of London. He was rescued by his father from his bondage as a clerk, entered at Lincoln's Inn, and was called to the Bar in November

The engraved title-page of Wilkie Collins' first book, *Memoirs of the Life of William Collins, Esq., R.A.*, 2 vols, 1848.

Size of page: 19.5 cm × 12 cm.

Wilkie Collins (1824–89), from the oil-painting by Sir John Millais.
Reproduced by courtesy of The National Portrait Gallery, London.

1851. His training in the law stood him in good stead when devising the legal arguments used in some of his later novels. His first literary work was a two-volume biography of his father, published in 1848, when the author was twenty-four years of age. Once he was launched on a literary career at least one full-length book a year appeared from his pen: *Antonina; or, The Fall of Rome*, 3 vols. 1850; *Rambles beyond Railways*, 1851; *Mr Wray's Cash-Box*, 1852; and a large number of works spanning almost all the categories of English literature, and occupying the author's lifetime.

It was in 1851 that Collins first met Charles Dickens, an event of considerable significance to both men. The two novelists, unequal as they were both in genius and reputation, nevertheless became firm friends and lifelong correspondents. Collins has also been accorded the distinction of being one of the very few writers to exert an influence over Dickens' subsequent literary work, and his impact on what later came to be known as detective fiction certainly surpassed that of his fellow author and close personal friend. Both set out to expose social evils and attack legal injustices, and both found a fascinating interest in the more notorious crimes of their day and in the methods employed by the uniformed and detective police.

They spent part of the spring of 1856 in France together, and it was here that Collins picked up a three-volume set of Maurice Mejan's *Recueil des Causes Célèbres* (1807–14), which was still in his library at his death. In his *Recollections of Wilkie Collins*, which he contributed to *Chamber's Journal*, Wybert Reeve quotes from a letter Collins wrote at that time to a personal friend:

> I was in Paris, wandering about the streets with Charles Dickens, amusing ourselves by looking into the shops. We came to an old book-stall, half shop and half store, and I found some dilapidated volumes and records of French crime – a sort of French *Newgate Calendar*. I said to Dickens, "Here's a prize!" So it turned out to be. In them I found some of my best plots.

Between the years 1853–56, he contributed a number of short stories to *Household Words*, later issued as a collection in a two-volume work entitled *After Dark*, 1856. In book form, the six stories had a connecting narrative, and all dealt with murderous crimes or other criminal activities. Several, including *The Stolen Letter* (a tale modelled in several respects on Poe's *The Purloined Letter*), and *The Lady of Glenwith Grange*, rely for an important part of their plots on a detective interest; while in *A Terribly Strange Bed*, the unfortunate inmate, with the heavy canopy slowly but inexorably descending on him, finds himself in much the same horrifying situation as the victim in Poe's *The Pit and the Pendulum*. A first edition of *After Dark*, complete with the 16-page catalogue at the end of Vol. I, the advertisement leaf at the end of Vol. II, and in its original publisher's cloth binding, would now be worth in the region of £50 ($125).

The first edition of the first book written by Eden Phillpotts, published by James Hogg, London, dated 1888. A prolific writer of plays, novels and romances, and of detective fiction, Phillpotts died in 1960 in his ninety-ninth year.

An 1871 poster design by Fred Walker for Wilkie Collins' *The Woman in White*.

THE WOMAN IN WHITE

The most difficult of B. L. Farjeon's many titles to find in acceptable condition as a first edition. The book is dated 1888.

48

A Railway Romance

About L.&N.W.

My Adventure in the Flying Scotsman

One Shilling Shares

Devlin the Barber

by B.L. Farjeon

WARD AND DOWNEY LONDON.

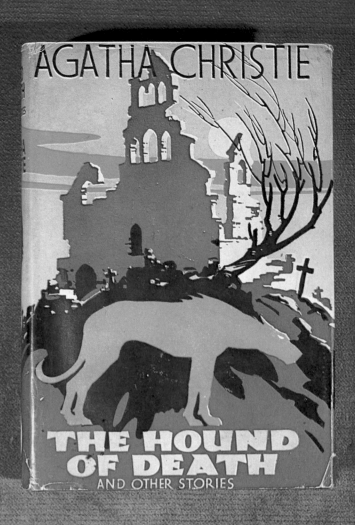

AGATHA CHRISTIE

THE HOUND OF DEATH
AND OTHER STORIES

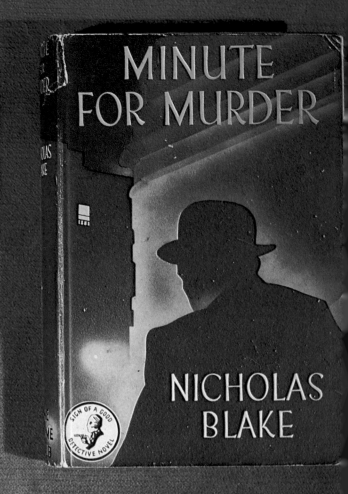

MINUTE FOR MURDER

NICHOLAS BLAKE

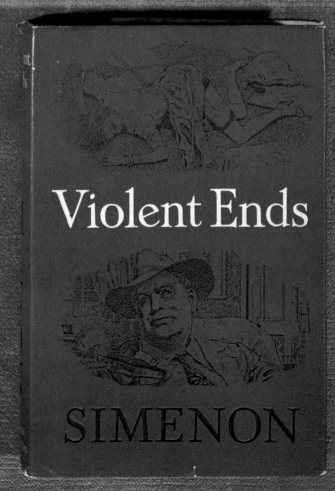

Violent Ends

SIMENON

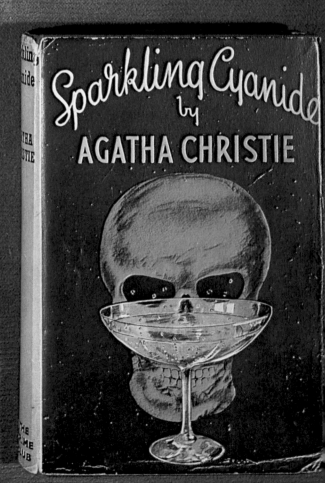

Sparkling Cyanide
by
AGATHA CHRISTIE

The skill Collins displayed in creating complicated plots could only be fully utilised in his full-length novels, and it is by these that he is remembered today, notably those woven around mysteries solved by logical deduction. It was his increasing interest in the processes of criminal detection and the factual assessment of a tangled web of clues that led to the production of the two books on which his present-day reputation is based. *The Woman in White*, 3 vols. 1860; and *The Moonstone*, 3 vols. 1868; both involve problems of detection. The latter, in the words of the late T. S. Eliot, is 'the, first, the longest, and the best of detective novels'.

The Woman in White was first published as a serial in *All the Year Round*, from 26 November 1859, and became one of the most popular novels of its age. As a book, the first large impression was completely sold out on the day of publication, while in the USA, a New York publisher boasted that his sales of the work had totalled more than 126,000 copies. It is a mystery story containing many elements of detective fiction, but without an acknowledged professional or amateur detective being personally involved. It is to Wilkie Collins' later classic tale of mystery and detective skills that the laurels must be awarded; it is a work deserving the most honoured place in any collection devoted to the history of detective fiction.

To attempt to describe in detail the wonderfully imaginative plot of *The Moonstone*, would destroy much of the pleasure for those readers who will one day be lucky enough to open the pages of the work for the first time. It is a book they will revisit many times, if my own taste is any guide. Descriptive writing and characterisation of a quality that has seldom been surpassed in any detective story make the work a joy to read. The extremely

The title-page of the first edition of one of the most important early works of detective fiction.

Size of page: 18 cm × 12 cm.

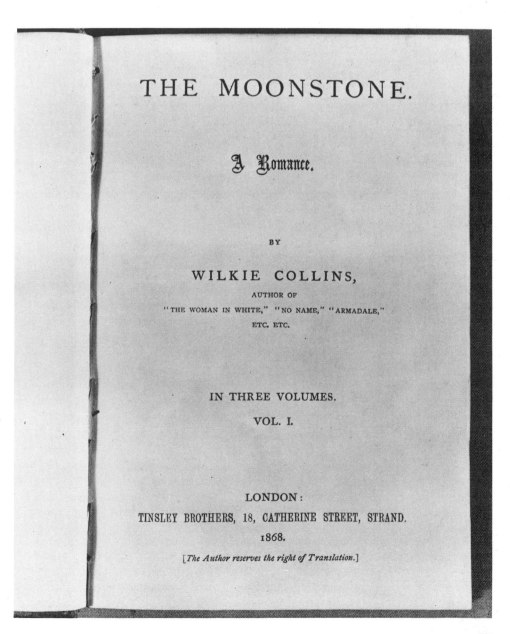

A selection of pictorial dust-jackets of 'modern' first editions.

intricate plot allowed Collins to confuse the issue and sidetrack his readers also helped to lift the work far above its nearest contemporary rivals in the field. One retains a vivid recollection of the underpaid and underprivileged Sergeant Cuff, the forerunner of a long line of odd, whimsical, commonplace, outlandish, suave, opera-loving, tone-deaf, pipe-smoking, martini-sipping sleuth-hounds:

> A fly from the railway drove up as I reached the lodge; and out got a grizzled, elderly man, so miserably lean that he looked as if he had not got an ounce of flesh on his bones in any part of him. He was dressed all in decent black, with a white cravat round his neck. His face was as sharp as a hatchet, and the skin of it was as yellow and dry and withered as an autumn leaf. His eyes, of a steely light grey, had a very disconcerting trick, when they encountered your eyes, of looking as if they expected something more from you than you were aware of yourself. His walk was soft; his voice was melancholy; his long lanky fingers were hooked like claws. He might have been a parson, or an undertaker – or anything else you like, except what he really was.

Cuff's passion for roses, and his other endearing eccentricities mask an incisive and razor-like intellect. But despite the care with which the author drew for his readers this spidery figure of a master-detective, he nevertheless allowed Cuff to make an exit from the pages of fiction when the last chapter of *The Moonstone* drew to a close. This was an error of a magnitude seldom equalled in the annals of English literature, and certainly not in the field of detective fiction. Sergeant Cuff was never to reappear, although his ghostly image haunted the chapters of the later novels of the genre throughout the 19th century and beyond.

In essence, the plot of *The Moonstone* centres around the disappearance of an enormous diamond that had once been set in the forehead of an image of the Indian moon-god. At the siege of Seringapatam it was stolen by an English officer, John Herncastle, who had cold-bloodedly stabbed to death the three Indian custodians of the treasure. Members of the Brahmin sect set to work, with the utmost determination, to recover the stone. In the story, the moonstone is handed to a Miss Verinder on her eighteenth birthday, but it mysteriously disappears that same night. Suspicion falls on three Indian jugglers who have been seen in the neighbourhood of the house, and on Franklin Blake, Miss Verinder's lover, who has come into possession of it while under the influence of opium. The story unfolds with a maze of false trails and changing suspicions, until, in the end, the final entrance of Sergeant Cuff unravels the tangled threads and presents a logical solution to the mystery.

Today, a copy of the first edition of *The Moonstone*, complete with its half-titles, the misprint 'treachesrouly' on page 129 in Volume 2, and with the leaves of advertisements in Volumes 2 and 3, will cost a collector in the region of £250 ($625). A good copy in the original cloth binding would not be overpriced at that figure, whereas a rebound half-calf or half-morocco specimen might well prove dear at less than a quarter of the price. But any text of the first edition is hard to come by, evidence of the many times the original volumes were read before they literally disintegrated in their final owner's hands. It is a fortunate collector who has any copy of the text of the first edition on his shelves.

Much of the credit for creating the modern detective novel belongs, in almost equal fashion, to Charles Dickens and Wilkie Collins. Dickens was the first to write in appreciative terms about the work of the English detective-police, and had he lived to complete *The Mystery of Edwin Drood*, it is possible that a detective story far exceeding even *The Moonstone* in quality of execution, originality of plot and characters, would have existed to delight the public. As A. E. Murch has pointed out in *The Development of the Detective Novel*, 1958, it was Wilkie Collins who bestowed a literary dignity on the emerging art with his books *The Woman in White* and *The Moonstone*. 'The plot in each of them is sensational but never incredible; the puzzle theme, intricate and well-sustained though it is, does not eclipse the human characters in interest or importance; and in these works Collins devised and presented the "fair play convention" which has had such far-reaching effects'.

The first (Australian) edition and the first English edition of a title that sold well over a million copies.

Size of front covers:
18.5 cm × 12.2 cm.

The Melbourne edition is reproduced by permission of The Mitchell Library, Sydney, Australia.

The Hansom Cab Era

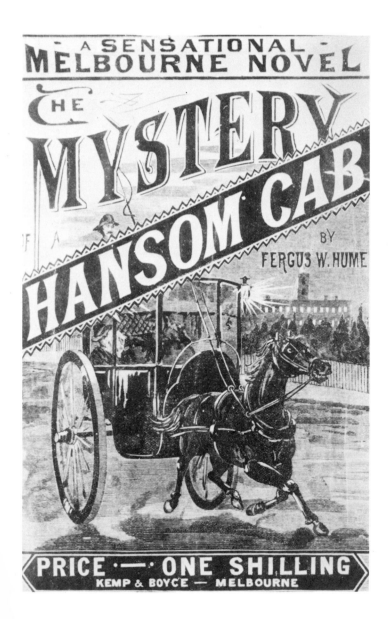

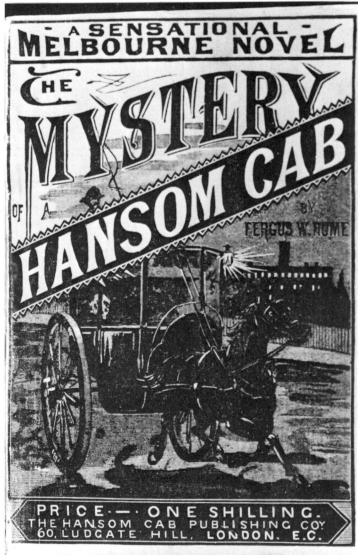

One of the most successful crime and mystery stories ever to be published was written by a New Zealand author. Ferguson Wright Hume (1859–1932), always wrote under the shortened name of Fergus Hume. He was born in England but educated at Otago University in his parents' native land. By the time he was 27 he was working in Melbourne, Australia, as a barrister's clerk, and intent on completing his first book. He dedicated it to the novelist James Payn (1830–98) whose latest work *The Luck of the Darrells*, 3 vols. 1885, he had read and admired. Hume submitted the manuscript to the Melbourne publishers Kemp & Boyce, who immediately accepted it. *The Mystery of a Hansom Cab*, had a first printing of 5,000 copies and was sold out within weeks of its first appearance in October 1886. The price was one shilling a copy. Another three impressions (each of 10,000 copies) were necessitated within a few months, and it has been stated that by the spring of the following year the vast majority of Australians already knew the entire plot by heart.

Hume had gripped his readers' imagination from the start of the first chapter, beginning the work with a dramatic series of action-filled paragraphs that ensured that any prospective purchaser who opened the book would be reluctant to put it down. He commenced with a supposed extract from the *Melbourne Argus*, taken from the issue for 28 July :

> Truth is said to be stranger than fiction, and certainly the extraordinary murder which took place in Melbourne on Thursday night, or rather Friday morning, goes a long way towards verifying this saying. A crime has been committed by an unknown assassin, within a short distance of the principal streets of this great city, and is surrounded by an impenetrable mystery. Indeed, from the nature of the crime itself, the place where it was committed, and the fact that the assassin has escaped without leaving a trace behind him, it would seem as though the case itself had been taken bodily out of one of Gaboreau's [*sic*] novels, and that his famous detective Lecoq only would be able to unravel it. The facts of the case are simple these :
>
> On the twenty-seventh day of July, at the hour of twenty minutes to two o'clock in the morning, a hansom cab drove up to the police station, in Grey Street, St. Kilda, and the driver made the startling statement that his cab contained the body of a man whom he had reason to believe had been murdered . . .

A good enough start to any detective story, with the victim lying dead in a cab at the station door, a silk handkerchief, soaked in chloroform, knotted tightly around his mouth.

> To think that the author of such a crime is at present at large, walking in our midst, and perhaps preparing for the committal of another, is enough to shake the strongest nerves. According to James Payn, the well-known novelist, fact is sometimes in the habit of poaching on the domain of fiction, and curiously enough, this case is a proof or the truth of his saying. In one of Du Boisgobey's stories, entitled *An Omnibus Mystery*, a murder closely resembling this tragedy takes place in an omnibus, but we question if even that author would have been daring enough to have written about a crime being committed in such an unlikely place as a hansom cab. Here is a great chance for some of our detectives to render themselves famous, and we feel sure that they will do their utmost to trace the author of this cowardly and daring murder.

The challenge was accepted, and it was Samuel Gorby, of 'the detective office, Melbourne City Police', that went into action. "I have been finding out things these last twenty years, but this is a puzzler, and no mistake."

The Mystery of a Hansom Cab eventually proved to be one of the biggest money-spinners in the history of fiction, but not for the unfortunate author. In the early part of 1887, after some 35,000 copies had already been printed in the original four Australian impressions, he foolishly parted with the copyright of the book to a sharp-eyed businessman called Frederick Trischler, for a paltry sum. Trischler promptly disappeared to London, and in the early summer of 1887 he and a small group of associates formed the Hansom Cab Publishing Company, with headquarters at 60, Ludgate Hill. They commissioned H. Blacklock & Company, 75, Farringdon Road, London E.C. to print 25,000 copies of *The Mystery of a Hansom Cab* every month, issuing it in pictorially-printed paper wrappers at a shilling a copy, headed on top of the front cover, 'A Sensational Melbourne Mystery'. Success appears to have been immediate. From July 1887 onwards the presses could hardly keep pace with public demand, despite the size of each month's printing. Within 18 months of the original appearance of the work in Melbourne more than a quarter of a million copies had been sold, a figure that has seldom been equalled up to the present day. By the turn of the century no less than twelve foreign translations had been made, and the book was still selling in a variety of formats in both England and the USA.

I searched for a copy to add to my own collection for many years. Once I was just beaten in a telephonic race to be the first to reserve the copy which a provincial bookseller had advertised for sale. "You've missed it by a matter of minutes, sir!" – and a bad-tempered morning to follow. The second time I was successful, but this was nearly three years later, after I had rejected rebound copies on several occasions. Now, at long last, I have an example of *The Mystery of a Hansom Cab*. It is of the second (or first English) edition, with the words 'One Hundreth Thousand' at the head of the title page. I am happy to say that the volume can be described as being in fine state (and I do not use the term 'fine' lightly), in its original, flimsy, pictorially-printed paper wrappers. I think it extremely unlikely that I shall ever discover an earlier or better copy of this ephemeral little publication. Few would have bothered to keep it in the age in which it first appeared, and no self-respecting bookseller would have preserved a secondhand copy at a time when one could have been purchased brand-new for as little as a shilling. The one I finally acquired must have remained unhandled and unread, in some attic chest, for it is as good as the day in which it first left the premises of Trischler's printers (see p. 52). What preserved it from the fate of its paper-wrappered shelf-mates we shall never know.

It is extremely unlikely that I shall ever be lucky enough to discover an earlier or better example, for if a first (Australian) edition should ever come on the market it would probably make well over £200 ($500). A good copy of a second (English) edition is worth in the region of £80 ($200) for very few examples have survived. A rebound copy would be worth only about a tenth of this amount, as much of the charm and character of the book is embodied in its luridly printed pictorial covers. Of the true first issue of the first edition only two copies are known. Both are in the collection of the Mitchell Library, Sydney, Australia.

It was not long before Fergus Hume heard about the phenomenal success of his first attempt at a detective story and promptly scraped together the fare, to take an immediate passage to England. During the months of voyage he appears to have written two further novels: *Madame Midas*, described as being a 'realistic and sensational story of Australian mining life', and *The Girl from Malta*. Both these were issued by The Hansom Cab Publishing Co., dated 1888, in pictorially-printed paper wrappers, the latter carrying a portrait of Hume on page seven. Both had lawyers acting the part of detectives, the first a Mr Calton, and the second Gerald Foster, barrister of the Middle Temple. After these two books, the author finally parted company with Frederick Trischler. His next novel was published by F. V. White, London, as *The Piccadilly Puzzle*, 1889, featuring Mr Dowker, a private detective, followed by another under the same publisher's imprint entitled *Miss Mephistopheles*, 1890, being a sequel to *Madame Midas*, with Detective Laball of the Melbourne Police acting as investigator.

In the meantime, the Hansom Cab Publishing Co., had changed its name to Trischler & Company, and from 1889 onwards continued printing about 5,000 copies a year of that perennial best-seller *The Mystery of a Hansom Cab*, without, as far as is known, paying Fergus Hume a penny in royalties. In 1895, Trischler finally disposed of the copyright to Jarrold & Son, a well-known London publishing house, and then disappeared from sight, and was not met with again in the literary world.

Hume settled in England, and began churning out as many as three full-length novels a year, changing his publishers almost as often as he changed his titles. In all, he is credited with over 140 different works, none of which reached anything like the popularity of his first book. Amongst his best detective stories are *The Fever of Life*, 2 vols. 1892; *The Black Carnation* (1892); *The Harlequin Opal*, 1893; *The Chinese Jar*, 1893; *The Lone Inn*, 1894; *The Crime of the 'Liza Jane'*, 1895; *The Masquerade Mystery* (1895); *The Silent House in Pimlico*, 1899; and *The Crimson Cryptogram*, 1900.

Hume acknowledged his indebtedness to Fortuné du Boisgobey in the opening chapter of his most famous book, and it is from the French author's story *An*

Omnibus Mystery, that he gleaned the idea that resulted in the fame by which he is still remembered today. *The Mystery of a Hansom Cab* was published at the end of what we may term the pre-Holmesian era. It appeared only a year before the first printing of *A Study in Scarlet*, the work which introduced the master-mind of logical deduction to a readership that soon spanned the English-speaking world. The name that gave Hume his title is believed to have been first used in 1847, the vehicle being described in *The Oxford English Dictionary* as 'a low-hung two-wheeled cabriolet holding two persons inside, the driver being mounted on a dickey behind, and the reins going over the roof'. Disraeli, in his novel *Lothair*, 3 vols. 1870, called the hansom cab 'the gondola of London'.

A number of minor writers, most of whose names are now forgotten by all except a handful of ardent bibliophiles, busied themselves with novels in which crime and detection were the central themes during the twenty-five years that preceded the advent of Sherlock Holmes in 1897. This was a period in which the influence of Poe and the French writers of detective fiction was all-pervading. Very few of their works passed the stage of first editions, and even less reached the dignified heights of acceptance by the circulating libraries with an issue in the mandatory three volumes. So, with few bibliographies to guide you, this is an exciting period in which to collect – even if prized volumes are but slowly acquired.

A generation or so ago a collector would have been venturing into almost untrodden territory : the books were on the shelves and at prices even the most impecunious could afford. There are still bargains to be picked up today, for in the field of detective fiction sometimes the most unpromising titles are rewarding.

A heavily-disguised detective of 1876. An illustration from *Where the Rail Runs Now: A Story of Coaching Days*, 1876, by F. Frankfort Moore.

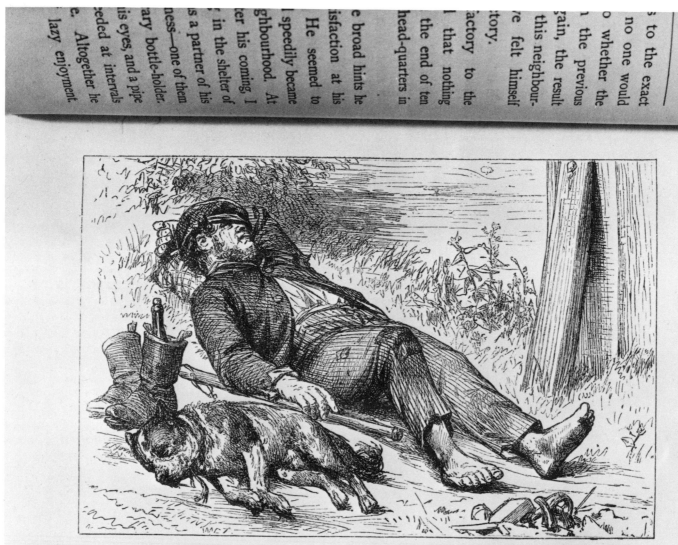

P. 36.

54

The murderer unmasked! The frontispiece of *Where the Rail Runs Now*.

Size of engraved surface: 13 cm × 9.5 cm.

BROUGHT TO BAY.—P. 238.

I remember taking down from the shelves of a small antiquarian bookseller's premises in Oxford a work called *Where the Rail Runs Now*, 1876, by F. Frankfort Moore, a writer who advertised himself as being the author of *Sojourners Together*, and *Flying from a Shadow*. The sub-title announced the book as 'A Story of Coaching Days', and it was as a novel of life on the road that I bought the little cloth-bound octavo. It was blocked on the red of its front cover with a picture of a four-in-hand, and below this, a long-funnelled railway engine belching steam and smoke. A few weeks later I picked it up as a volume for bedtime reading and discovered that it was a first-class tale of detective fiction. There was even a heavily-disguised Scotland Yard officer to carry out the final arrest, as I have shown in the illustration. Not surprisingly, with a title as misleading as this, it is a work that has escaped the notice of bibliographers, and there are countless others produced during the same period, 1870–1900, that still await recognition.

A few of the titles in my collection that follow the earlier yellow-backs include the stories by James M'Govan, such as *Brought to Bay; or, Experiences of a City Detective*, 1878; *Hunted Down; or, Recollections of a City Detective*, 1878; *Strange Clues; or, Chronicles of a City Detective*, 1881; and *Traced and Tracked; or, Memoirs of a City Detective*, 1884. A representative selection of other titles include *In the Dead of Night*, 3 vols. 1874, by T. W. Speight; *Fast and Loose*, 3 vols. 1885, by Major Arthur Griffiths, who also wrote *The Rome Express*, 1896, and *Ford's Folly Ltd*, 1900; *The Cliff Mystery*, 1888, by Hamilton Aïde; *A Recoiling Vengence*, 1888, by Frank Barrett, whose *Under a Strange Mask*, 2 vols. 1889, is also a detective story; and *Bazi Bazoum; or, A Strange Detective*, 1889, by Charles Matthews.

In 1874 the first of the Pinkerton detective stories, *The Expressman and the Detective*, appeared in Chicago, USA, under the imprint of Keen, Cooke & Company. The author, Allan Pinkerton (1819–84), was born in Glasgow, Scotland, and settled in Illinois, USA, early in the 1840s. From the time he stepped ashore in his adopted country he seems to have made crime, or rather the unmasking of the criminal, his vocation, for within a few months he had trapped a gang of counterfeiters and brought them to justice. He was so good at detection that by 1846 he had succeeded in being promoted to deputy sheriff of Kane County, Illinois. Four years later he became chief of the detective division of the Chicago police force. The same year (1850) he established the world-famous private detective agency that still bears his name.

It was in the 1870s, the middle of the hansom cab era, that Pinkerton conceived the idea of a series of detective tales based on the factual backgrounds of his more sensational cases. Soon he was churning out story after story of the profession he knew so well, nearly always with himself as the master detective, or with a Pinkerton agent as investigator. He never missed a chance to advertise his agency, and most of his volumes were illustrated with engravings and had as a front cover design an unblinking eye, accompanied by his firm's slogan 'We Never Sleep'. *Claude Melnotte as a Detective*, 1875; *The Detective and the Somnambulist*, 1875; *The Model Town and the Detectives*, 1876; *Criminal Reminiscences and Detective Sketches*, 1878; *The Gypsies and the Detectives*, 1879, are some of his better-known titles. There was also a later series by his son Frank, issued monthly from March, 1887, by Laird & Lee, Chicago. The embracing title was *The Frank Pinkerton Detective Series*, and included stories such as *Dyke Darrel the Railroad Detective*; *$5,000 Reward*; and *Jim Cummings; or, the Great Adams Express Robbery*. Fine copies of any of them are exceedingly scarce, but this observation applies to nearly all early editions of detective fiction of the period before the end of the first quarter of the 20th century. The mixture of fact and fiction in Pinkerton's books made them extremely popular in the USA, and to a lesser extent in Britain. Few copies survived the succession of readers who battered the books with the enjoyment of reading in the first decade of their existence. Like other popular novels, they passed from the hands of the original purchaser to those of his family and friends, which left the books dog-eared and dejected. Library copies suffered the same fate in about a quarter of the time.

John R. Coryell had a different approach from that employed by Pinkerton. He modelled his techniques on those employed by the London publishing firm of Hogarth House, sponsors of the famous series of *Jack Harkaway Stories*, written by Bracebridge Hemyng, the first of which appeared in the July 1871, issue of *Boys of England Magazine*. Hogarth House ran a special section of their *Gem Pocket Library*, which offered detective stories of '128 pages of new and original text, illustrated, in coloured wrappers' at the bargain price of twopence a volume. In the USA that type of cheap literature came to be known as the Dime Novels. These made their original appearance in the mid-1860s (the term is believed to have been first used in 1865). The public enjoyed reading novelettes and luridly illustrated magazines, and was now to have its insatiable appetite for detective fiction catered for by a long series of single-volume novels. Cowboys and Red Indians were rapidly being supplanted in public favour by more sophisticated crime and detection stories set in urban surroundings, and the credit for the change of taste must be accorded in large degree to the exploits of the John R. Coryell's ubiquitous investigator Nick Carter.

The Adventures of Nick Carter derived many themes from the French novelists discussed in a previous chapter, but the tales were nearly always set in America. The hero first appeared in a long-running serial called *The Old Detective's Pupil*, published in the *New York Weekly* during 1884. Carter himself is introduced as a young orphan whose father had just been killed by gangsters, and he decides forthwith to devote his life to the task of bringing the murderers to justice. Most of the early paper-backed novels carried an announcement on their back covers which was surprisingly frank about the similarity of

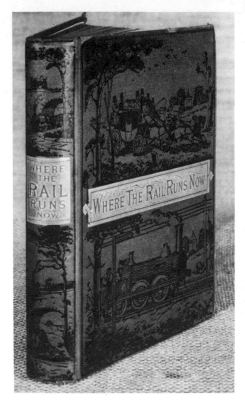

An important early work of detective fiction, with a most unlikely-sounding title: shown here in the first edition, dated 1876, and discussed on page 55.

Height of spine: 17.5 cm.

Opposite, top left
The Sexton Blake stories started as far back as 1894, the first appearance of this legendary hero being in the magazine *Union Jack* in the issue dated 4 April of that year. The *Sexton Blake Library*, shown above, was still cataloguing his adventures well into the 1960 s.

Size of front cover: 18 cm × 13.5 cm.

Sexton Blake's junior partner 'Tinker', his next-door neighbour in Baker Street, London, and a young man endowed with all the enviable attributes.

Bottom left
One of the many magazines that featured the Sexton Blake stories. The three issues shown were published in 1912–5.

Size of front cover: 27.7 cm × 19.4 cm.

Bottom right
One of the Aldine Library's juvenile detective stories, published in 1895. Other titles included *Joe Phoenix, the Police Spy*; and *Buffalo Bill's Double; or, The Desparate Detectives*.

Size of front cover: 22 cm × 14 cm.

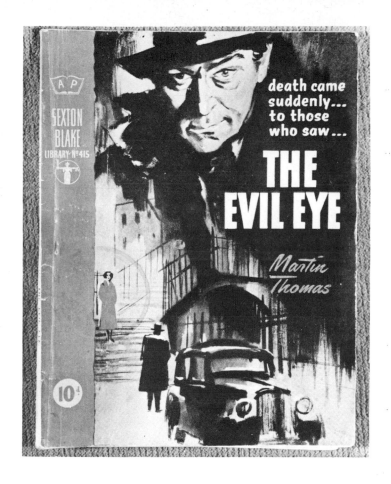

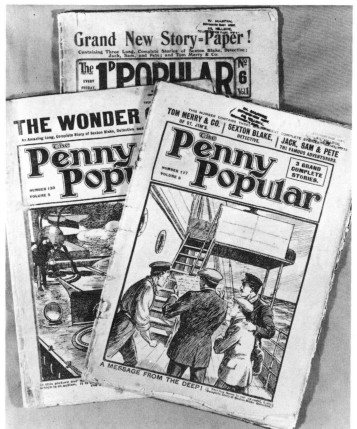

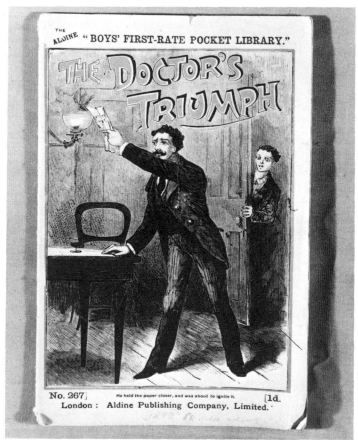

the newly-printed tales with all that had gone before :

Nick Carter stands for an interesting detective story. The fact that the books in this line are so uniformly good is entirely due to the work of a specialist. The man who wrote these stories produced no other type of fiction. His mind was concentrated upon the creation of new plots and situations, in which his hero emerged triumphantly from all sorts of trouble, and landed the criminal just where he should be – behind bars. If your dealer cannot supply you with exactly the book you want, you are almost sure to find in his stock another title by the same author which you have not read.

Coryell's detective stories won such an immense following that at one time he was commissioned to write a million words a year featuring the exploits of Nick Carter. With a team of hack-writers churning out story after story from his own series of basic plots, he achieved this target with little difficulty.

In England they were almost equally popular. They first appeared in *The People's Pocket Story Books*, selling at threepence apiece, before the founding of *Nick Carter's Magazine*. As a detective hero he ran our own immortal Sexton Blake a close second in popular favour. The long series of *Sexton Blake Stories*, comprising *The Adventures of Sexton Blake*, and scores of other titles, led to the formation of *The Sexton Blake Magazine*, which enjoyed an enviable circulation for many years. He appears to have been a compilation of several writers and it is not known who originally created a character who was as widely popular in his day as James Bond, in a later age.

The century drew to a close with The Parlour Car Publishing Company in New York issuing a series of several hundred pictorially-printed paper-wrapped detective tales under the general title of *Old Sleuth's Own*, each at a dime (see illustration p. 57). In London, The Aldine Publishing Company was just as industrious, and by 1900 its series of *Detective Tales*, selling at twopence, had exceeded the three hundred mark. They all chronicled the exploits of those fearless investigators, Mr Pulcher, and his assistant Thrash, the cleverly disguised Harry Hunter, known as 'The Bootblack Detective', and of course the pert and precocious Daisy Bell, known to her readers without a blush as 'The Pavement Detective'.

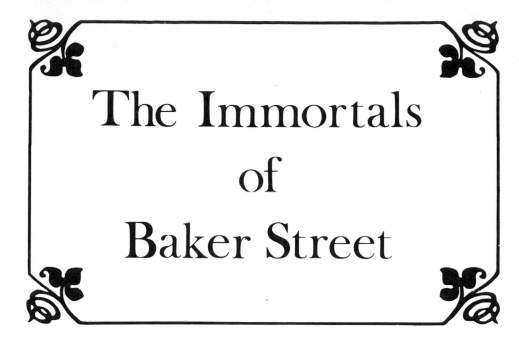

The Immortals of Baker Street

As to my companion neither the country nor the sea presented the slightest attraction to him. He loved to lie in the very centre of five millions of people with his filaments stretching out and running through them, responsive to every little rumour or suspicion of unsolved crime.

SPECIMEN OF THE MS. OF "THE ADVENTURES OF SHERLOCK HOLMES.

A specimen of the original manuscript of one of *The Adventures of Sherlock Holmes*, by Conan Doyle.

It is only about once in every generation that a fictional character assumes a life of his own and steps out from the pages of literature into our day to day existence. These *genii* of the printed page do not age as ordinary men – they are the familiars who by sheer force of personality attain immortality and undying fame. Tens of thousands of ordinary mortals, who may not have read a single paragraph of the stories which gave their heroes birth, conjure up their image, correct in every detail, as soon as they hear their name. To speak the magic words unfolds a wide panorama – an exotic way of life totally divorced from everyday existence, yet somehow as intimately familiar in general aspect as one's closest friend. From Robinson Crusoe to James Bond is a long way; but each has secured his honoured place in this select band. In the most honoured place in the hierarchy stands Sherlock Holmes.

The consulting rooms at Number 221b, Baker Street, Marylebone, where fearful and distracted clients brought their problems to be solved by the master, and where their stories were preserved for posterity by his stubbornly faithful friend and chronicler, Dr Watson, have been known and visited in the mind's eye for nearly a hundred years by readers throughout the world. During the Festival of Britain in 1951, the local borough council debated whether to stage a display showing the progress of St. Marylebone throughout the ages, or to plan a Sherlock Holmes Exhibition in order 'to honour our most distinguished resident'. They carried out the latter plan, to the unbounded delight of enthusiasts from all parts of the world, many thousands of whom flocked to the restored 'Number 221b, Baker Street' in order to inspect the master's lodgings for themselves. The personality of the greatest of detectives lived on : the consulting room was as he left it on the day of the fatal trip in which he encountered his arch-enemy Professor Moriarty face to face on the ledge overhanging the precipitous Reichenbach Falls. Everything was as he and Watson had left it – 'his cigars in the coal-scuttle, his tobacco in the toe of a Persian slipper, and his unanswered correspondence transfixed by a jack-knife into the very centre of his wooden mantlepiece'. There, too, were what now amounted to the insignia of his amateur profession – his silk dressing-gown, his Inverness cape, and the inevitable deer-stalker cap. On the table were his newspapers, dated April 1891, his magnifying-glass, and one of his curly-stemmed briars. Discarded hypodermic-syringes still lay in a drawer in his desk, and the beloved companion of his leisure hourse, his Stradivarius, lay silent in its velvet-lined case. Sherlock

Left
This montage depicting the Sherlock Holmes stories appeared in *The Bookman Special Christmas Number 1929*, an issue largely devoted to detective fiction and the supernatural.

Holmes seemed very much alive.

His personal creator, the man who gave birth to a legend that will endure far beyound our present day, was Arthur Conan Doyle (1859–1930). Born in Edinburgh, Scotland, the eldest son of a clerk in the Board of Works, he was educated at Stonyhurst and at Edinburgh University. He studied medicine, and qualified as a doctor in 1881, setting up his practice in Southsea, near Portsmouth in Hampshire, where he lived and worked until 1890. It was while he was still a student in Edinburgh that he came under the influence of Joseph Bell, an eminent consulting surgeon, who was to act as his tutor. It was Bell who later gave him the idea that revolutionised his whole life, and inspired the figure that was to make his name a household word.

By 1886, Conan Doyle had already published several short stories, and had finally completed a full-length novel, *The Firm of Girdlestone*, which was returned with polite rejection slips by every publishing house to whom he submitted it. His medical practice earned him little or nothing, his writing even less. But he had by no means given up hope of one day earning a living by his pen. His own comments, contained in his *Memories and Adventures*, 1924, reveal the sudden decision that marked the turning point in his fortunes:

> I felt now that I was capable of something fresher and crisper and more workmanlike. Gaboriau had rather attracted me by the neat dove-tailing of his plots, and Poe's masterful detective, M. Dupin, had from boyhood been one of my heroes. But could I bring an addition of my own? I thought of my old teacher, Joe Bell, of his eagle face, of his curious ways, of his eerie trick of spotting details. If he were a detective he would surely reduce this fascinating but unorganised business to something nearer to an exact science.

I would try if I could get this effect . . . It is all very well to say that a man is clever, but the reader wants to see examples of it, such examples as Bell gave us every day in the wards. The idea amused me. What should I call the fellow? First it was Sherringford Holmes – then it was Sherlock Holmes. He could not tell his own exploits, so he must have a commonplace comrade as a foil. A drab, quiet name for this unostentatious man. Watson would do. So I had my puppets and wrote my *Study in Scarlet*.

Despite Conan Doyle's confidence in his latest creation, for many weary months this second story suffered much the same fate as his earlier (and so far unpublished) novel. It shuttled backwards and forwards between author and publishing houses, until finally, after a longer than usual interval, he opened a letter containing an outright offer of £25 for the copyright. Even then there was

" Lestrade and Holmes sprang upon him like so many staghounds." (Page 116.)

The frontispiece for a late (1901) edition of *A Study in Scarlet*, with the likeness of Sherlock Holmes by George Hutchinson quite differently portrayed from the well-loved character created in pictorial form by Sidney Paget.

Size of page: 18.8 cm × 12 cm.

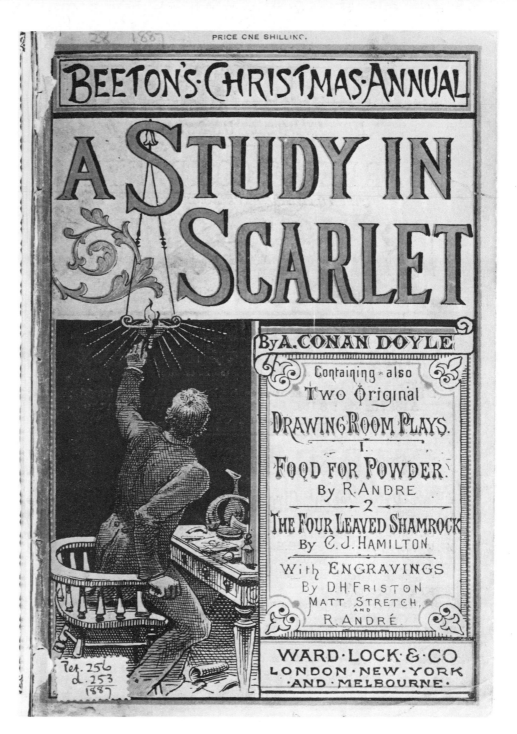

The first appearance of Sherlock Holmes. A copy of one of the few surviving paper-wrappered 1887 editions of *Beeton's Christmas Annual*.
Reproduced by courtesy of *The Bodleian Library, Oxford*.

a snag. He was asked to agree to a delay amounting to some fifteen months before publication of the work. For a writer expecting at least a three-figure offer for his manuscript, for a story he was convinced would quickly become a best-seller, this paltry sum was almost a personal insult. Nevertheless, he badly needed the money, and, as he kept assuring himself, he would at least have the satisfaction of seeing his own name in print. The words, 'Author of . . .' would look impressive on any future title page. That same night he wrote to Messrs. Ward, Lock & Co., and accepted their terms.

It was November 1887 before *A Study in Scarlet* actually appeared in print. It occupied the leading position in the 28th issue of *Beeton's Christmas Annual*, a periodical that appeared in pictorial paper wrappers at the end of each succeeding year. It was here, in this ephemeral little annual, that Sherlock Holmes first made his bow. The issue sold at one shilling a copy. An estimate of the value set on it by collectors of detective fiction in our own day and age can be gauged by the few copies to change hands in recent times. In its original pictorially printed paper wrappers a copy of the 1887 issue of *Beeton's Christmas Annual* is today worth well over £1,000 ($2,500).

The story received little praise from contemporary critics, despite its appearance as a novel in hard covers later the following year. The book did, however,

EDITORIAL OFFICE OF " THE STRAND MAGAZINE."

result in an offer of a substantial advance being made to Doyle by the American publishing house responsible for issuing *Lippincott's Magazine.* They commissioned him to write a second detective story, including his investigators Sherlock Holmes and Dr Watson – an offer the writer gratefully accepted. In February, 1890, *The Sign of Four* made its appearance in the magazine as a serial, to be published in volume form under a London imprint in the same year. Conan Doyle's fortunes were turning. 1890 also saw the publication of his long-delayed *The Firm of Girdlestone,* and another story : *The Captain of the Polestar, and other Tales,* (neither of which contain any elements of detective fiction). But *The Sign of Four* soon became a popular success on both sides of the Atlantic ; fame and fortune were at last knocking at his door.

In London, the owner of the newly-born *Strand Magazine* was eager for fresh literary talent. George Newnes (1851–1910), had made a fortune as the founder of *Tit-Bits,* a magazine wholly devoted to the lightest of reading and most sensational of anecdotes. Now he was aiming to capture a larger share of the middle-class market with an illustrated periodical of a popular nature but of higher literary and artistic quality. The first issue appeared early in January 1891, in pictorial paper wrappers, priced at sixpence a copy. In June and December of each year a bi-annual volume of the monthly parts was issued, each bound in light blue cloth over bevelled boards, blocked pictorially in black and gold. The first two volumes, dated 1891, bore the address 'Burleigh Street, Strand' on their title-pages and on the street-sign on their front covers. In all the later issues, this was changed on title pages and binding to read 'Southampton Street'.

From the first issue in January, Newnes set out to give the public its money's worth, promising in his preface that the magazine would 'contain stories and articles by the best British writers, and special translations from the first foreign authors. These will be illustrated by eminent artists'. He kept his word, and the first bi-annual volume listed in its index the names of Grant Allen,

H. Greenhough Smith, literary editor of *The Strand Magazine,* the man to whom the creator of Sherlock Holmes first submitted his manuscripts.

Gentlemanly murder committed in a dignified manner, in a more leisurely age. The illustration shows the frontispiece of *The Missing Delora,* 1910, by E. Phillips Oppenheim, one of the few titles of detective fiction of the period to have all its plates colour-printed.

WHEN BARTOT SAW US HE FELL BACK WITH A THEATRICAL START

LE GRAND JOURNAL
KIDNAPPED
ECE
DARING
ISTERY
LUPIN
TEST NEWS

The decision to change the name of the thoroughfare from Burleigh Street to Southampton Street, and the building numbers, is reflected on these early and later paper-wrappered monthly issues of *The Strand Magazine*.

CLEVER DETECTIVES.

" GIVE THEM A CHANCE."

Have you a clue? Do you miss anything? Is anything wrong? Was the first look into the mirror this morning productive of a satisfactory murmur something akin to "Why was I born so beautiful"? or was it followed by a miserable, moaning "I'm a little off colour again"? If the latter, there's a clue. Do not procrastinate. The detectives should at once be called in to play their part. Now, the "Sherlock Holmes" in cases of this kind is "Beecham's Pills"; no fear of them getting on the wrong scent. They will soon discover the lost appetite, and restore the Rosebud of Health. These private inquiry agents will let you know if your friend, liver, has again "sold you a spotted dog" so to speak, and they will have a full report to make before they have done with you.

RELIABLE INFORMATION.

Inspector:—"Here you have something to start with : I always maintain Beecham's Pills are worth a Guinea a Box : they have often been of great assistance to me."

Advertisers were quick to exploit the popularity of Sherlock Holmes. This advertisement lauding the detective qualities of Beecham's Pills appeared in *The Strand Magazine* in May 1894.

Suave and impenetrable, the great French detective Arsène Lupin on the way to solving yet another case of wilful murder. The illustration is from the front cover of the first English edition of *The Hollow Needle*, 1911, by Maurice Leblanc.

Alexander Dumas, Bret Harte, E. W. Hornung, Michael Lermontoff, Prosper Mérimée, Alfred de Musset, Alexander Pushkin, and Stanley Weyman, among a host of other writers. Gordon Browne, Paul Hardy, A. Ludovici, Sidney Paget, W. Rainey, W. S. Stacey, and G. F. Watts, were the chief illustrators. The editor (in fact, though not in name) was Greenhough Smith, whose strong interest in police and detective work was reflected in some of the stories printed in the first issues, with *A Night with the Thames Police* as a leading piece. *Three Birds on a Stile*, by B. L. Farjeon, was the first story of detective fiction he printed, but both Newnes and Smith had read and admired *The Sign of Four* and a personal letter was sent to Doyle offering him attractive terms for a series of tales featuring his Baker Street characters.

The first of the series of six short detective stories made its appearance in the issue for July 1891, and all were incorporated in the second cloth-bound volume issued at the end of that year. *A Scandal in Bohemia* was soon followed by *The Red-Headed League*, and then *A Case of Identity*. By the time that *The Boscombe Valley Mystery* and *The Five Orange Pips* had appeared, public interest was intense and the circulation figures of the magazine were rocketing. *The Man With the Twisted Lip* completed the six contracted Sherlock Holmes stories, and the editor immediately asked for more. Conan Doyle just as promptly refused. He was determined to write a new historical novel to complement his earlier *Micah Clarke*, 1889. Smith, prompted by Newnes, wrote again, asking Conan Doyle to name his own terms, and with public interest at its height, and a shoal of fan-mail arriving by every post, the author found it difficult to resist the pressure. He decided to ask a price he felt sure would be refused. But almost by return of post came a reply accepting and enclosing a substantial cheque in part-payment. The historical researches were reluctantly abandoned for the time being, and six more Sherlock Holmes adventures were conceived and written.

By this time, Conan Doyle's story, *The White Company* was appearing in *The Cornhill Magazine*, and was later issued as a three-volume novel, dated 1891. He had acquired a literary agent, A. P. Watt, who he afterwards admitted 'relieved me of all the hateful bargaining, and handled things so well that any immediate anxiety for money soon disappeared'. But, just as things seemed to be going along really well, he was suddenly struck down with a severe attack of influenza. In many ways this was the turning point in Conan Doyle's life. As he lay ill, and at one point close to death, he had time to think :

> For a week I was in great danger, and then found myself as weak as a child and as emotional, but with a mind as clear as crystal. It was then, as I surveyed my own life, that I saw how foolish I was to waste my literary earnings in keeping up an oculist's room in Wimpole Street, and I determined with a wild rush of joy to cut the painter and trust for ever to my power of writing. I remember in my delight taking the handkerchief which lay upon the coverlet in my enfeebled hand, and tossing it up to the ceiling in my exultation. I should at last be my own master. No longer would I have to conform to professional dress or try to please any one else. I should be free to live how I liked and where I liked. It was one of the great moments of exultation of my life. The date was in August, 1891 . . . I settled down with a stout heart to do some literary work worthy of the name. The difficulty of the Holmes work was that every story really needed as clear-cut and original a plot as a longish book would do. One cannot without effort spin plots at such a rate. They are apt to become thin or break. I was determined, now that I had no longer the excuse of absolute pecuniary pressure, never again to write anything which was not as good as I could possibly make it, and therefore I would not write a Holmes story without a worthy plot and without a problem which interested my own mind, for that is the first requisite before you can interest any one else.

When he discussed the text of these stories with his mother, whom he always quoted as his shrewdest critic, he told her in a letter (printed by John Dickson Carr in *The Life of Sir Arthur Conan Doyle*, 1949): 'I think of slaying Holmes in the last, and winding him up for good and all. He takes my mind from better things'. This confession absolutely appalled her : 'You won't! You can't! You mustn't!' she angrily stormed in reply. He hesitated but finally altered his mind, and the second series of six tales, which had commenced with *The*

Conan Doyle and his wife, photographed July 1892, outside their home in South Norwood, London.

A Day with Dr. Conan Doyle.

BY HARRY HOW.

From a Photo, by] DR CONAN DOYLE AND MRS. CONAN DOYLE. *[Elliott & Fry.*

DETECTIVISM up to date— that is what Dr. Conan Doyle has given us. We were fast becoming weary of the representative of the old school; he was, at his best, a very ordinary mortal, and, with the palpable clues placed in his path, the average lock Holmes entered the criminal arena. He started on the track. A clever fellow; a cool, calculating fellow, this Holmes. He could see the clue to a murder in a ball of worsted, and certain conviction in a saucer of milk. The little things we regarded as nothings were all and everything to Holmes. He was an artful fellow, too;

Adventure of the Blue Carbuncle, continued with one of his best and most thrilling stories – *The Adventure of the Speckled Band* – and finally ended with *The Adventure of the Copper Beeches.*

Conan Doyle was also lucky with his illustrator, in much the same manner as Lewis Carroll with John Tenniel. The *Adventures* which appeared in *The Strand Magazine* were accompanied by a brilliant series of illustrations from the pen of the talented young artist, Sidney Paget (1860–1908), whose pictures exactly captured the atmosphere of the text. His portraits of Holmes have been accepted as speaking likenesses ever since, and have moulded our image of the master detective.

The last of the *Adventures of Sherlock Holmes* appeared in the *Strand* in June 1892, but if Conan Doyle thought that a round dozen of Holme's exploits would be enough to satisfy his readers he was very much mistaken. For some of the monthly issues, queues of prospective purchasers had formed outside the offices of the magazine and the latest exploits of the Baker Street detective and his faithful aide were discussed in homes and offices throughout the country. The one fear of the editor of *The Strand* was that a rival publisher would offer better financial terms, and he lost no time asking Conan Doyle to submit further stories. 'They have been bothering me for more Sherlock Holmes tales', the author wrote to his mother in February, 1892. 'Under pressure I offered to do a dozen for a thousand pounds, but I sincerely hope they won't accept it.' But accept it they did, and his terms were agreed immediately.

66

In December 1892, the thirteenth story appeared, entitled *The Adventure of Silver Blaze*, and formed part of volume IV in the cloth-bound issue of the magazine. Volume V contained six more tales, and volume VI, covering the period July to December 1893, a further five, making a total for the two series of 24. It was the last story, *The Adventure of the Final Problem*, that caused a furious outcry from thousands of readers who had been avidly following every move of Sherlock Holmes throughout the series. In it, Watson sadly related the events leading to his friend's fatal meeting with his arch-enemy Professor Moriarty, an encounter which culminated in a death-grapple on a narrow ledge overlooking a sheer drop of several hundred feet into the pool below the Reichenbach Falls. Watson's final words to his readers were explicit:

> An examination by experts leaves little doubt that a personal contest between the two men ended, as it could hardly fail to end in such a situation, in their reeling over, locked in each other's arms. Any attempt at recovering the bodies was absolutely hopeless, and there, deep down in that dreadful cauldron of swirling water and seething foam, will lie for all time the most dangerous criminal and the foremost champion of the law of their generation.

Not only the *Strand Magazine*, but the author himself was deluged in an avalanche of letters of protest from grief-stricken readers. Clerks in London offices took to wearing black arm bands as a sign of mourning, and several letters Conan Doyle received were frankly abusive. One, from a young lady in her late 'teens, started with the words 'You beast!' It was months before the clamour died down. Newnes had previously hastened to assure his many subscribers:

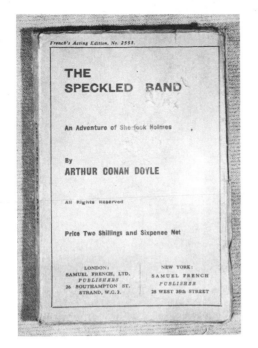

The first separate printing of *The Speckled Band*, published undated in 1910. The play opened at The Adelphi Theatre, London, on 4 June 1910, and was revived at The Strand in February 1911, and at The St. James's in September 1921.

Size of front cover:
19 cm × 13 cm.

Right
Monthly issues of *The Strand Magazine* were also issued biannually in pictorially-printed cloth-bound volumes.

Size of front cover:
25 cm × 17 cm.

There will be only a temporary interval in the Sherlock Holmes stories. A new series will commence in an early number. Meanwhile, powerful detective stories will be contributed by eminent writers.

This assurance had been given in the interval between the end of the first series and the commencement of the second, and had been printed as early as July 1892. This time Conan Doyle remained adamant, refusing to write any further detective adventures and concentrating on finishing *The Stark Munro Letters*,

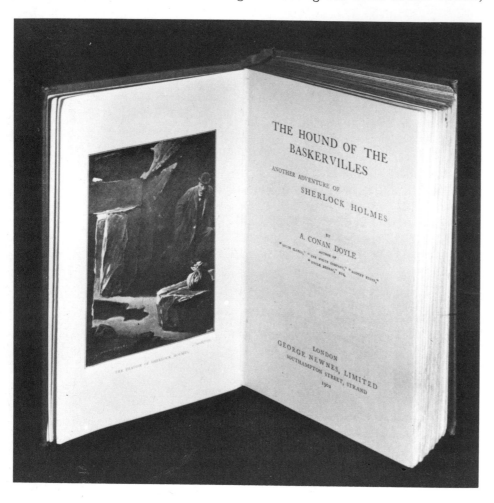

The most famous of Conan Doyle's full-length detective stories.

Size of title-page: 18.5 cm × 12 cm.

then appearing in *The Idler Magazine*, while *The Strand* had to be content with *The Exploits of Brigadier Gerard*. *Rodney Stone* was published in 1896, and *Uncle Bernac* the following year, and it was not until 1901 that *The Strand* commenced serialising *The Hound of the Baskervilles*, later published as a novel, dated 1902. Originally, the author did not contemplate making it a Sherlock Holmes story, but as the plot gradually took shape and the characters took command of the action it was Holmes that dominated the scene and Watson that once again chronicled events. The story was set 'in the 'eighties', to allow for the later tragedy at the Reichenbach Falls, and Watson carefully explained that the events he related ante-dated that regretful affair. The public's appetite had once again been whetted by savouring one of the best detective stories ever written, and amid the general acclaim and plaudits of the crowd the author's resolution not, under any circumstances, to resurrect his hero, weakened like a New Year's pledge.

In the meantime, two of the great cornerstones of any worthwhile collection of first editions of detective fiction had been published in book form. *The Adventures of Sherlock Holmes*, 1892, appeared as a tall and heavy octavo, bound in smooth blue cloth over bevelled boards, the leaf edges gilded, and with the front cover and spine blocked in black and gold. *The Memoirs of Sherlock Holmes*, 1894, was issued in exactly similar format, but in a dark blue cloth, and contained eleven (of the original twelve) Holmes stories that comprised the second collection of *Adventures* in *The Strand Magazine*. The author dedicated the first of the two volumes to his old tutor on whom he had modelled his now world-famous detective – Joseph Bell, M.D. The first issue of this title

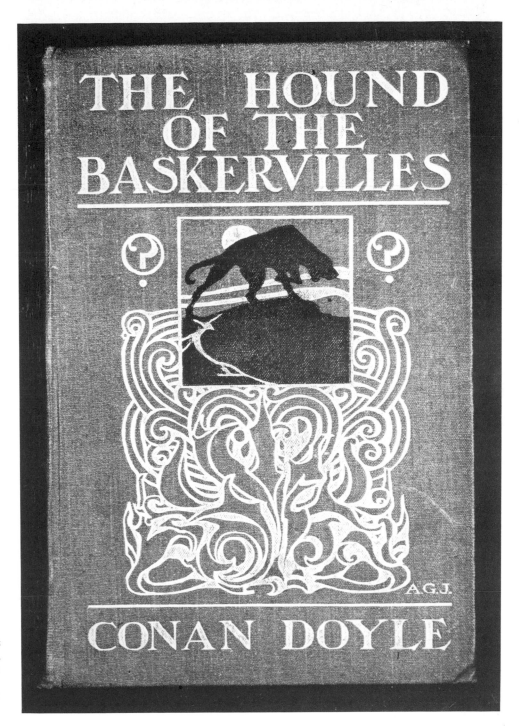

THE HOUND OF THE BASKERVILLES

CONAN DOYLE

A.G.J.

The first edition of one of Conan Doyle's most successful Sherlock Holmes stories, published in 1902. A copy in good condition now fetches about £50.

Size of front cover:
19 cm × 12 cm.

has the oblong street-sign left blank (high on the wall in the picture of the Strand on the front cover). In later issues of the first edition the name 'Southampton Street' has been filled in. The reason for this can be seen when the cloth-bound volumes of the magazine are examined. The first two bi-annual volumes carry the name 'Burleigh Street' in this position, but on volume three this is changed to 'Southampton Street', at a time when *The Adventures of Sherlock Holmes* was about to be issued in book form. Until the re-named street had its sign in place the artist was correct in leaving it blank, so that the first few hundred copies have no street name. A set of the two first editions in as fine condition as the pair shown in the coloured plate would now be worth in the region of £200 ($500).

It was in the spring of 1903 that Conan Doyle at last consented to restore Holmes to life. As soon as a preliminary announcement to this effect was made there was a rush to obtain copies of *The Strand* containing the first of the new series of stories. *The Adventures of the Empty House* appeared in the issue for October, 1903, and by lunch time on the day of publication, long queues had formed outside Newnes' offices in Southampton Street. The printing presses had to be kept going night and day to keep pace with the demand, and, according to eye-witnesses, 'the scenes at the railway bookstalls were worse . . . than a

Not all the Conan Doyle stories that appeared in *The Strand Magazine* featured Sherlock Holmes. *The Story of the Brazilian Cat*, a tale of attempted murder, appeared in the December 1898 issue, illustrated by Sidney Paget.

bargain sale'. In the USA the series of stories appeared in *Collier's Weekly*, with the famous Frederic Dorr Steele illustrations, and the tales later appeared in book form with the predictable title of *The Return of Sherlock Holmes*, 1905.

In response to the continuing demand, Conan Doyle eventually produced three more Holmes books. The first, a long novel, was titled *The Valley of Fear*, 1915, and ran as a serial in *The Strand Magazine* during 1914–15. Thirty-three more short stories were later collected as *His Last Bow*, 1917, and *The Case-Book of Sherlock Holmes*, 1927. This last title appeared only a year or two before the author's death, and in his preface to the work, Conan Doyle, now in his 69th year, reflected on the way the character he had created in 1887 had gradually assumed a personality stronger than his own.

> I fear that Mr Sherlock Holmes may become like one of those popular tenors who, having outlived their time, are still tempted to make repeated farewell bows to their indulgent audiences. This must cease and he must go the way of all flesh, material or imaginary . . . His career has been a long one – though it is possible to exaggerate it; decrepit gentlemen who approach me and declare that his adventures formed the reading of their boyhood do not meet the response from me which they seem to expect.
>
> I was fully determined at the conclusion of *The Memoirs* to bring Holmes to an end, as I felt my literary energies should not be directed too much into one channel. That pale, clear-cut face and loose-limbed figure were taking up an undue share of my imagination. I did the deed, but, fortunately, no coroner had pronounced upon the remains, and so, after a long interval, it

was not difficult for me to respond to the flattering demand and to explain my rash act away . . . Had Holmes never existed I could not have done more, though he may perhaps have stood a little in the way of the recognition of my more serious literary work. And so, reader, farewell to Sherlock Holmes!

The immense popularity of his detective stories stems from Conan Doyle's fortuitous amalgam of several contrasting elements, which created a figure that almost exactly equated with middle-class Victorian ideas of a contemporary hero. He was, first and foremost, an Englishman, in complete contradiction to European literary predecessors, and, more important, an English gentleman of the correct social and financial background, clothed with the respectability that would ensure his membership of the most exclusive London clubs. Intellectually, he was the superior of his fellow men, and markedly so when compared with his foreign rivals in the same field. A handsome batchelor appearance, rooms in Baker Street, a private income of comfortable proportions, mannerisms and eccentricities that set him apart from lesser mortals, an enviable scientific ability, inpenetrable disguises, accomplished acting abilities, combined with great physical strength concealed in a sinewy frame – who amongst his vast audience of commonplace readers leading commonplace lives could match these qualities, or resist an imaginary hero-translation into the role he played? His exploits opened for the rapidly growing readership of middle- and working-class families an exciting new vista of an everyday world spiced with romance and danger in which their own wits might ultimately bring them fame and fortune commensurate with his own. From the time when the first series of *Adventures* made their appearance in *The Strand Magazine*, the reading public took Holmes to their heart, and to an equal extent his indefatigable comrade-in-arms Dr Watson, according them both an affection that has lasted to the present day.

Those collectors eager to amass a complete set of first editions of Sherlock Holmes stories have still a sporting chance of realising their objective, providing they discount the almost legendary first appearance of *A Study in Scarlet*. Even here hope need not be abandoned. A copy of the correct issue of *Beeton's Christmas Annual* could as easily turn up at your local jumble sale, or even a market bookstall, priced at 50p, as it could at about £1,000 ($2,500) in the catalogue of an experienced antiquarian bookseller or under the hammer of a specialist auctioneer. The seller either knows as much as you do, or remains in blissful ignorance. There is no half-way house.

Although *A Study in Scarlet* was the principal item in this annual it also contained several other stories not by Conan Doyle. The tale's first appearance in book form was as a paper-wrapped publication issued by Ward, Lock & Co., in 1888. This first separate issue is almost as rare as the work's first appearance in print. *The Sign of Four*, the second story to feature Sherlock Holmes, after its appearance in *Lippincott's Magazine*, was published as a hardback by Spencer Blackett, London, dated 1890. *The Adventures of Sherlock Holmes*, 1892, and *The Memoirs*, 1894, have already been discussed; but the next on the list, *The Return of Sherlock Holmes*, 1905, published in a binding of smooth blue cloth, blocked in gold, is far rarer than either of these latter two titles. It was issued by George Newnes Ltd., and contains thirteen Holmes adventures, the illustrations being once again by Sidney Paget. Fine copies are seldom met with and usually command about £100. Why the title should be so rare is difficult to elucidate, but in all my years as a book-collector I have only seen a single example in fine original condition complete with all its sixteen full-page tipped-in plates. *The Valley of Fear*, 1915, *His Last Bow*, 1917, and *The Case-Book of Sherlock Holmes*, 1927, are comparatively easy to find and should not present much difficulty to the collector. A finely-produced collected edition of *The Adventures of Sherlock Holmes*, 3 vols., *Later Adventures*, 3 vols., and *Final Adventures*, 2 vols., edited by Edgar W. Smith, was published by the Limited Editions Club in 1950–53.

Ardent devotees of the cult can still join The Baker Street Irregulars, a club that has flourished in the USA for a great many years and has chapters in London and most capital cities in Europe. The society has one rigid rule: *never*, under any circumstances, must the name of Conan Doyle be mentioned. To do so is to incur a heavy fine, and persistent offenders may be expelled from membership. If, however, he *must* be referred to it can only be as 'Dr Watson's literary agent'.

After Holmes

Things were never to be quite the same again. The public appetite had been whetted to a degree that had publishers clamouring for detective stories from authors whose literary calibre varied in quality as widely as the themes of the plots they submitted.

Even before Sherlock Holmes had established his pre-eminence over every rival in the field, the number of detective fiction stories had been increasing with each passing year. Writers of the standing of Robert Louis Stevenson (1850–94), had already tried their hands. He and his stepson Lloyd Osbourne contributed *The Wrong Box*, 1889, with the detective-lawyer Michael Finsbury painstakingly tracing the misadventures of a rapidly decomposing corpse. Stevenson's interest in mystery and crime stories was of long standing. *Markheim*, a short story featuring the murder by stabbing of an antique dealer, had appeared in *Unwin's Christmas Annual*, 1886 before being included in *The Merry Men and Other Tales and Fables*, 1887. Its original appearance in print coincided with the publication of *Strange Case of Dr Jekyll and Mr Hyde*, 1886, a book which has provided a common phrase for describing 'a dual personality. This justly celebrated work was published in a humble binding of paper wrappers, printed in red and blue. The price was a shilling a copy. In the first issue the date on the front cover was altered by the publishers from '1885' to the following year by changing the final figure from '5' to '6' in ink. The date on the title-page remained at '1886'. It had been intended to publish the work in December 1885, but publication was delayed to January 1886, when it was discovered that the bookstalls were already exceptionally full of Christmas numbers of shilling novels. The New York edition actually gained priority of issue by a lead of five days. The sheets were also published in a binding of orange cloth, with the title-page dated 1886 as in the first issue. Both are illustrated on p. 73.

A later work in which Stevenson and Osbourne collaborated was *The Wrecker*, 1892, published by Cassell & Company at six shillings a copy in a binding of smooth blue cloth. The investigator in the story is the narrator himself, and it is in the epilogue that Stevenson confesses that he and Lloyd Osbourne:

> had long been at once attracted and repelled by that very modern form of the police novel or mystery story, which consists in beginning your yarn anywhere but at the beginning and finishing it anywhere but at the end; attracted by its peculiar interest when done, and the peculiar difficulties that attend its execution; repelled by that appearance of insincerity and shallowness of tone, which seems its inevitable drawback. For the mind of the reader, always bent to pick up clues, receives no impression of reality or life, rather an airless, elaborate mechanism; and the book remains enthralling, but insignificant, like a game of chess, not a work of human art.

The Wrecker itself fell between two stools. As a tale of adventure set in the wide Pacific it has fascinated a large number of readers. But as a detective story it must be accounted a failure; partly because of the technical difficulties caused by a nautical setting, with seafaring arguments beyond the comprehension of landlubbing readers, so that the clues are effectively submerged beneath a tangle of ropes, spars and bilge-water.

Lesser figures that deserve a notice are H. F. Wood, whose *The Passenger*

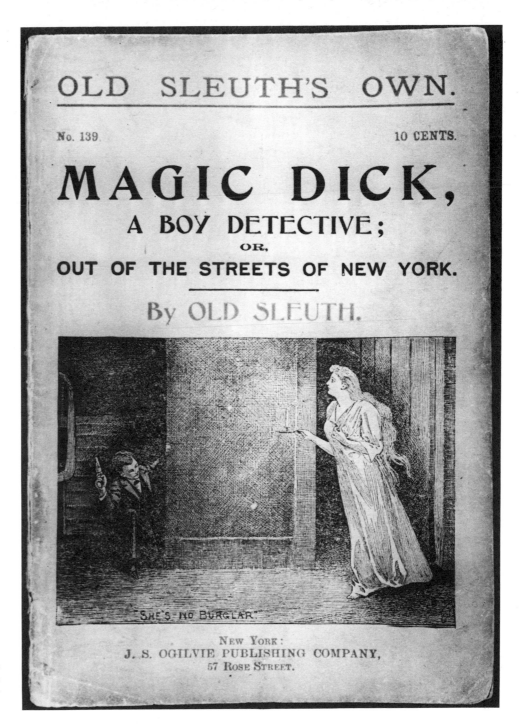

OLD SLEUTH'S OWN.

No. 139.   10 CENTS.

MAGIC DICK,
A BOY DETECTIVE;
OR,
OUT OF THE STREETS OF NEW YORK.

By OLD SLEUTH.

"SHE'S NO BURGLAR."

NEW YORK:
J. S. OGILVIE PUBLISHING COMPANY,
57 ROSE STREET.

Published in pictorial paper-wrappers in 1894 by the Parlour Car Publishing Company, the series of *Old Sleuth's Own* finally comprised several hundred titles.

from Scotland Yard, 1888, and *The Englishman of the Rue Cain*, 1889, were both published by Chatto & Windus, London, in pictorial paper-covered boards; and Richard Arkwright, whose *The Queen Anne's Gate Mystery*, 2 vols. 1889, was issued by F. V. White. But the best of the minor authors of the period leading up to the full-scale appearance of Sherlock Holmes was probably Joyce Emmerson Preston Muddock (1843–1934), whose only detective story under his own name seems to have been *Whose was the Hand?* 1901, published by Digby, Long & Co. Fifty or more appeared written under his pseudonym of 'Dick Donovan', with some of the best being *The Man-Hunter*, 1888; *Who Poisoned Hetty Duncan?* (1889); *Tracked and Taken*, 1890; *A Detective's Triumphs*, 1891; *The Man from Manchester*, 1891; *From Clue to Capture* (1893); *The Records of Vincent Trill of the Detective Service*, 1899; and *The Crime of the Century*, 1904. Many of his earliest tales were published simultaneously in two different bindings of pictorial paper-covered boards or full cloth and it is impossible to accord priority of issue to either format. Cecil Courteney had published his detective story *Link by Link* in 1886, and, surprisingly this same title was used by Dick Donovan for a series of short stories issued in 1893.

By the time the first series of *Adventures of Sherlock Holmes* appeared in *The*

A Romance from a Detective's Case-Book by Dick Donovan made its first appearance in *The Strand Magazine* in July 1892.

Strand Magazine in 1891, a number of authors had made their vocation detective story writing and many seemed capable of little else. A notable exception was Arthur Morrison (1863–1945), a journalist employed on the staff of the *National Observer*, whose first book, *The Shadows Around Us*, appeared in 1891. His second, *Martin Hewitt: Investigator*, 1894, set the seal on his career as a writer of detective fiction, and was first published as a serial in *The Strand* before being issued in book form under the imprint of Ward, Lock & Co. *Chronicles of Martin Hewitt*, 1895, was followed by the third in the series, *Adventures of Martin Hewitt*, 1896, all three titles being published by Ward, Lock & Company, London, after first running as serials in *The Strand Magazine*. Other detective stories from his pen were *The Dorrington Deed Box* (1897), with the unscrupulous Horace Dorrington acting as private detective, and *The Red Triangle*, 1903, the last of the Martin Hewitt books. Morrison had spent years as a journalist in the East End of London, and his experiences there were reflected in his penetrating and realistic studies of the squalor, crime, and

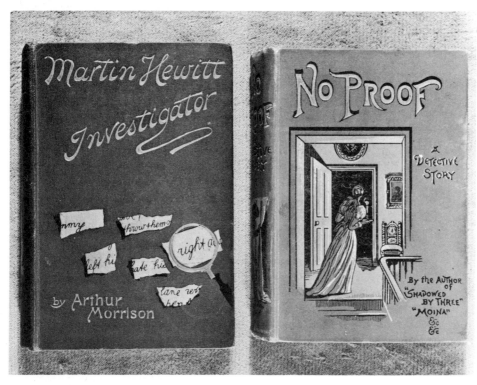

Two detective novels first published in 1895. Height of *Martin Hewitt*: 19 cm.

Frontispiece by Sidney Paget for *Martin Hewitt – Investigator*, 1895, by Arthur Morrison.

Size of page: 18.5 cm × 12 cm.

A refreshing change from the body in the library! The dramatic frontispiece by E. Fairhurst to *An Ocean Secret*, 1904, by Guy Boothby.

Size of plate: 19 cm × 12.3 cm.

"THERE WAS MIRSKY, STARING STRAIGHT AT ME." [*Page* 181.

"Lying upon his back was the body of a man, a white man, pinned to the deck by a knife through his throat."

"An Ocean Secret." (Page 62.)

the degrading social conditions of the 1890s, in *Tales of Mean Streets*, 1894, and *A Child of the Jago*, 1896, both of which passed through several editions. His last book, *Fiddle O'Dreams*, was published as late as 1933.

Another author whose literary interests transcended those of detective fiction and yet was an influence of importance in this sphere was Guy Newell Boothby (1867–1905), an Australian novelist, born in Adelaide where he later became private secretary to the mayor. His first book, *On the Wallaby*, 1894, recounted his experiences in the Australian outback, and this was a theme he returned to in his fictional works, *A Lost Endeavour*, 1895; *Bushigrams* (1897); and *Billy Binks – Hero* (1898). But his main success came when he turned his hand to crime and detection stories and introduced the public, through the pages of the *Windsor Magazine*, to his anti-hero Dr Nikola. He wrote a total of five novels featuring the dark and ruthless Nikola, and the first was probably the best of the series. *A Bid for Fortune; or, Dr Nikola's Vendetta*, 1895; *Doctor Nikola*, 1896; *The Lust of Hate*, 1898; *Dr Nikola's Experiment*, 1899; and '*Farewell, Nikola*', 1902; comprise the set, and it is a fortunate man who has found them all in the form of first editions. In his short and startlingly sudden literary career,

Part of the author's collection of the first editions of Guy Boothby.

Average height of volumes: 20 cm.

This is the second of the series of Doctor Nikola stories by Guy Boothby, first published in 1896.

Size of title-page: 19.2 cm × 12.5 cm.

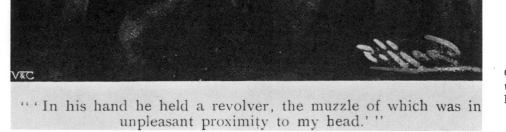

"'In his hand he held a revolver, the muzzle of which was in unpleasant proximity to my head.'"

One of Harold Piffard's dramatic illustrations for *My Strangest Case*, 1902, by Guy Boothby.

Size of plate: 19.2 cm × 12 cm.

Boothby wrote fifty full-length books, many of which were detective novels. Amongst the best of these were: *A Prince of Swindlers* (1898), serialised in *Pearson's Magazine* the previous year; *The Mystery of the Clasped Hands*, 1901; *The Childerbridge Mystery*, 1902; *My Strangest Case*, 1902; *The Curse of the Snake*, 1902; *A Queer Affair*, 1903; *The League of Twelve*, 1903; *A Consummate Scoundrel*, 1904; *A Brighton Tragedy*, 1905; *A Crime of the Under-Seas*, 1905; and *A Stolen Peer*, 1906; this last title being published after his sudden death in Bournemouth at the age of 38. He was a friend of Rudyard Kipling, who wrote:

> Mr Guy Boothby has come to great honours now. His name is large upon the hoardings, his books sell like hot cakes . . . I've met him several times in England, and he added to my already large respect for him.

Today, the name of Guy Boothby, one of the most successful of the early Australian novelists, is remembered by only a handful of bibliophiles and students of literary history. He did at least secure a place in the columns of *The Dictionary of National Biography*, an honour not accorded to his contemporary Arthur Morrison, who survived him by 40 years. An indication of the modern assessment of their respective roles in the field of English literature can be derived from the fact that Boothby gained a place in the original *Cambridge Bibliography of English Literature*, from which the name of Arthur Morrison is absent; but in *The New C.B.E.L.* Boothby has been banished while Morrison has half a column to himself. We can take comfort that the decision-makers themselves do not claim to be infallible, and Boothby's name may yet be reinstated in a future revision.

As the 1890s drew to a close, nearly every publishing house of note seemed to use the services of several specialist detective-fiction writers. Except for their names on the title-pages of the books they wrote, we know little about the vast majority of these shadowy figures, some of whom are remembered in the catalogues of National Libraries by only a single work, woven around a plot that was probably years in the hatching and more years in the accepting. But this was the beginning of the first of the Golden Ages of detective fiction, brought to a temporary decline with the outbreak of World War I, and which entered its second phase during the 1920s and 1930s. The public appetite for crime novels was voracious. They consumed all that was set before them, and many a book that would not in less hectic times have been accorded shelf space in the circulating libraries now found itself cased and labelled and even subject to reviews.

Many of the writers I have here on the shelves in my study, I more easily recognise as romantic novelists, biographers, poets, or specialists in juvenile literature. George R. Sims (1847–1922), considered by many contemporary enthusiasts to be an English poet worth remembrance, (although neither in the *D.N.B.* or the *C.B.E.L.* is there a mention of his name), gave us *Rogues and Vagabonds*, 1885; *Life Stories of Today*, 1896; *Dorcas Dene, Detective*, 1897; *The Case of George Candlemas*, 1899; and *In London's Heart*, 1900; all novels of detective fiction. He is remembered today almost exclusively for a line we can all recite: 'It is Christmas Day in the Workhouse, and the cold bare walls are bright . . .' constantly misquoted (even by *The Oxford Dictionary of Quotations*) as 'It *was* Christmas Day in the Workhouse . . .' No music-hall comedian ever reached the final stanza of the first verse:

> For with clean-washed hands and faces,
> In a long and hungry line
> The paupers sit at the tables
> For this is the hour to dine.

without the inevitable interruption from his straight-man – 'I say! I say! I say! A funny thing happened to me on the way to the theatre . . .' *In the Workhouse: Christmas Day*, and such other classics as *Billy's Rose*, and *The Lifeboat*, made their first appearance in book form in *The Dagonet Ballads*, 1881, before Sims turned to novel writing. His detective stories are largely neglected, but with the publication of *Parlour Poetry*, 1967, by Michael R. Turner (Michael Joseph, London), there has been a revival of interest in his other literary work.

Another who drew his financial strength from diverse literary activities was

Robert Leighton, better known as a writer of boy's adventure stories in the manner of R. M. Ballantyne and G. A. Henty. In collaboration with his wife, Marie Connor Leighton, he worte *Convict 99*, 1898, and *Michael Dred, Detective*, 1899, (possibly the first story in which the murderer turns out to be the detective himself). Matthais M'Donnell Bodkin, Q.C., whose *Recollections of an Irish Judge*, 1914, tells of his birthplace and vocation, was responsible for *Paul Beck, the Rule of Thumb Detective*, 1898; and also for *Dora Myrl, the Lady Detective*, 1900. David Christie Murray (1847–1907), who started his journalistic career under George Dawson on *The Birmingham Morning News*, before emigrating to London and the pages of *The Times*, began his long series of novels with *A Life's Atonement*, 1879. Fifteen years later, he gave us *The Investigations of John Pym*, 1895; *A Race for Millions*, 1898; in which Inspector Prickett of Scotland Yard makes his debut; and, with Henry Herman, *He Fell Among Thieves*, 2 vols. 1891.

Sir Max Pemberton (1863–1950), one time editor of *Cassell's Illustrated Family Paper*, and the author of numerous romantic novels, turned his attention briefly to the activities of his newly-created private detective Bernard Sutton when he wrote *Jewel Mysteries I Have Known*, 1894. Frank Richardson (1871–1917), is credited with being the first novelist to title a book with a telephone number, *2835 Mayfair*, (*c*.1905), which he started in classic fashion:

> The body of a man in evening-dress lay on the dull, crimson carpet. The black eyes were staring fixedly at the electric light hanging from copper shades . . .

– a dramatic curtain raiser employed on numerous occasions ever since.

One of the most distinguished of 19th-century fictional detectives was undoubtedly Prince Zaleski, created in the book of that name by Matthew Phipps Shiel (1865–1947), journalist and poet, whose best known work is probably *The Purple Cloud*, 1901. *Prince Zaleski*, 1895, was published by John Lane, London, as No. VII in their famous *Keynotes Series*, and in the USA by Roberts Bros, Boston. Each volume had a title-page and cover design by Aubrey Beardsley; all are now difficult to procure in anything approaching original condition. In the creation of his hero, Shiel acknowledged his debt to Edgar Allan Poe, and to Eugene Sue, whose Prince Rodolphe bears a striking resemblance to Zaleski. Other critics have noticed a similarity with several of Dupin's characteristics, so the Prince was obviously a man of many parts. Reclining languidly on a *chaise-longue* in a darkened room, in his remote country mansion, Zaleski occupies occasional moments of *ennui* in solving crime mysteries brought to him by his only contact with the outside world. As A. E. Murch has pointed out in his book on the development of the detective novel:

> There is no one quite like Zaleski. He is the quintessence of the inductive, analytical reasoner, a student with an immense store of learning, created for readers capable of grasping clues derived from a Latin quotation, a couple of words in Greek, or some inconsistency in a sketch of mythological figures. He is the detective for the intelligensia, the greatest possible contrast to Nick Carter, who is the detective of the uneducated. Each of them could appeal only to a limited section of the reading public, and neither could compare in popularity with their illustrious contemporary, Sherlock Holmes, who attracted readers of all classes of society and every educational level.

Shiel occasionally collaborated with Louis Tracy (1863–1928), who used the pseudonym, 'Gordon Holmes', in many of the books he wrote jointly or alone. With Shiel's help he wrote *The Late Tenant*, 1907, and *By Force of Circumstance*, 1909. But *The Arncliffe Puzzle*, 1906, was Tracy's work alone, and his detective, Inspector Furneaux, had some claim to fame before being eclipsed by the rising generation of streamlined private investigators. Many of Tracy's books are mystery stories rather than examples of detective fiction, but in several the demarcation line between one and the other can barely be discerned. Among the best of his works were *The Strange Disappearance of Lady Delia*, 1901, in which Inspector Furneaux first makes his bow; *A Mysterious Disappearance*, 1905; *The Silent House*, 1911; *The Feldisham Mystery*, 1911; *The Case of Mortimer Fenley*, 1915; *Number Seventeen*, 1919; and *The Lastingham Murder*, 1929.

One of the few fictional characters to rival Holmes in popularity was Raffles, a celebrated cricketer in the highest social bracket, apparently endowed with a

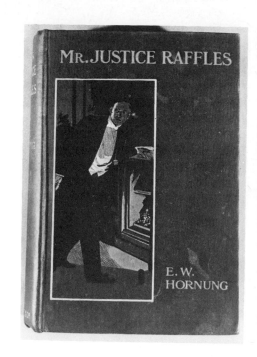

None of the Raffles books are easy to find in first edition form. This is one of the later titles, published by Smith, Elder & Co., London, dated 1909.

Size of front cover:
19.6 cm × 12.6 cm.

Frontispiece by E. Fairhurst for *The League of Twelve*, 1903, by Guy Boothby.

Size of pictorial surface: 13 cm × 9 cm.

considerable private income – most of which was actually derived from the audacious burglaries he carried out with the aid of his faithful lieutenant Bunny. Raffles was created by E. W. Hornung (1866–1921), brother-in-law to Conan Doyle, and the author may well have borrowed the name of his gentleman-burglar from the latter's story, *The Doings of Raffles Haw*, 1892. *Hornung's* first book, *A Bride from the Bush*, 1890, was the result of a two-year stay in Australia, but fame did not come to him until the appearance of *The Amateur Cracksman*, 1898, published by Methuen, London, a work in which Raffles was introduced to the public. His further adventures are recorded in *Raffles*, 1901; *A Thief in the Night*, 1905, which concludes with the hero's death as a soldier in the Boer War; and *Mr Justice Raffles*, 1909. Hornung also wrote *Dead Men Tell No Tales*, 1899; *The Shadow of the Rope*, 1902; and *The Crime Doctor*, 1914; all of which have some claim to be included in this present work. After the author's death, Barry Perowne obtained permission to continue the saga, and was responsible for *The Return of Raffles*, 1933; *She Married Raffles*, 1936; and *Raffles and the Key Man*, 1940.

Looking at the shelves where my collection of detective fiction is housed I can see a number of important writers still awaiting recognition and an

This was probably Miss Van Snoop's one and only case, for I have been unable to trace the lady detective's next appearance. The story, by Clarence Rook, made its appearance in the first volume of *Harmsworth's Magazine*, 1900.

THE STIR OUTSIDE THE CAFÉ ROYAL.
A STORY OF MISS VAN SNOOP, DETECTIVE.
By Clarence Rook.
Illustrated by Hal Hurst.

COLONEL MATHURIN was one of the aristocrats of crime; at least Mathurin was the name under which he had accomplished a daring bank robbery in Detroit which had involved the violent death of the manager, though it was generally believed by the police that the Rossiter who was at the bottom of some long firm frauds in Melbourne was none other than Mathurin under another name, and that the designer and chief gainer in a sensational murder case in the Midlands was the same mysterious and ubiquitous personage.

But Mathurin had for some years successfully eluded pursuit; indeed, it was generally known that he was the most desperate among criminals, and was determined never to be taken alive. Moreover, as he invariably worked through subordinates who knew nothing of his whereabouts and were scarcely acquainted with his appearance, the police had but a slender clue to his identity.

As a matter of fact, only two people beyond his immediate associates in crime could have sworn to Mathurin if they had met him face to face. One of them was the Detroit bank manager whom he had shot with his own hand before the eyes of his fiancée. It was through the other that Mathurin was arrested, extradited to the States, and finally made to atone for his life of crime. It all happened in a distressingly common-place way, so far as the average spectator was concerned. But the story, which I have pieced together from the details supplied—firstly, by a certain detective sergeant whom I met in a tavern hard by Westminster; and secondly, by a certain young woman named Miss Van Snoop—has an element of romance, if you look below the surface.

It was about half-past one o'clock, on a bright and pleasant day, that a young lady

"HE SHOT THE BANK MANAGER BEFORE THE EYES OF HIS FIANCÉE."

or anybody else. He generally does the deed in a more open, if more brutal, way. But it is to be feared that a great many more people get rid of undesirable contemporaries in this manner than is popularly supposed.

committing suicide, or that someone else, perhaps his wife or son, is committing murder. And, after all, the signs in the living are very obscure. Of course, if a person is foolish enough (as many are) to drink sulphuric or nitric acid, his mouth and throat are

THE DETECTIVE—NEW STYLE—IN THE LABORATORY.

No. 2.—AUGUST, 1898.   K

The appearance of the first of the 'scientific' detectives; an illustration in *Harmsworth's Magazine*, August 1898.

honourable mention in this chapter. No self-respecting history devoted to the cause would ignore the contribution R. Austin Freeman made, or the influence his work exerted on later writers. Freeman (1862–1943), introduced his readers to a figure who in many ways epitomises the art of scientific investigation and logical deduction. Dr John Evelyn Thorndyke was the leading figure in a long sequence of detective stories, and displayed his skill as a scientist far more efficiently (and far more plausibly) than his rival Sherlock Holmes. Like Conan Doyle, Freeman had abandoned the profession of medicine for that of an extremely successful writer of popular fiction. He based his hero Thorndyke, again like Conan Doyle, on his former tutor at medical school, Dr Alfred Swayne Taylor, a specialist in medical jurisprudence and forensic science. These were the skills that Thorndyke displayed to the full, and many critics have remarked on the likeness he bore to that impressive expert witness in matters scientific, Sir Bernard Spilsbury (1877–1947). Spilsbury featured in many sensational real-life murder trials in his capacity as a pathologist; but, as Freeman had written the earliest Thorndyke stories several years before Spilsbury became a well-known public figure, the likeness is merely coincidental.

Dr Thorndyke made his entrance in the pages of *The Red Thumb Mark*, 1907, published by Collingwood in variant binding of paper wrappers or full cloth. Each style of binding was embellished with a large red thumb-mark on its front cover, and first editions of this famous work are prizes eagerly sought by collectors on both sides of the Atlantic Ocean. The second edition, published in 1911 by Hodder and Stoughton, is the one most commonly found, but even this now fetches in the region of £5 ($12.50). The original title in the series was

THE · CASE · OF
MISS · ELLIOTT

· BARONESS · ORCZY ·

The Hollow
Needle

The
Radium Terrors

The Old Man
in the Corner

Baroness Orczy

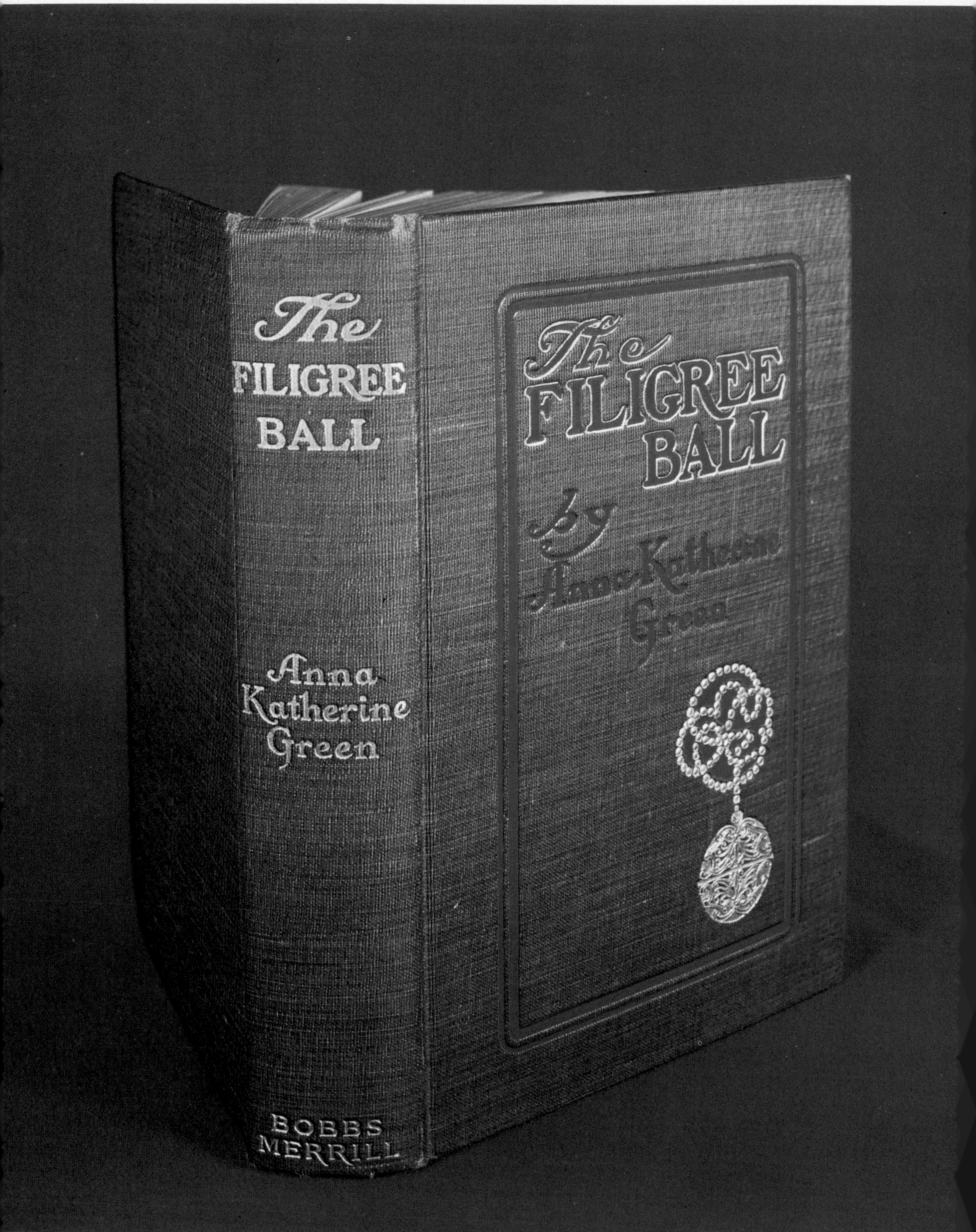
The FILIGREE BALL
Anna Katherine Green
BOBBS MERRILL
The FILIGREE BALL
by
Anna Katherine Green

followed by *John Thorndyke's Cases*, 1909 (Chatto & Windus); *The Eye of Osiris*, 1911; which Hodder & Stoughton published in brown cloth with Egyptian style decoration. (They issued most of the later Thorndyke books.) *The Mystery of 31 New Inn*, 1912; *The Singing Bone*, 1912; and *A Silent Witness*, 1914; followed successively, and stories continued to appear at regular intervals until Freeman's death in 1943. In *The Singing Bone*, the author discovered a new technique of plot construction. In this series of stories, he waived the advantages of suspense and dramatic *dénouement* in order to allow the reader to witness the crimes being committed. He then permitted him to accompany Dr Thorndyke as he gradually gathered his evidence, the reader enjoying the novelty of always knowing the facts in advance of the great detective, until his proofs were complete enough to allow him to make an arrest. It was a method often imitated by later writers.

In Europe, there had been few detective stories of any note since Boisgobey's death in 1891. Translations of the various adventures of Sherlock Holmes had proved very popular indeed, especially in France, where the tales of Raffles had also met with considerable success. They had been appreciated by two French writers, both journalists, who set out to produce detective stories in similar vein. Maurice Leblanc (1864–1941), was the author of half a dozen inconsequential novels by 1906, and was then asked by the editor of the magazine *Je Sais Tout* to contribute a crime story as a serial. The result was the appearance of *Arsène Lupin, gentleman-cambrioleur*, a story published in book form in 1907. It made its first appearance in English translation as *The Seven of Hearts*, 1908, published under a Cassell, London, imprint. Leblanc was determined to endow Lupin with greater powers of intellect than those possessed by his foremost English rival, and in his second story of the series, *Arsène Lupin contre Herlock Sholmès*, 1908, Lupin soon manages to outwit 'the great detective'. The work was a sarcastic parody of Conan Doyle's creations, 'Herlock Sholmès' acting with the slow emphasis of a country yokel, while his colleague 'Wilson' was more like an aggressive whisky-swilling squire. Leblanc admitted later that he had borrowed both characters from stage Englishmen depicted in French vaudeville productions of some fifty years earlier. The work appeared in England as *The Fair-Haired Lady*, 1909 (Grant Richards), a name taken from the longest story in the book, but the title was changed later the same year to *Arsène Lupin versus Holmlock Shears*. The same inserted catalogue of advertisements, dated 'Spring, 1908', occurs in both versions, but the first-named title is the earlier.

Throughout his 25 years as a fictional detective, Arsène Lupin adopted a Robin Hood–Raffles scheme of living, and was, first and foremost, the mastermind behind a long succession of burglaries and jewel thefts which completely outwitted the police. It was not until the appearance of *Le Bouton de Cristal*, 1912, (published in England by Hurst & Blackett in 1913, as *The Crystal Stopper*) that Lupin agreed (for motives of his own) to assist the police, and from that time onwards he seemed shorn of some of his previous glamour. Other titles in the series are *L'Aiguille Creuse*, 1909, translated as *The Hollow Needle*, 1911 (Eveleigh Nash, London); *813*, 1910, translated as *813; A New Arsène Lupin Adventure*, 1910 (Mills & Boon, London); *Les Confidences d'Arsène Lupin*, 1914; and *Les Trois Crimes d'Arsène Lupin*, 1917. *The Arrest of Arsène Lupin*, 1911, was published by Eveleigh Nash, but this completely failed to jeopardise his highly successful career, and he was still going strong in the 1930s.

The second of the French writers who made a substantial contribution to the genre was Gaston Leroux (1868–1927), who was as well known as Leblanc in the journalistic world. He, too, commenced his career as a writer of sensational novels, but while reporting notable criminal trials for *Le Matin*, he conceived the idea for the plot of his most successful detective novel, *Le Mystère de la Chambre Jaune*, 1907, which appeared earlier that year as a serial in the magazine *L'Illustration*. It is in this mystery of a sealed room that the young reporter-detective Joseph Rouletabille is introduced. The story was an immediate success, an English translation appearing in New York as *The Mystery of the Yellow Room*, 1908 (Brentano), and under the same title in London as number 54 in the *Daily Mail Sixpenny Novels* series, in paper wrappers, illustrated by Cyrus Cuneo. A slightly different translation was issued by Edward Arnold, London, as a hard-back edition, dated 1909. A murder taking place in a room that to all outward appearances was completely sealed proved a popular

One of John Williamson's illustrations for
The Beetle, 1897, by Richard Marsh.
Size of plate: 18.4
cm × 12 cm.

THEY STARED AT ME IN SILENCE AS I DRAGGED THESE OUT AND
LAID THEM ON THE FLOOR.

innovation, and had been used by Edgar Wallace in *The Four Just Men*, 1905,
and by Israel Zangwill (1864–1926), in *The Big Bow Mystery*, as early as 1892.
Leroux set out to challenge the detective skill of his readers from the first
chapter, presenting them with clue after clue that has to be set aside as fresh
evidence is revealed by young Rouletabille, reporting the mystery for his paper,
L'Epoque. A sequel, *Le Parfum de la Dame en Noir*, 1907, stretched coincidence too far, and lacked much of the excitement of the earlier story. It
appeared in England, under the title *The Perfume of the Lady in Black* (1909),
as number 72 in the *Daily Mail Sixpenny Novels* series. The only other of
Leroux's works to achieve international fame was *The Phantom of the Opera*,
1910, produced as a most successful film in the early 1930s.

One of the fictional French detectives of the period to achieve popularity in
Britain was Eugène Valmont, created by Robert Barr (1850–1912), in his
collection of short detective stories, *The Triumphs of Eugéne Valmont*, 1906
(Hurst & Blackett). Contained in this collection is *The Absent-Minded Coterie*,
an elegantly-told tale of a confidence trick, perpetrated by simple yet cunningly
contrived means, that has deservedly been reprinted on many subsequent
occasions.

On another shelf devoted to writers whose first editions of detective fiction

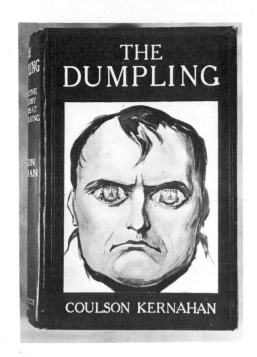

Modelled on a latter-day Napoleon, *The Dumpling*, 1906, one of the most readable of Edwardian detective fiction titles, owed its dramatic front-cover illustration to Stanley L. Wood.

Size of front cover:
20 cm × 13 cm.

One of Stanley L. Wood's illustrations for *The Dumpling*, 1913.

Size of plate: 20 cm × 13 cm.

" THERE PEERED THROUGH A BROKEN PANE OF GLASS . . . THE WHITE AND WICKED FACE OF THE DUMPLING."

are difficult to find and about whom little is known in a biographical or bibliographical way, I can see works by A. Eric Bayly, author of *The Secret of Scotland Yard*, 1900 (Sands & Co., London); and *The House of Strange Secrets*, 1899. 'Grant Allen' (1848–99), i.e. Charles Grant Blairfindie Allen, remembered today principally for *The Woman Who Did*, 1895, wrote at least one first-class collection of detective stories in *An African Millionaire*, 1897, a work first serialised in *The Strand Magazine*; and also contributed *Ivan Greet's Masterpiece*, 1893; and *Hilda Wade*, 1900. This latter title's only association with the genre stems from the fact that Conan Doyle wrote the last chapter at the request of his dying friend and near neighbour. A title I have searched for over many years, but have yet to find, in first edition, is that spine-chilling horror story *The Beetle*, 1897, by Richard Marsh, a writer who contributed a number of detective tales around the turn of the century. These included *The Crime and the Criminal* (1897); *The Datchet Diamonds* (1898); and *Philip Bennion's Death*, 1899; none of which are easy to find.

Coulson Kernahan published *Scoundrels and Co.*, 1894, anonymously, and then went on to give his readers *Captain Shannon*, 1897. Both these works were surpassed by his sensational tale, *The Dumpling – A Detective Love Story*, 1906 (see illustration, left), written, according to his publishers, after the author had incurred great personal risk. The blurb inserted at the end of the book is worth repeating :

> The scene of the first chapter is laid in the most dangerous opium den in East London, which Mr Kernahan visited personally, quite alone, and in disguise, in order to smoke opium, so that his vivid description is drawn from actual knowledge. At great personal risk Mr Kernahan contrived to gain entrance to Anarchist Meetings, so is not ignorant of their methods. His pictures of life amongst the Submerged Tenth in East London are in each case actual personal experiences . . . *The Dumpling* is a very bomb-shell of a story.

It is a title, apparently until now unrecognised by bibliographers, that deserves a prominent place in any collection, and is as readable today as it was in the Edwardian era. It is worth finding for its vivid series of illustrations by Stanley L. Wood, who also designed the cover.

Sitting next to the handful of Kernahan's works on the same shelf is *Murder by Warrant*, 1898, by E. T. Collis; and works by B. L. Farjeon (1838–1900), represented by *Great Porter Square; A Mystery*, 3 vols. 1885; *The Mystery of M. Felix*, 3 vols. 1890; and *Samuel Boyd of Catchpole Square; A Mystery*, 1899. Another difficult favourite is Francis Edward Grainger (1893–1924), whose books always appeared under his pseudonym 'Headon Hill'. *Guilty Gold*, 1896, in which the detective is Inspector Heron, of Scotland Yard; *By a Hair's Breadth*, 1897; *The Spies of Wight*, 1899; *Caged; The Romance of a Lunatic Asylum*, 1900; *Tracked Down*, 1902; and *The Comlyn Alibi*, 1916; are some titles I have been able to locate. His earlier detective stories, such as *Clues from a Detective's Camera* (1893) published by Arrowsmith, Bristol; and *Zambra the Detective*, 1894 (Chatto & Windus), have so far eluded me.

Hume Nisbet was another author who regularly employed Scotland Yard officers to do his detective work, as in *A Singular Crime*, 1894; *Comrades of the Black Cross*, 1899; and *Children of Hermes*, 1901, in which latter title Nicodemus Dove Turtle, of the CID officiates. Henry Hawley Smart (1833–1893), established a reputation as a horse-racing novelist whose vocation (like Edgar Wallace) was largely centred in writing tales of adventures on the Turf. Many of his works contain elements of crime and detection, such as *Struck Down* (1885); '*The Plunger*', 2 vols. 1891; and *Without Love or License*, 3 vols. 1890. The majority of his titles were later issued in pictorially-printed boarded bindings in the form of yellow-backs.

E. Phillips Oppenheim (1866–1946), lived to the age of 80, and had a literary career which spanned a period extending from the start of the Sherlock Holmes stories to the end of World War II. Most of his large output does not concern us here, but from the appearance of his first novel, *Expiation*, 1887, followed by *The Mysterious Mr Sabin* (1898), he interspersed his work with a number of spy thrillers and several detective novels which passed through numerous editions. Amongst the best of these were *The Mystery of Mr Bernard Brown*, 1901; *The Long Arm of Mannister*, 1908, first published in the USA

"I saw the thing steal out below his cuff."

The Master Mummer]

[*Page* 32.

"It was Mr. Watson of New York."

The Mysterious Mr. Sabin.]

[*Page* 394.

(the British edition appeared the following year as *The Long Arm*); *The Illustrious Prince*, 1910; *A Maker of History*, 1906; *The Great Impersonation*, 1920; *The Honourable Algernon Knox, Detective* (1920); *Nicholas Goade, Detective* (1927); and *Inspector Dickins Retires* (1931), (published in the USA as *Gangsters' Glory*).

William le Queux (1864–1927), wrote in much the same vein as Oppenheim, contributing over 140 novels and short stories, the most famous being *The Invasion of 1910*, published in 1906, a book that was said to have predicted the outbreak of World War I. *The Mystery of a Motor Car*, 1905, is one of his most sought-after titles; but *The Tickencote Treasure*, 1903; and *The Mysterious Mr Miller*, both run it close.

Barry Pain, (1864–1928), is remembered more as a humourist than as a writer of detective tales, and his short stories in *The Cornhill Magazine* in the 1890s made his name widely known. But his *The Memoirs of Constantine Dix*, 1905 (T. Fisher Unwin), with its dramatic pictorial front cover (see illustration p. 85) is a title eagerly sought by collectors of detective fiction. Another writer of diverse talents was A. C. Fox-Davies, an international authority on heraldry, who contributed *The Dangerville Inheritance*, 1907, and *The Mauleverer Murders*, 1907 (both published by John Lane, London), and was then heard of no more.

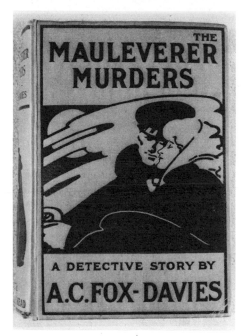

Above
Another of the motorised detective novels, published by John Lane, London, dated 1907.

Size of front cover:
19.5 cm × 13 cm.

Above
A difficult first edition detective novel to find in good condition. It was published by T. Fisher Unwin, London, in 1905.

Size of front cover:
18.7 cm × 12.5 cm.

Above right
The dramatic front cover of the first edition, dated 1912, of a title that was to remain in print until the 1930's.

Size of front cover:
19.7 cm × 13.5 cm.

Above far right
Published in 1909, this first edition features one of the earliest American motorised detectives.

Size of front cover:
20.7 cm × 14.5 cm.

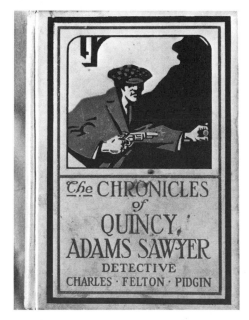

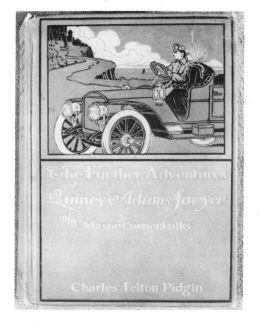

In the USA Jacques Futrelle (1875–1912), enjoyed considerable success with his series of detective stories employing the talents of a 'thinking machine'. The character he designed for this task was Professor Augustus S.F.X. Van Dusen, whose method was an instant application of cold, clear logic to the solution of any unsolvable mystery presented to him. He made his first appearance in *The Chase of the Golden Plate*, 1906; but it was in a collection of short stories issued as *The Thinking Machine*, 1907, (later issued by Chapman & Hall, London, also dated 1907), and *The Thinking Machine on the Case*, 1908 (published in Britain by Nelson, as *The Professor on the Case*, 1909), that he was allowed full scope to perform his feats of mental wizardry. The first-named title was later reissued in 1918 as *The Problem of Cell 13*, after the name of the first story in the book. This was undoubtedly Futrelle's most successful and best-remembered tale, with Professor Van Dusen, in his 'No. 8 hat', locked in a death-cell that appears to be escape-proof. In this most ingenious *tour de force*, which impressed me immensely when I first read it as a teenager, Futrelle succeeds in devising a method by which, for a wager, the Professor makes good his escape. *The Master Hand*, 1914 (Hodder & Stoughton), was the last of his stories to be published in Britain.

Another American writer, Melville Davisson Post (1871–1930), gave us *The Strange Schemes of Randolph Mason*, 1896; *The Man of Last Resort*, 1897; and *The Corrector of Destinies*, 1909; stories recounting the exploits of an unscrupulous lawyer who devised means of bending the criminal code for his own ends. Mason's most popular detective stories, however, centred on the activities of Uncle Abner, whose adventures ran for several years in magazines and periodicals before being collected in book form as *Uncle Abner: Master of Mysteries*, 1918. This work is still in print today.

I have a particular affection for the works of Charles Felton Pidgin (1844–1923), the American inventor and statistician who conceived the idea which resulted in the assembly of one of the earliest mechanical tabulation machines. He was also, in his spare time, a writer of detective stories, and the covers of his books are invariable blocked in vivid pictorial presentations of incidents that occur in the pages of the volume, some of which are illustrated here (see page 86). He made his name as a writer with the first of the series, *Quincy Adams Sawyer and Mason's Corner Folks*, 1900; and this was followed by *The Further Adventures of Quincy Adams Sawyer*, 1909, with Miss Mary Dana playing the part of detective; and *The Chronicles of Quincy Adams Sawyer, Detective*, 1912; all published by L. C. Page & Company, Boston. Each story centres on the intrigues and sometimes sinister goings-on in the village of Mason's Corner (later renamed Fernborough) near Boston, Massachusetts, with the series taking on the character of a saga as the younger generations grow up and gradually replace the older personages of the earlier tales.

I have only recently acquired examples of the first editions of another

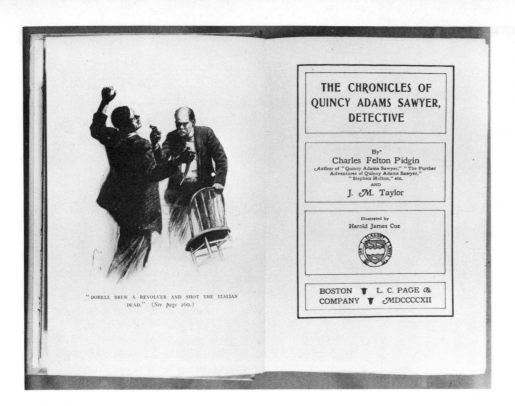

"DOBELL DREW A REVOLVER AND SHOT THE ITALIAN DEAD." (*See page 260.*)

THE CHRONICLES OF
QUINCY ADAMS SAWYER,
DETECTIVE

By
Charles Felton Pidgin
*Author of "Quincy Adams Sawyer," "The Further
Adventures of Quincy Adams Sawyer,"
"Stephen Holton," etc.*
AND
J. M. Taylor

Illustrated by
Harold James Cue

BOSTON ▼ L. C. PAGE &
COMPANY ▼ *MDCCCCXII*

All Pidgin's detective novels centre on the intrigues and sinister happenings in the village of Mason's Corner, near Boston, Mass., in which Quincy Adams Sawyer, the local sleuth-hound, tackles the problems in a direct and forthright manner.

Size of title-page:
19 cm × 13 cm.

American writer – Thomas W. Hanshew (1857–1914), the inventor of *Cleek, the Man with the Forty Faces*, 1910, a Raffles-type character who usually escapes from his pursuers because of the extreme mobility of his features. *Cleek of Scotland Yard*, 1914; *Cleek's Government Cases*, 1917; and, (written with his wife Mary), *The House of the Seven Keys* (1921); are among similar titles, in all of which the india-rubber Cleek plays a prominent part.

Other American writers for whom I have space for only a brief mention are Arthur B. Reeve (1880–1936), the creator of Craig Kennedy, who first appeared in *The Silent Bullet*, 1912; and Julian Hawthorne (1846–1934), son of the novelist Nathaniel Hawthorne, who edited and compiled one of the earliest, and certainly the most comprehensive anthologies of detective fiction. This six-volume work, issued under the imprint of *The Review of Reviews*, New York, dated 1908, was titled *Library of the World's Best Mystery and Detective Stories*, and comprised 'One Hundred and One Tales of Mystery by Famous Authors of East and West'. A complete set in its original buckram binding, blocked pictorially on each front cover with a bull's-eye lantern, now fetches in the region of £60. ($150).

Edwin Balmer and William MacHarg collaborated to write *The Achievements of Luther Trant*, 1910, in which the principle of a 'lie-detector' is used in a fictional tale for the first time; while Samuel Hopkins Adams published *Average Jones*, 1911, in which his detective of that name made his first and final appearance. *The Mystery of the Boule Cabinet*, 1912, by Burton E. Stevenson; *The Master of Mysteries*, 1912, published anonymously by Gelett Burgess; and *Through the Wall*, 1909, by Cleveland Moffett, are possibly the best available in a very lean period in this field, in the USA. As Howard Haycraft states in his *Murder for Pleasure*, 1942, 'It can not be pretended that the American detective story revealed anything like the quantity or the level of quality of its English counterpart in the years up to the first world conflagration'.

During the decade that spanned the Edwardian era detective fiction attained a new respectability. Writers distinguished in other fields now recognised it as an acceptable literary occupation and were quick to take advantage of the financial rewards it had to offer. G. K. Chesterton (1874–1936), accelerated the process by the publication of the article in which he championed the cause, *The Defence of the Detective Story*, 1901, and by his essays on Sherlock Holmes which appeared in *The Daily News* in 1901 and 1907. In *The Club of Queer Trades*, 1905, he wrote a series of adventure stories in the style of Conan Doyle, with the author himself cast in the role of Watson. *The Man Who Was Thursday*, 1908, has some detective interest; but it was in his series of Father Brown stories that Chesterton gave life to one of the most famous and best-loved of

One of the earliest collected editions of detective stories. It appeared as a six-volume work in 1908, edited by Julian Hawthorne, son of the novelist Nathaniel Hawthorne.

Size of title-page:
18.4 cm × 12.3 cm.

fictional detectives, even though some of the tales in which he appeared cannot truly be classed as *bona fide* detective fiction.

The Innocence of Father Brown, 1911, has been described as 'one of the finest volumes of detective short stories ever written . . .' by Ellery Queen. This was followed by *The Wisdom of Father Brown*, 1914; *The Incredulity of Father Brown*, 1926; *The Secret of Father Brown*, 1927; and the belated and less praiseworthy, *The Scandal of Father Brown*, 1935. Chesterton revealed in his *Autobiography*, 1949, that he had based his priestly little detective's intellectual and spiritual qualities (although not, he tells us, his personal appearance) upon 'my friend, Father John O'Connor, of Bradford'. Therefore, it is not surprising that the little Roman Catholic priest's main preoccupation is with the moral and religious aspects of the crimes he is solving, rather than the apprehension of the criminal and the administration of legal punishment. With his psychological approach to the problems of human frailty, and his endowment of the guilty with good as well as bad qualities, Chesterton's works of detective fiction assume a special importance in the genre, while Father Brown, whose most 'conspicuous quality was not being conspicuous', will be remembered as one of its most endearing characters.

The overlap in time between many of the writers mentioned in this chapter and those listed in that devoted to the Hansom Cab Era is considerable. The literary careers of a few of the most hardy even spanned the several years which encompassed the period bounded by the two World Wars. Those whose output was centred mainly in the inter-war years are discussed in a later chapter, but there are a few, such as Chesterton, whose early contributions must be mentioned here. In the case of Eden Phillpotts (1862–1960), the difficulties are obvious in

Only a few of Phillpotts' works concern us here, but his first book, which set

To satisfy the public appetite for murder mysteries, contemporary newspapers and periodicals made use of the services of detective fiction writers in many ways. Lincoln Springfield's article in *Harmsworth's Magazine* dealt with most of the sensational London murders, from Jack the Ripper onwards.

any attempt to keep strictly to an ordered, chronological sequence of chapter headings. Despite the fact that he was 26 years of age at the time of the publication of his first book, his career as a writer extended well over 60 years. After a shaky start, his output became prolific, as many as eight full-length works making their appearance in a single year – embracing poetry, novels, collections of short stories, plays and essays, retold stories from the classics, and detective fiction.

87

a style for the hundreds that were to follow, deserves a place in the library of any enthusiast, although the task of finding a copy in its original first issue binding may take him several years. *My Adventure in the Flying Scotsman: A Romance of London and North-Western Railway Shares*, 1888, was issued by James Hogg and Sons, London, at a shilling a copy, the author himself paying the costs of publication. The small number of copies sold help to account for its rarity today, and also acted as a dampener on Phillpotts' hopes of making a successful career as a writer. It was three years before he ventured to appear again. The slim little book of some 64 pages was first issued in a full cloth orange binding, the front cover being blocked in a rainbow hue of colours overprinted in black (see illustration on p. 88). The misprint 'breaks' for 'brakes' appears on page 47. The remaining sheets were later reissued in light pink paper-covered boards, printed on the front cover in black, and priced this time at only sixpence a copy. Although *My Adventure in the Flying Scotsman* displays the newly-fledged author's lack of literary style, to say nothing of his difficulty with both grammar and syntax (faults later overcome), the story has the merit of a dramatic ending as the swaying train nears Carlisle, notwithstanding the fact that the identity of the potential murderer is never in doubt. The 'small, seedy-looking' detective from Scotland Yard plays little part in the story, the final act of which can be seen depicted on the end-papers of *Victorian Detective Fiction*, 1966, edited by Eric Osborne (Bodley Head Ltd., London).

Amongst the best of Phillpotts' later detective works are those he wrote under the pseudonym 'Harrington Hext'. The first of these was *Number 87*, 1922; but he also used the name for *The Thing at their Heels*, 1923, (first published by The Macmillan Company, New York, and later by Thornton Butterworth, London); *Who Killed Diana?* (1924), first published in the USA under the title of *Who Killed Cock Robin?*; and *The Monster*, 1925, (Macmillan, New York, there being no British edition of this title). Of these the best is possibly *The Thing at their Heels*, in which Phillpotts used his intimate knowledge of the English countryside and the conflicting emotions of a rural community to write a convincing tale of a series of murders investigated by one Inspector Midwinter. The work has been acclaimed as a masterpiece of detective fiction by Jacques Barzun and W. H. Taylor in their *A Catalogue of Crime* (1971). Other titles in the genre written by Phillpotts under his own name are *The Grey Room*, 1921 (Macmillan, New York); *The Red Redmaynes*, 1922 (Macmillan, New York, the first British edition being published undated the following year by Hutchinson, London); *A Voice from the Dark*, 1925 (with same imprint details as preceding title); *Jig-Saw*, 1926, later published undated in London under the title *The Marylebone Miser; The Jury*, 1927 (Macmillan, New York); and *"Found Drowned"*, 1931 (Macmillan, New York). These first editions, published in the USA, are difficult for British collectors to find, but at the moment none of Phillpotts' works fetch more than a few pounds apiece, with the notable exception of *My Adventure in the Flying Scotsman* which is now valued at over £50 ($175).

It is with one of Chesterton's closest friends, Edmund Clerihew Bentley (1875–1956), that we close this chapter, which traces the history of detective fiction as far as the outbreak of World War I. He was educated with the great 'G.K.C.' at St Paul's School, London, before going up to Oxford, and it was at St Paul's that their lifelong friendship began. As he sat in the science class at the age of sixteen, he devised the metrical form later designated by Chesterton as that 'severe and stately form of free verse known as the Clerihew'. It owed its birth to the lines:

> Sir Humphry Davy
> Abominated gravy.
> He lived in the odium
> Of having discovered Sodium.

His *Biography for Beginners*, 1905, with illustrations by G. K. Chesterton, was eventually published under the pseudonym of 'E. Clerihew'. Bentley had earlier been one of the first to recognise the merits of *The Wallet of Kai Lung*, 1900, by 'Ernest Bramah' (Ernest Bramah Smith, 1868–1942), while he was working for the magazine *The Speaker*, and contributing regular features to *Punch*. The encouragement he gave to Bramah was instrumental in the later appearance of a series of famous detective stories from the pen of that writer, in which Max

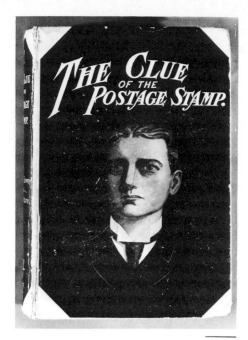

Sought by philatelists as well as collectors of early detective fiction, this first edition of Arthur Bray's novel was published in Dublin, dated 1913, in a binding of pictorially-printed paper-covered boards.

Size of front cover:
19.6 cm × 13 cm.

Carrados, the first sightless investigator, was introduced. *Max Carrados*, 1914; *The Eyes of Max Carrados*, 1923; and *Max Carrados Mysteries*, 1927, complete the trio of collections of short stories in which the blind detective figures. Meanwhile, Bentley was working on the story that was to bring him fame and fortune. He had conceived the novel idea of a detective's convincing solution to a crime ultimately being proved wrong. The result was *Trent's Last Case*, (1913), published by Nelson's in their series of two shilling novels, in a blind-stamped binding of blue cloth. The book was dedicated by the author to G. K. Chesterton, who in his turn had previously dedicated to Bentley *The Man Who Was Thursday*, 1908.

Trent's Last Case immediately established itself as a bestseller, and has remained in print ever since its original appearance, besides being translated into a number of foreign languages. Unlike most detective fiction of the period, the author concentrated much of his attention on making his characters true to life, giving his readers authentic portraits of people they could recognise in the street, at home, or at work. Trent himself appears as a cultured man of leisure, who finally builds up a watertight case. But there is something wrong somewhere. What Trent deduced was true, but it was not the whole truth. The complete revelation is reserved, with effective artistry, for the final chapter. Bentley had achieved a rare success, that of a detective story that can still be read with pleasure despite the fact that the secret is already known. His later stories featuring the same investigator, *Trent's Own Case*, 1936 (Constable), and *Trent Intervenes*, 1938, cannot rank with his masterpiece, in which he had broken all the conventions inherited from Edgar Allan Poe.

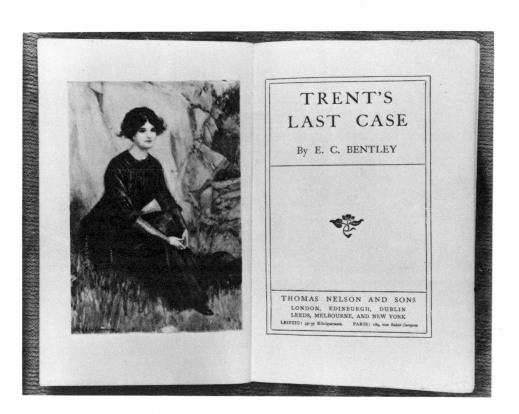

Issued with a coloured frontispiece, this first edition of one of the most famous of detective stories appeared undated in 1913.
Size of title-page:
18.4 cm × 12 cm.

The Lady Sleuths

It was Edgar Allan Poe who earned the title of the Father of the Detective Story, and to his compatriot, Mrs Anna Rohlfs, go the family honours and the corresponding title of the Mother of the Detective Story.

Born Anna Katharine Green (1846–1935), which was the name she used as an authoress, she grew up in Brooklyn, New York, and graduated from the Green Mountain Junior College in 1866. Her father was a well-known criminal lawyer, and this was the only reason she was able to give, in later years, as an explanation of her unprecedented invasion of the masculine field of detective fiction. In 1884 she married Charles Rohlfs, a somewhat prosaic character whose interest was in the designing and manufacture of furniture. Anna's married life was spent in Buffalo, where she died in her ninetieth year.

With her first attempt at a fictional work she achieved a remarkable success, and gave the world a book that has been in print ever since. It was to exercise a considerable influence on detective fiction for many years to come. *The Leavenworth Case*, 1878, was published by Putnams, New York, as were her next seven titles. Its sub-title, 'A Lawyer's Story', did much to reveal its intent – but nothing of its secrets. From the first chapter, the drama and mounting tension holds the reader in its grip, and the atmosphere of the story is so modern that only the candle-lit rooms and the hissing gas chandeliers give a clue to its date. From the time when the news of the murder of Mr Leavenworth is hurried to his lawyer, Everett Raymond, who relates the story, the excitement steadily increases, with the author's investigator, Mr Ebenezer Gryce, 'one of our city detectives . . . a portly, comfortable personage with an eye that never pounced . . .' beavering away at the clues that finally lead to the guilty party's unmasking. All the ingredients beloved by later writers of the school are introduced: the rich old dignitary, struck down just as he is about to make out a new will; the silent-footed butler; the body stretched prone in the library; the ballistics expert; and the coroner's inquest with its detailed medical evidence. Miss Green even included a folding facsimile letter in the volume, and a sketch-map of the scene of the crime. *The Leavenworth Case* was published in London early in 1879. After reading a later British edition, Prime Minister Stanley Baldwin described the work as 'one of the best detective stories ever written'.

With the immediate success of this book, her aspirations as a poet were relegated to second place in her literary career, although she published *Defence of the Bride, and other Poems*, 1882, and *Risifi's Daughter, a drama*, 1887. But nearly all of her 40 or more titles, the last of which, *The Step on the Stair*, was published by Dodd, Mead & Co., New York, as late as 1923, were works of mystery and detective fiction. Her first book was quickly followed by *Strange Disappearance*, 1880; *X Y Z; a Detective Story*, 1883; *Hand and Ring*, 1883; *The Mill Mystery*, 1886; *7 to 12; a Detective Story*, 1887; *Behind Closed Doors*, 1888; *The Forsaken Inn* (1890); *A Matter of Millions* (1891); *The Old Stone House*, 1891; *Cynthia Wakeham's Money*, 1892; *Marked "personal"*, 1893; and so on, to the end of her career. Amongst the best of her later works were *A*

The Mother of the Detective Story. A rare photograph of the American novelist Anna K. Green, author of *The Leavenworth Case*. *Reproduced by permission of The New York Public Library.*

Difficult Problem, 1900; *A Circular Study*, 1900; *The Filigree Ball*, 1903; and perhaps *The Golden Slipper*, 1915, because of the interest in her woman detective, Violet Strange, whose success stems largely from her interpretation of the clues unearthed by her sagacious and suspicious bloodhound. All Anna Katharine Green's titles appeared as first editions under American imprints, and most were published in Britain a few months later.

Several critics have attributed detective themes to women writers whose works were published long before Miss Green appeared on the stage, but in nearly every case there are only oblique references to the art or the unravelling of a mystery contained in a short story. G. K. Chesterton credited Charlotte Brontë, stating that '*Jane Eyre* remains the best of her books, because while it is a human document written in blood, it is also one of the best blood-and-thunder detective stories in the world'. *Jane Eyre* was published in three volumes in 1847, but it was while the controversy about what contemporary critics termed 'Sensation Novels' was rampant in the mid-1850s that they were further outraged by the discovery that many had been written by seemingly straight-laced and moral figures of womanhood. Publishers were often reluctant to encourage women writers, and many used pseudonyms, especially when recounting tales which figured crimes and the criminal underworld. Elizabeth Cleghorn Gaskell

(1810–1865), who was later to contribute *The Life of Charlotte Bronte*, 2 vols. 1857, one of the finest biographies in the history of English literature, published *Cranford*, 1853, as a serial in the weekly magazine *Household Words*, edited by Charles Dickens. It was in this periodical that *The Squire's Story* first appeared, modelled as a tale of mystery and detection on Dick Turpin's final unmasking as a highwayman while living under cover in the city of York, a story quoted earlier in this work.

With Mrs Henry Wood (1814–1887), we are perhaps on a little firmer ground. His first book *Danesbury House*, 1860, attracted little comment; but with the appearance of her internationally famous *East Lynne*, 3 vols. 1861, she achieved a phenomenal success, despite having had the work rejected out of hand by three well-known London publishing houses. It finally appeared under the imprint of Richard Bentley, and was continually in print until the mid-1930s. As a serial, it appeared in *Colborn's New Monthly Magazine*, commencing in 1860, but it was as a three-decker in Mudie's and other circulating libraries that sales rocketed, selling more than a million copies during the authoress's lifetime. Woven into the romantic pathos of the story, there is á carefully constructed murder mystery. An innocent man has been convicted on circumstantial evidence, fresh clues are unearthed, alibis established, missing witnesses traced, and the process of logical detection is finally brought to a successful conclusion with the discovery of the real murderer. Although there is no detective in the modern sense, the book ends with a neat array of evidence being placed before the court in a manner that would not discredit Erle Stanley Gardner himself.

In the same year, 1861, an equally famous title first made its appearance as a serial in the insolvent magazine *Robin Goodfellow*. It finished in September 1861, with the printing of Chapter XVIII. The whole book was published during 1861–63 in *The Sixpenny Magazine*, published by Ward & Lock. *Lady Audley's Secret*, 3 vols. 1862 (Tinsley Bros, London), was the product of Mary Elizabeth Braddon (1837–1915), a novelist even more prolific than Mrs Henry Wood. Afterwards, she always prefaced each of her works with the words 'By the author of Lady Audley's Secret', but never achieved anything like the same success. She admitted later that she owed much of her inspiration for this, her first three-volume novel, to Wilkie Collins's *The Woman in White*. *Lady Audley's Secret* is a dramatic story of blackmail, bigamy, and cold-blooded murder, with the heroine of the title revealed as the perpetrator of the heinous misdeeds. She is brought to justice more by the long arm of coincidence than by the exercise of any detective skill, but there are elements of logical deduction in the story, especially in her elderly husband's methods of proving her guilt.

In 1874 Miss Braddon married John Maxwell, a publisher and founder of several periodicals. She later edited *Belgravia* from 1866, and *Mistletoe Bough* from 1878, in both of which some of her own stories appeared. Several of these later works contained elements of detective interest, and the majority of them were concerned with unsolved crimes. *A Strange World*, 3 vols. 1875; *Dead Men's Shoes*, 3 vols. 1876; *An Open Verdict*, 3 vols. 1878; *Just as I Am*, 3 vols. (1880); *The Missing Witness* (1880); *Wyllard's Weird*, 3 vols. (1885); *Like and Unlike*, 3 vols. 1887; and *The Fatal Three*, 3 vols. (1888); are the titles most likely to interest the collector of detective fiction, but all are now extremely difficult to find in their original cloth bindings and usually fetch well over £50 ($175) each as first editions. A copy of *Lady Audley's Secret* in its original publisher's binding of royal blue dot-and-line-grain cloth, blocked in blind on front and back covers, would be worth well over £100 ($250) today. As I have pointed out in *The Collector's Book of Books*, the market price of three-volume novels, like all classes of books, is intimately linked to the condition in which they are offered for sale. A work in pristine original state may well be worth £200 ($500): the same title in the same issue of the same edition, rebound in half-calf, the text soiled and dogeared, and lacking its half-titles, may well be an expensive purchase at less than £10 ($25).

It was not long before other women writers followed the lead given by Miss Braddon. Miss Florence Alice Price (1857–1929), who wrote under the pseudonym 'Florence Warden', gave her public *A Prince of Darkness*, 3 vols. 1885, in which the detective is Gerald Staunton, a lawyer's clerk; while *The House on the Marsh* (1884) featured Detective Maynard of Scotland Yard. Other detective stores that appeared from her pen were *A Sensational Case*, 1898; *The Mystery* of *Dudley Horne*, 1897; and *No. 3, the Square*, 1903. Mary Cholmondeley (1859–1925), achieved a sudden reputation with the publication of *The Danvers Jewels* (1887), first issued in a binding of blue-grey pictorial wrappers, although she did not admit the authorship until the second edition appeared (this time in diagonal fine-ribbed cloth), dated 1898. A sequel, *Sir Charles Danvers*, 2 vols. 1889, was followed by another detective story, *The Hand on the Latch*, 1903, which was later reissued in a collection of short stories, under the title, *The Lowest Rung*, 1908.

Helen Mathers (1853–1920), who later became Mrs. Reeves, published a work of crime and detection as early as 1878. This tale, which she called *As He Comes up the Stair*, is related from the condemned cell by a woman wrongly convicted of the murder of her husband. It appeared as number 5 in the series of Bentley's Half-Crown Empire Library. *Eyre's Acquittal*, 3 vols. 1884, by the same author, is yet another murder story in a court-room setting, a theme she first used in *The Land O' Leal*, 1878. *Murder or Manslaughter*, 1885, and *Blind Justice*, 1890, followed much the same pattern. But a collector must be very lucky if he can find any of her first editions today.

Miss Elizabeth S. Drewry used a private detective to solve the murder mystery in *The Death Ring*, 1881, while Catharine Louisa Pirkis is remembered solely for her much-sought-after *The Experiences of Loveday Brooke, Lady Detective*, 1894. The book is notable for the use of a detective's visiting-card, which is pasted down at an angle on the front cover. It gives her address as Lynch Court, Fleet Street, and the volume contains seven of her adventures in the world of crime.

Few other women writers in Britain contributed to the genre in the years leading up to the outbreak of World War I. Exceptions to this rule were Beatrice Heron-Maxwell, who wrote *The Adventures of a Lady Pearl-Broker*, 1899, which has some detective interest; and the important series of works written by Elizabeth Thomasina Meade (1854–1914), who later became Mrs. Toulmin Smith. All her works appeared under the signature 'L. T. Meade', and she is credited with well over 250 stories for children and teenage girls. Women writers of detective fiction suffered from the serious disadvantage of having been denied any scientific, medical or legal training. This made it almost impossible for them to create convincing detectives who made professional use of these attributes. Most of the investigators in their novels depended more on an assessment of the psychological aspects of the cases and suspects before them, with their instinctive reactions often displaying distinctive feminine traits. Intuition and character assessment played a disproportionate part in arriving at the correct solution to a mystery – talents not to be underestimated, as any erring husband will readily confirm.

L. T. Meade compensated for her lack of scientific and medical knowledge by using the services of at least two male collaborators who were skilled in both these fields. These were 'Clifford Halifax' (Dr Edgar Beaumont), and 'Robert Eustace' (E. Rawlins), who later wrote *Hidden Treasures of Egypt* (1925), using the same pseudonym. Several of the earlier jointly-written stories made their first appearance in the pages of periodicals such as *The Strand Magazine* or *The Harmsworth Magazine*. It was in the former that her *Stories from the Diary of a Doctor* was issued, running concurrently with the second series of *The Adventures of Sherlock Holmes*, and commencing with *My First Patient* in issue Number 31 in July 1893. The earlier stories dealt mainly with the sensational mysteries which her fictional Dr Halifax encountered in his country practice, and in which he acted the part of an amateur detective. With the second series of *Stories from the Diary of a Doctor*, commencing in *The Strand* in January 1895, Meade concentrated on presenting detailed investigations into murder cases, nearly all of which had a medical flavour. *Adventures of a Man of Science* followed, a series of stories again written with 'Clifford Halifax', in which Paul Gilchrist scientifically investigates in a manner very reminiscent of Sherlock Holmes. This series of tales appeared in 1896, at a time when the magazine was serialising Conan Doyle's *Rodney Stone*. But it was with *The Brotherhood of the Seven Kings*, serialised in *The Strand* from January 1898, and later published in book form, dated 1899, by Ward, Lock & Co., that she achieved real success as a writer of detective stories, relying for medical and scientific advice on 'Robert Eustace'. In this daring series of adventures, in which the recluse and philosopher, Norman Head, acts the part of detective, L. T. Meade created a new

An illustration from *The Brotherhood of the Seven Kings*, 1899, by L. T. Meade and 'Robert Eustace', in which the hero is sentenced to decapitation by having his feet roped to a heavy raft. The ebbing tide does the rest.

Size of plate: 19 cm × 12 cm.

"The moon rose presently, and its pale beams struck across my dungeon."

species of quarry – that of a woman gang-leader who cold-bloodedly plans the crimes which her underlings commit. The researches of Ellery Queen later led him to announce this as 'the earliest appearance of a femal felon in a series of short stories'. The rarity of the first edition, dated 1899, complete with all its 16 full-page tipped-in plates by Sidney Paget, has forced up the price of fine copies of the title to something in the region of £40 ($100). *Stories from the Diary of a Doctor*, 1894 (Newnes); and the second series of the same title, published in 1896 (Bliss, Sands & Foster) change hands at less than a quarter of this amount. Among her other detective books are *A Son of Ishmael*, 1896 (F.V. White & Co.), with a Mr Crossley as private detective; *The Sanctuary Club*, 1900, in which the hero, Mr Bell, is called in to investigate a series of deaths at first thought to be from supernatural causes; *A Race with the Sun*, 1901; and *This Troublesome World*, 3 vols. 1893, in which the detective police-officer is William Green.

One of *Strand Magazine's* illustrations in the series *Stories from the Diary of a Doctor* by L. T. Meade, which commenced publication in July 1893.

"THE HORROR OF STUDLEY GRANGE."
(See page 15.)

This was the period during which Miss Emma M. Murdoch, later Mrs. E. Murdoch Van Deventer, was publishing her series of detective novels in the USA all under the pseudonym of 'Lawrence L. Lynch'. Most of her titles appeared under London imprints within a few months of their being published in the USA, and included *Shadowed by Three*, 1879; *The New Detective Story: The Diamond Coterie*, 1884; *A Mountain Mystery*, 1886; *A Slender Clue; or, The Mystery of the Mardi-Gras*, 1890; *Moina: A Detective Story*, 1891; *A Dead Man's Step*, 1893; *Against Odds*, 1894; *No Proof. A Detective Story*, 1895; and *The Unseen Hand*, 1898. Nearly all her works first appeared under the imprint of Chicago publishing houses before being issued in England by Ward, Lock & Co.

Her compatriot, Carolyn Wells (1870?–1942), later Mrs. Hadwin Houghton, did much to stimulate renewed interest in tales of detective fiction in the USA and created a vogue for the subject at a time when other styles of sensational novels were increasingly in favour with the reading public. Born in Rahway, New Jersey, she was educated at home, because a severe attack of measles as a child left her with defective hearing. She stated later that she had never read any detective stories until her interest was stimulated by having one of Anna Katharine Green's novels read to her. This was in 1909, and from then onwards she tirelessly turned out a series of novels and romances – some 170 full-length books in all, over 70 of them mystery stories. Most of the latter related to the exploits of Fleming Stone, whose score of solving nearly eighty separate murder cases has seldom been equalled. Her detective made his bow in *The Clue*, 1909, having first appeared in a short story in *Lippincott's Magazine* the same year. Amongst the best of her many tales are *Faulkner's Folly*, 1917; *The Room with the Tassels*, 1918 (both issued by George H. Doran & Co.); *The Diamond Pin*, 1919 (Lippincott); and *Feathers Left Around*, 1922 (Lippincott). Miss Wells also edited *American Detective Stories* and *American Mystery Stories*, both collections being published by the Oxford University Press, 1927. She is also remembered for her pioneering work of criticism in which she discusses every aspect of the subject: *The Technique of the Mystery Story*, 1913 (revised edition 1929).

The works of Isabel Ostrander (1885–1924), who wrote under her own name as well as using the pseudonyms 'Robert Orr Chipperfield', 'David Fox', and 'Douglas Grant', pointed the way to the later crime thrillers, although her work owed much to the influence of Anna K. Green. *Suspense*, 1918, has an Alfred Hitchcock ring about it; but *The Heritage of Cain*, 1916; *The Clue in the Air*, 1917; and *How Many Cards?* 1920; showed her indebtedness to those who had gone before. *Ashes to Ashes*, 1919, was praised by Dorothy L. Sayers as 'an almost unique example of the detective story told from the point of view of the hunted rather than the hunter'. *Twenty-Six Clues* (1919), with its two murders in a private museum; its rivalry between Terhune, the scientific detective, and his opposite number McCarty, who operates by the police rulebook; as well as the twenty-six lettered clues, is a finely worked-out piece of detective fiction that influenced later writers. *The Man in the Jury Box*, 1921; *The Doom Dealer*, 1923; and *The Handwriting on the Wall*, 1924; were among her later work, all of which were first published in the USA.

Amongst the most popular of the American women writers of detective fiction was Mary Roberts Rinehart (1876–1958), whose work has been said to bridge the gap between that of Anna Katharine Green and 'Leslie Ford'

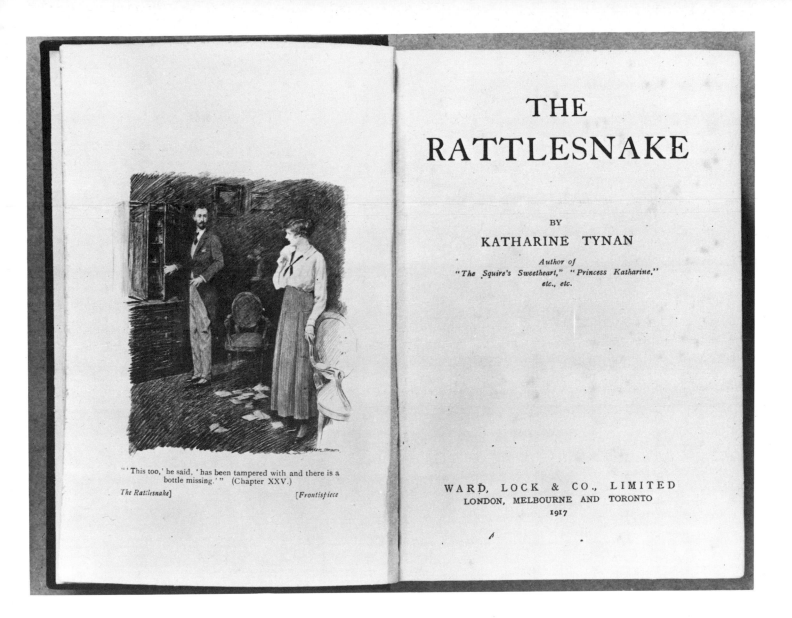

"'This too,' he said, 'has been tampered with and there is a bottle missing.'" (Chapter XXV.)

The Rattlesnake]   *[Frontispiece*

THE RATTLESNAKE

BY

KATHARINE TYNAN

Author of
"The Squire's Sweetheart," "Princess Katharine,"
etc., etc.

WARD, LOCK & CO., LIMITED
LONDON, MELBOURNE AND TORONTO
1917

One of the rare detective stories written by Katharine Tynan (1861–1931), better known as poet, novelist, and contemporary historian.

Size of title-page:
18.8 cm × 12.5 cm.

who will be mentioned shortly. She was born in Pittsburgh and became the wife of Dr Stanley Rinehart in 1896. With her first novel, *The Circular Staircase*, 1908 (Bobbs–Merrill Co.), she established a reputation that her later work consolidated, and many of her titles are still selling well in the present day. Yet, with the single exception of Nurse Pinkerton, no detective appears in more than one of her 20 full-length works. She also published a very successful series of humorous novels in which the heroine is an eccentric spinster who glories in the name of Tish. Mary Rinehart's autobiography, *My Story*, appeared in 1931.

Her masterpiece of detective fiction is generally considered to be *The Man in Lower Ten*, 1909, a tale told in the first person singular, which originally appeared as a serial some two years earlier. Few of her stories owe anything to French or English influences, and represent a refreshingly new aspect of American detective fiction. *The Amazing Adventures of Letitia Carberry*, 1911; *The Case of Jennie Brice*, 1913; *The After House*, 1914; *The Amazing Interlude*, 1917; and *The Red Lamp*, 1925; are amongst her best works. *The Circular Staircase* was later dramatised (with the collaboration of Avery Hopwood), and enjoyed a long run on Broadway, New York, under the title *The Bat*, opening at the St James's Theatre, London, in January 1922.

Among the last of the American women novelists of the period which I have space to discuss must be Mrs Zenith Jones (Brown), who was born in 1898, and has since been a prolific contributor to the best-selling lists of detective fiction in the USA. The wife of Dr Ford K. Brown of St John's College, Annapolis, she has said that a visit to Oxford was responsible for the production of six or more 'Mr Pinkerton' tales, all published under the pseudonym 'David Frome'. Pinkerton is a henpecked little detective, seemingly always stuffed with cold, who blunders after his companion, Inspector Bull, stumbling over and accidently exposing well-hidden clues. Her titles include *The Hammersmith*

95

Murders, 1930; *In at the Death*, 1930; *By the Watchman's Clock*, 1932; *The Man from Scotland Yard*, 1932; and *Mr Pinkerton finds the Body*, 1934. Using her other pseudonym of 'Leslie Ford', a name she has employed for at least 20 of her novels, Mrs Zenith Brown has written (amongst many other titles): *The Sound of Footsteps*, 1933; *The Clue of the Judas Tree*, 1933; *The Strangled Witness*, 1934; *Ill-Met by Moonlight*, 1937; and *Murder in Maryland*, 1942. First editions of her works all bear the imprint of American publishing houses.

During the Edwardian era, the most important woman writer of detective fiction in England was undoubtedly Baroness Orczy (1865–1947). She was born in Hungary, the daughter of Baron Felix Orczy, a talented musician and scion of an ancient landowning family, and moved to London with her parents at the age of fifteen. Here she studied painting, and later met Montague Barstow, an artist and illustrator, whom she married in 1894. With her husband, Emma Orczy wrote and illustrated children's stories, and for those who like to collect their authors in as a complete a state as possible, her first book, *The Enchanted Cat* (1895), will be extremely difficult to find. Her earliest work of detective fiction is also an elusive title to acquire as a first edition, but it is an important book in the history of the art of suspense and ractiocination and well deserves a place in every self-respecting collection. *The Case of Miss Elliott*, 1905 (T. Fisher Unwin), named after the first of the twelve short stories which the work contains, is a landmark in the genre, introducing for the first time in any language an 'armchair detective' – a thin and bony old man who solves his cases without stirring from his habitual seat in a London tea-shop. The narrator is a young lady, a reporter on a London paper:

> Quite by chance I found myself one morning sitting before a marble-topped table in the ABC shop. I really wondered for the moment what had brought me there, and felt cross with myself for being there at all.
>
> "A glass of milk and cheesecake, please," said a well-known voice.
>
> The next moment I was staring into the corner, straight at a pair of mild, watery blue eyes, hidden behind great bone-rimmed spectacles, and at ten long bony fingers, round which a piece of string provokingly intertwined.
>
> There he was as usual,, wearing – for it was chilly – a huge tweed ulster, of a pattern too lofty to be described. Smiling, bland, apologetic, and fidgety, he sat before me . . . His long bony fingers had caught the end of the bit of string, and he was at it again, just as I had seen him a year ago, worrying and fidgeting, making knot upon knot, and untying them again, whilst his blue eyes peered at me over the top of his gigantic spectacles.

In her autobiography, *Links in the Chain of Life*, 1947 (Hutchinson), Emma Orczy told how the idea of her fictional detective came to her while she was sitting, fog-bound, in a London horse-omnibus. Through the gloom she caught sight of a placard advertising the latest Sherlock Holmes story, and then and there she decided to write a series of detective tales which would be 'built round an original character whose personality must in no way be reminiscent of Sherlock Holmes'. The first six stories were published in *The Royal Magazine* and created such interest that a further six were demanded. A collection of a dozen was then issued in book form as *The Case of Miss Elliott*. Four years later a long series of stories centred around the same character was published as *The Old Man in the Corner*, 1909 (Greening & Co.), and illustrated by H. M. Brock.

By this time, Baroness Orczy was a familiar name throughout the land. In 1902 she had completed the manuscript of the tale that was to bring her both fame and fortune – *The Scarlet Pimpernel*, 1905, a novel of the French Revolution, only to have the book rejected by at least twelve well-known London publishers. With her husband as collaborator, she wrote a dramatised version under the same name. The play opened in Nottingham in 1903, before being transferred to the New Theatre, London, on 5 January 1905, with Fred Terry and Julia Neilson in the leading parts. Within a few days publishers were clamouring for the right to publish the book, and she finally selected Greening & Co., who issued the work in a binding of blue cloth, blocked on the front cover in gold and colours, with a central illustration of pimpernel flowers. As a first edition it commands about £25 ($37.50) today. *I Will Repay*, 1906; and *The Elusive Pimpernel*, 1908; were two of the many sequels.

Lady Molly of Scotland Yard, 1910 (Cassell), of which three editions appeared

Part of the author's collection of first editions of Agatha Christie titles.

Pride of place in any collection of detective fiction must be given to the Sherlock Holmes stories, shown here in fine copies, first editions of the two most-sought-after titles.

Collected today as much for their lurid pictorial covers as for their texts, the two titles shown epitomise publishers' binding styles for the sensational novel at the turn of the century.

THE SECRET ADVERSARY — AGATHA CHRISTIE

THE MAN IN THE BROWN SUIT — AGATHA CHRISTIE

THE MURDER OF ROGER ACKROYD — AGATHA CHRISTIE

THE LISTERDALE MYSTERY — AGATHA CHRISTIE

THE ABC MURDERS — AGATHA CHRISTIE

CARDS ON THE TABLE — AGATHA CHRISTIE

TEN LITTLE NIGGERS — AGATHA CHRISTIE

FIVE LITTLE PIGS — AGATHA CHRISTIE

AFTER THE FUNERAL — AGATHA CHRISTIE

4·50 FROM PADDINGTON — AGATHA CHRISTIE

A CARIBBEAN MYSTERY — AGATHA CHRISTIE

ENDLESS NIGHT — AGATHA CHRISTIE

A Daughter a Daughter — MARY WESTMACOTT

The SILENT HOUSE IN PIMLICO

Fergus Hume

AUTHOR OF "THE MYSTERY OF A HANSOM CAB"

THE CRIME AND THE CRIMINAL

RICHARD MARSH

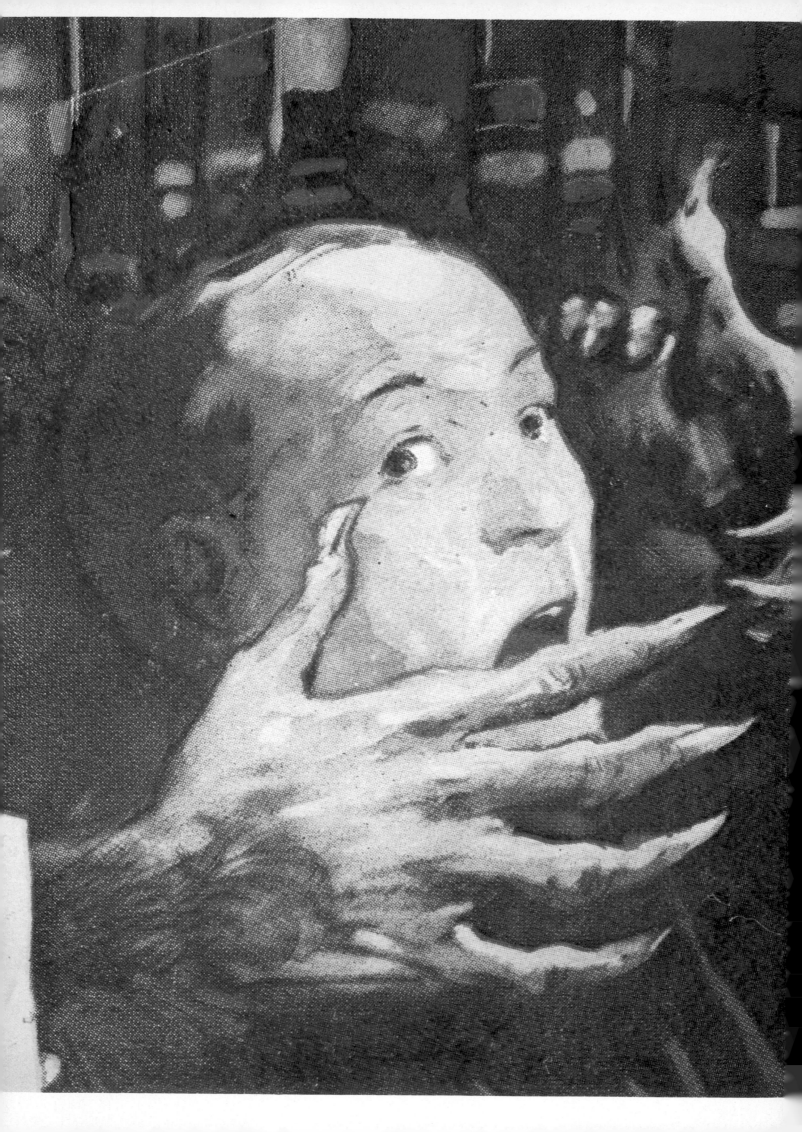

"He held out his hands for the irons" (*see page 319*).

in the same year, has been a target for collectors for many years. Complete with its sixteen tipped-in full-page plates by Cyrus Cuneo, it is a most desirable possession, redolent of the Edwardian age, but a most difficult book to find in anything approaching original condition. Baroness Orczy's other works of detective fiction are *Unravelled Knots*, 1925, and *Skin o' my Tooth*, 1928; but it is with the old man in the corner that a collector's main interest will lie. The final story in the series, entitled *The Mysterious Death in Percy Street*, reveals for the first time that the elderly armchair detective had more than a mere passing interest in at least some of the murder cases he solved so convincingly. Whenever there was a dearth of crime, he made sure that there were sufficient ingenious and carefully contrived deaths to keep his mental faculties fully engaged – or, at least appear so to his young and attractive listener. Suddenly, in the final story, she became suspicious :

"[The murderer] was never seen or heard of again?" Polly asked.
"He has disappeared off the face of the earth. The police are searching for

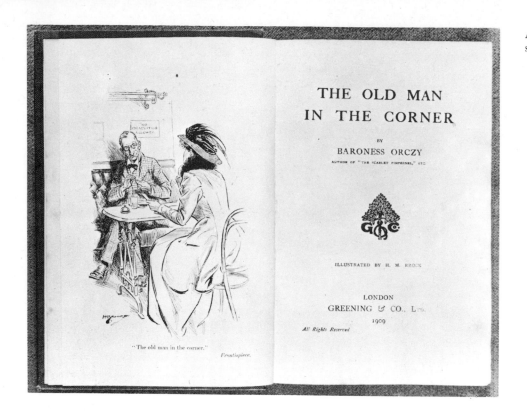

A title now avidly sought by collectors, showing the first of the armchair detectives. Size of title-page: 18.2 cm × 12 cm.

him, and perhaps some day they will find him – then society will be rid of one of the most ingenious men of the age."

He was watching her through his great bone-rimmed spectacles, and she could see the knuckles of his bony hands, just above the top of the table, fidgeting, fidgeting, fidgeting, till she wondered if there existed another set of fingers in the world which could undo the knots his lean ones made in that tiresome piece of string.

Then suddenly – the whole thing stood before her – Mrs Owen lying dead in the snow besides her open window; one of them with a broken sash-line, tied up most scientifically with a piece of string. She remembered the talk there had been at the time about this improvised sash-line . . .

"If I were you," she said, without daring to look into the corner where he sat, "I would break myself of the habit of perpetually making knots in a piece of string."

He did not reply, and at last Polly ventured to look up – the corner was empty . . . She has never set eyes on the man in the corner from that day to this.

Shades of the Reichenbach Falls! In so gentle a manner did the Baroness dispose of her outworn sleuth before turning her attention to the historical and romantic novels she continued to write for another thirty years.

The only title of detective interest written by Lady Kitty Vincent appears to be *"No. 3"*, 1924, a tale woven around the mysterious death of a King's Messenger. Mrs Belloc Lowndes (1868–1947), wrote a number of short stories featuring her French detective, Hercules Popeau; but she is remembered today for her book *The Lodger*, 1913. In it, she expertly reproduced the horror and suspense surrounding the Jack the Ripper murders that terrorised the East End of London in 1888–89, viewed through the eyes of a suburban landlady who gradually comes to suspect that her new lodger is the murderer. This was a fictional reconstruction of an actual series of murders, a theme she returned to in *Lizzie Borden*, 1939, and *An Unrecorded Instance*, a short story based on the 'Brides in the Bath' murders.

Suddenly we have arrived in time among the 'modern', contemporary writers whose new titles are still appearing today. Of these, Agatha Christie (*b.* 1891), now Lady Mallowan, is surely the best-loved and one of the most widely-read detective fiction writers of all time. Born in Torquay, Devon, daughter of Frederick Alvah Miller of New York, she was christened Agatha Mary Clarissa, and educated privately by her mother at home. Later she became the wife of Col Archibald Christie and then of Sir Max Mallowan. Her paperback sales in

An illustration by H. M. Brock for *The Old Man in the Corner*, 1909, by Baroness Orczy. Size of page: 18.2 cm × 11.8 cm.

"It looks as if he had been strangled."

Great Britain alone have been computed at over one-and-a-half million copies per annum, rivalling those achieved by the Belgian writer Georges Simenon.

Agatha Christie's first book was written when she was serving in a Voluntary Aid Detachment in Torquay Hospital towards the end of World War I. She has told us that, during this period, she had read many detective novels, 'as I had found they were excellent for taking one's mind off one's worries. After discussing one with my sister, she said it was almost impossible to find a *good* detective story, where you don't know who had committed the crime. I said I thought I could write one. She was doubtful about it. Thus spurred on, I wrote *The Mysterious Affair at Styles*'.

She had a very difficult time in finding any publisher willing to risk the expense of issuing the work to the public, but finally, with the help of her father, the volume at last made its appearance under the imprint of John Lane, New

York, dated 1920. Her most inspired fictional character, the little Belgian detective with the sharply waxed moustaches, was introduced to her readers as M. Hercule Poirot. With the aid of his 'little grey cells', he has been instrumental in solving countless mysteries ever since. The critic Sutherland Scott has called this novel 'one of the finest firsts ever written', and with it began Agatha Christie's long and continuing literary career. In this first work, she paints a particularly vivid portrait of upper-class Britain in the immediate postwar years, and the title has been a coveted collector's piece for several decades. The first English edition, (John Lane, 1921) is also a difficult 'first' to secure and has recently been catalogued as high as £25 ($37.50).

The Secret Adversary, 1922, which first introduced that dynamic couple Tommy and Tuppence Beresford : *The Murder on the Links*, 1923; *Poirot Investigates*, 1924; and *The Man in the Brown Suit*, 1924; (all published by John Lane, London), were followed by the title which brought her immediate fame and which is still her most widely discussed book even today. *The Murder of Roger Ackroyd*, 1926 (Collins), issued in a binding of blue cloth lettered on the spine and front cover in red, (as were her next two titles – *The Big Four*, 1927, and *The Mystery of the Blue Train*, 1928), was a brilliantly written detective novel and caused a sensation amongst reviewers and the public alike. It was a *tour de force* in the widest sense, and the final relevation of the true identity of the murderer provoked an outcry which turned into the most violent and long-lasting debate in the history of detective fiction. The device the author employed was, in fact, perfectly legitimate. 'Some readers have cried indignantly "Cheating!",' wrote Mrs Christie, 'an accusation that I have had pleasure in refuting by calling attention to various turns of phrasing and careful wording'. This best-selling novel was afterwards dramatised by Michael Morton under the title *Alibi*, opening at the Prince of Wales's Theatre, London, in May 1928. Agatha Christie is one of a select handful of writers who have successfully brought detective themes to the stage, and one does not have to be reminded of such plays as *Ten Little Niggers*, *Witness for the Prosecution*, and of the marathon *Mousetrap*, which, in 1972, has been running continuously in London for a staggering total of twenty years, to realise the phenomenal success she has achieved in this medium.

Among her later books, mention must be made of *The Murder at the Vicarage*, 1930; *Peril at End House*, 1932; *Lord Edgware Dies*, 1933, (published in the USA as *Thirteen at Dinner*); *A.B.C. Murders*, 1936; *Cards on the Table*, 1936; *Ten Little Niggers*, 1939 (published in the USA as *And Then There Were None*); *Five Little Pigs*, 1942; *The Body in the Library*, 1942; *4.50 from Paddington*, 1957; and *By the Pricking of my Thumbs*, 1968; all issued under the imprint of Collins, London. This is merely a selection of her many titles, and Mrs Christie has also written several novels containing neither crime nor detective, such as *A Daughter's Daughter*, 1952 (William Heinemann), using the pseudonym 'Mary Westmacott'. But it is by her diverse and subtly contrived tales of detective fiction that she has attained literary fame; as has Miss Marple, her gentle little spinster detective, and the precise and dignified Hercule Poirot, whose adamant refusal to descend to his knees in Holmes-like fashion, to search for clues, stamps him as one of the great.

Dorothy Leigh Sayers (1893–1957), was the only child of the Revd. H. Sayers, headmaster of Christ Church Choir School, and of Helen Mary Leigh. After attending Godolphin School, Salisbury, she took a first class honours degree in modern languages at Somerville College, Oxford. It was early in 1920, while working as an advertisement agency's copy-writer, that she conceived the plan of writing detective stories aimed at a class of reader who would enjoy a demanding intellectual content. In this scheme her academic training was of immense advantage, but she had also to master the art of imparting a literary flavour to her mystery stories.

That she had succeeded in this aim was obvious from the date of the publication of her first detective novel, *Whose Body?*, 1923, (Fisher Unwin) which introduced the aristocratic figure of Lord Peter Wimsey, a suave and well-groomed amateur detective, lavishly equipped with learned and artistic traits of character and an insatiable interest in unsolved crimes. His cases are related in *Clouds of Witness*, 1926 (Gollancz); *Unnatural Death*, 1927 (Ernest Benn); *The Unpleasantness at the Bellona Club*, 1928 (Benn); and *Lord Peter Views the Body*, 1928 (Gollancz). It was at this point in her career that Miss Sayers said that she became fascinated with detective fiction as a literary form. Later, she edited anthologies of titles she considered amongst the best work in the field, which was issued as *Great Short Stories of Detection, Mystery and Horror*, 3 vols. 1928, 1931, 1934. These were published in the USA as *The Omnibus of Crime*, 3 vols.

In *The Documents in the Case*, 1930 (Benn), she relied for her scientific knowledge on her collaborator 'Robert Eustace', who, it will be remembered, had assisted L. T. Meade in similar manner some 32 years earlier. This novel has been described as a technical masterpiece, with its division into two separate sections, headed 'Synthesis' and 'Analysis'. But it lacked the fascination of Lord Peter Wimsey's well-bred nonchalance, as he delicately pierces the web of mystery. He made a welcome reappearance in *Strong Poison*, 1930 (Gollancz), where he meets for the first time Miss Harriet Vane, a murder suspect he eventually makes his wife (in *Busman's Honeymoon*, 1937). In the intervening years, Dorothy L. Sayers wrote some of her most famous detective novels, including *The Five Red Herrings*, 1931; *Have His Carcase*, 1932; *Hangman's Holiday*, 1933; *Murder Must Advertise*, 1933; *The Nine Tailors*, 1934; and *Gaudy Night*, 1935; all published by Gollancz in bindings of black cloth lettered third set in a thinly-disguised version of her Oxford college. It was in these three in red. The last three titles mentioned are the most important of her works of detective fiction, the first authenticated by her early life in an advertisement agency office, the second relying on her knowledge of campanology, and the books that she came nearest to achieving her ambition of writing a 'literary' detective novel.

Ngaio Marsh was born in Christchurch, New Zealand, in 1899, where her maternal grandfather had been an early coloniser. Her first name (pronounced 'Ny-o') is the Maori word for a flowering tree. She spent the years between 1928 and 1932 in England, and before returning to New Zealand left the manuscript of her first book with a London publishing house. *A Man Lay Dead*, 1934, was issued two years later, to be followed by such titles as *Enter a Murderer*, 1935; *Death in Ectasy*, 1936; *Artists in Crime*, 1938; *Death at the Bar*, 1940; *Death and the Dancing Footman*, 1942; *Colour Scheme*, 1943; *Died in the Wool*, 1945; *Final Curtain*, 1947; *Singing in the Shrouds*, 1959; *Death at the Dolphin*, 1967; and *Clutch of Constables*, 1968. This is only a representative selection of her many stories of crime and detection, in which her personal backgrounds of art and the theatre have served her well. Both themes figure in many of her books. Her experience of the theatre, in which she has worked as actress, producer and lecturer, has enabled her to fashion an authentic backcloth of realistic detail. Her detective, Inspector Roderick Alleyn, son of the aristocratic Lady Alleyn, exhibits many of the well-poised idiosyncrasies of Lord Peter Wimsey. High-society doors which would otherwise remain closed to him are frequently opened through 'family connections'. Many of Miss Marsh's books portray vividly aspects of life in her native country, and in *Died in the Wool* she tells the story of life on a New Zealand sheep farm and of the wool trade, giving a new setting to a detective story. Perhaps her best-known work and the one with which she first sprang to fame is *Artists in Crime*, 1938, which made her name familiar in the USA as well as in Britain.

Other women writers of detective fiction were at work during the second Golden Age of the genre in the 1920s and '30s. Gladys Mitchell (*b.* 1901), many of whose mystery thrillers feature her raucously-dressed detective Mrs Bradley, portrays middle-class life in the suburbs of the larger English cities, under such titles as *The Mystery of a Butcher's Shop*, 1929; *The Saltmarsh Murders*, 1932. Her later works include *Watson's Choice*, 1955, and *Spotted Hemlock*, 1958. Mrs George Ronald Rougier (*b.* 1902) who writes under the pseudonym 'Georgette Heyer', is perhaps best known for her historical romances, but she has written a number of first-class detective novels, including *Footsteps in the Dark*, 1932; *Why Shoot a Butler*, 1933; *The Unfinished Clue*, 1934; *Death in the Stocks*, 1935, (published in the USA as *Merely Murder*); *They Found Him Dead*, 1937; *A Blunt Instrument*, 1938; *Duplicate Death*, 1951, a return to detective fiction after a ten year break; and *Detection Unlimited*, 1953. In the mid-1950s, most of her detective works were republished – some twenty years after their first appearance – which has led Barzum and Taylor to assert, in *A Catalogue of Crime*, 1971, that this 'attests to the sterling merits of this inadequately prized writer. She ranks with Sayers, Allingham, and Marsh, possessing the sure touch of the first and avoiding the occasional bathos of the other two'.

Margery Allingham (1904–66), (Mrs Philip Youngman Carter), was encouraged by her parents to write stories while still a child. Her first published work, *Blackkerchief Dick: A Tale of Mersea Island* (1923) was published when she was only nineteen, and her first detective story, *White Cottage Mystery*, was printed as a newspaper serial in 1927, and as a book in 1928. It was a story she came to dislike and one she has never listed amongst her works. Her literary career began in earnest with the appearance of *The Crime at Black Dudley* (1929), published undated by Jarrolds, London, and this was followed by a series of detective tales that soon made her name a household word. Her major success stemmed from the first appearance of her mild-mannered amateur detective, Albert Campion, in *Death of a Ghost*, 1934, although before this she had produced such titles as *Mystery Mile* (1930); *Look to the Lady* (1931); *Police at the Funeral*, 1931; and *Sweet Danger*, 1933. From the world of artists, introduced in *Death of a Ghost*, Miss Allingham chose a scene of a London publishing house in *Flowers for the Judge*, 1936; then came *Case of the Late Pig*, 1937; with the setting later altering to a Mayfair dressmaking salon for *The Fashion in Shrouds*, 1938. In *Black Plumes*, 1940, the author created a new detective, Inspector Bridie; but her earlier investigator was recalled in *Traitor's Purse*, 1941, a spy thriller set in war-time London. Her later titles include *The Beckoning Lady*, 1955 (published in the USA as *The Estate of the Beckoning Lady*); *Hide My Eyes*, 1958; *China Governess*, 1963; and several omnibus volumes of her collected stories.

Moving to the present, we can acknowledge the success of Lucy Malleson (b. 1899) with her detective heroes, although only the *nom de plume* 'Anthony Gilbert' appears on her title-pages. *Something Nasty in the Woodshed*, 1942, a title she may have borrowed from Stella Gibbons' *Cold Comfort Farm*; *A Nice Cup of Tea*, 1951; *A Question of Murder*, 1955; *And Death Came Too*, 1956; *Out for the Kill*, 1960; and *Looking-Glass Murder*, 1966; represent a cross-section of her works, in some of which her knight-errant is a coarse and none-too-highminded lawyer, Arthur Crook.

Dr Doris Bell Collier Ball (b. 1897), known to her readers as 'Josephine Bell', was a practising physician in London until 1954. Besides her many detective novels, she has written a valuable factual study – *Crime in Our Time*, 1962, (Vane, London), an account of modern crime and the criminal. Her fictional detective, as might be imagined, is a doctor. He first interrupts his medical duties to investigate the circumstances surrounding a *Murder in Hospital*, 1937; and continues the hunt in *Fall Over Cliff*, 1938; *Death at Half Term*, 1939 (published in the USA as *Curtain Call for a Corpse*); and *From Natural Causes*, 1939. Among her later works are *Death at the Medical Board*, 1944, in which the same Dr David Wintringham again features; *Death in Retirement*, 1956; and *Death on the Reserve*, 1966.

Others which should be mentioned include Elizabeth Mackintosh (1896–1952), who wrote under the pseudonyms of 'Josephine Tey' and 'Gordon Daviot'. *The Man in the Queue*, 1929; *A Shilling for Candles*, 1936; *Miss Pym Disposes*, 1946; *The Franchise Affair*, 1948; *Brat Farrar*, 1949, published in the USA as *Come and Kill Me*, 1950; and *The Daughter of Time*, 1951; are amongst the best of her works. *The Singing Sands*, 1953, was published posthumously. Margot Bennett (b. 1903) started her career with *Time to Change Hats*, 1945; and continued with *Away Went the Little Fish*, 1946; *The Widow of Bath*, 1952; *Farewell Crown and Goodbye King*, 1953; and *Someone from the Past*, 1958. Nancy Hermione Bodington (b. 1912) writes under the name 'Shelley Smith', and has produced, amongst other titles, *Come and be Killed*, 1946; *He Died of Murder*, 1947; *The Woman in the Sea*, 1948; *An Afternoon to Kill*, 1953; and *The Lord Have Mercy*, 1956.

Joan Fleming (b. 1908) started as a writer of children's books: *Dick Brownie and the Zagabog* (1943), was followed by several other 'Reward Books' as they were then called. Her first adult novel, *Two Lovers Too Many*, 1948, had a scientific theme centring on the action of radio-active isotopes. Amongst her many other titles are *You Can't Believe Your Eyes*, 1957, published by Collins, London, (as are all her later works); *When I Grow Rich*, 1962, which brought her the Critic's Award; and *Young Man I Think You're Dying*, 1970, for which she gained the coveted literary prize of The Golden Dagger, awarded by the Crime Writer's Association. With well over thirty novels to her credit, she has recently written *Screams from a Penny Dreadful*, 1971 (Hamish Hamilton), telling the story of the trials and tribulations of earlier generations of her family, caught in the toils of the Industrial Revolution.

In the USA several women writers were active in the interwar years. Phoebe Attwood Taylor (*b.* 1909), in her Cape Cod novels featured the homespun, pipe-smoking detective Asey Mayo. *The Cape Cod Mystery*, 1931; *Spring Harrowing*, 1939; *The Hollow Chest*, 1941; and *Dead Ernest*, 1944; have all passed through several editions, each written under her pseudonym of 'Alice Tilton'. The best of her later novels is possibly *Diplomatic Corpse*, 1951.

Georgina Ann Randolph (1908–57), who employed the pseudonym 'Craig Rice' (as well as those of 'Daphne Sanders' and 'Michael Venning'), used the wiles of her lawyer-detective John J. Malone to extricate the innocent from the electric chair, in the tough and fiery Dashiell Hammett tradition. *Trial by Fury*, 1941; *The Lucky Stiff*, 1945; *The Fourth Postman*, 1948; was followed by *Forty-Five Murderers*, 1952, a book which passed through several editions on both sides of the Atlantic. At the time of her sudden death she was engaged in writing *The April Robin Murders*, later completed by 'Ed McBain' (Evan Hunter, *b.* 1926), whose own detective stories attract a wide audience under such titles as: *The Con Man*, 1957; *Killer's Choice*, 1957; *Lady Killer*, 1958; and *Killer's Wedge*, 1959.

Mignon G. Eberhart (*b.* 1899), used a hospital setting for several of her detective novels, including *The Patient in Room 18*; and *From This Dark Stairway*, 1931. Her large output has included *The Cases of Susan Dare*, 1934; *Five Passengers from Lisbon*, 1946; *Another Man's Murder*, 1957; and *Run Scared*, 1963.

No doubt, I shall be taken to task by the critics for the omission of several deserving names, not only in this chapter, but in all those devoted to the 20th century. To list every author who has made a worthwhile contribution to the genre would fill at least four volumes the size of this present book, so there must be many whose efforts cannot be acknowledged here. It appears that nearly every writer of novels, whose output could be numbered in double figures, made at least one attempt at creating a detective whose exploits might capture the public's imagination. Few amongst the lady sleuths succeeded in the full measure of their hopes, yet the outstanding names listed in this chapter there are many whose contribution to the annals of detective fiction will ensure them permanent remembrance among lovers of the art form.

The Modern Writers

The world war of 1914–18 stands an arbitrary dividing-line in time between the old-style detective story, tinged with the romanticism of the Victorian era, and the works of the post-War writers, looking at the world about them through less charitable and more discerning eyes. Inevitably, there was an overlap between the new school of 'modern' writers, originating fresh and often surprisingly unexpected trends, and those whose earliest works had appeared in Edwardian times but who were still giving fresh life to well-tried forms of the detective novel well into the 1930s.

Probably the most prolific writer of mystery thrillers, several of which can be classed as detective fiction, was that likeable, flamboyant spendthrift, Edgar Wallace (1875–1932). His earliest works, such as *The Mission that Failed!*, 1898; *Writ in Barracks*, 1900; and *Unofficial Dispatches* (1902); chronicled his experiences in South Africa during the period of the Boer War, during which he became a Reuters correspondent and later a correspondent for the *Daily Mail*. These particular books, and many of his later works, have no real place in this present volume, but are of the utmost concern to those collectors who seek out every title of the authors they prize. They have a formidable task ahead of them with Edgar Wallace, a writer whose prodigious output left a bibliography of several hundred titles.

It was with *The Four Just Men*, 1905, that he achieved his first success, a book that rapidly became a bestseller. But any profits that the author may have expected from the novel scheme he devised were eaten up by the sensational offer he made, printed in large type on the front cover of the book. He offered £500 reward (First Prize £250 – the balance shared) to any reader who could

The stage production of Edgar Wallace's play *On the Spot*, at the Theatre Royal, Birmingham, after its successful run at Wyndham's Theatre, London.

One of the most sought-after collection of detective short-stories, *Carrington's Cases*, 1920, originally published by William Blackwood, Edinburgh at five shillings a copy, now fetches in the region of £20.

Size of front cover: 18.8 cm × 12.6 cm.

'furnish on the form provided the explanation of Sir Philip Ramon's death'. The plot centres around the murder, 'in No. 44 Downing Street', of the British Foreign Secretary, the man responsible for piloting a new Aliens Extradition Bill through Parliament. His life had been threatened by 'The Four Just Men', an international coterie who have sworn to avenge injustice wherever it may be found, and who are known to have committed several assassinations during the previous few months – always at the time and place notified in their letters to their victims. Wallace builds the excitement and tension to a climax at the end of the book when Ramon is killed, at exactly eight o'clock as predicted, despite a police guard of several hundred men posted in the streets outside and in the rooms and corridors of the building where he is sheltering. All the clues are carefully displayed, but the reader is left to find his own solution to the mystery of how the crime was actually committed. The winning entries were finally paid out, having submitted their solutions on the competition slip which was tipped-in on perforated paper at the end of the book. This numbered entry form, together with the folding frontispiece, must still be present in complete copies of the first edition. The work was issued by the Tallis Press, London, in a binding of smooth orange cloth, printed in black on the front cover and spine. Due to the large printing of the 1905 edition, it is by no means a difficult 'first' to find, but copies have recently been catalogued as high as £20 ($50).

Of the author's countless thrillers, only a few qualify as *genuine* detective stories. These include the series featuring Mr J. G. Reeder – that likeable character complete with his mutton-chop whiskers, a square pre-Churchillian bowler-hat, and tight-rolled umbrella. *The Mind of Mr. J. G. Reeder* (1925); *Terror Keep* (1927); *The Murder Book of Mr. J. G. Reeder*, 1929; *Red Aces* (1929); and *Mr. J. G. Reeder Returns*, 1933; feature the best of his appearances in the role of an apologetic investigator, although most of his detective triumphs seem to hinge more on luck than an intellectual appraisal of the facts. Despite the author's manifest faults as a writer, for too many of his stories are marred by lack of revision and bear obvious signs of the haste in which he churned them out, by 1928, Wallace was earning some £50,000 a year. One critic has worked out that one in every four books printed and sold in Britain during his heyday was an Edgar Wallace title, yet such was his zest for life and contempt of financial law and order, that at his death in Hollywood, USA in 1932, (where the first of his motion-picture stories, *King Kong*, was produced shortly afterwards), his estate totalled £150,000 worth of debts. But this burden was cleared in only two years by his accruing royalties, a source of income for his heirs that has gone on increasing ever since. Amongst the most popular of his other works were his early African stories, such as *Sanders of the River*, 1911; *People of the River*, 1912; *Bosambo of the River*, 1914; *"Bones"*, 1915; and *The Keepers of the King's Peace*, 1917. Apart from these titles, there are other works in which crime and detection figured. These include *Angel Esquire* (1908); *The Fourth Plague*, 1913; *Melody of Death*, 1915; *The Clue of the Twisted Candle* (1918); *Green Rust*, 1919; *The Daffodil Mystery*, 1920; *The Clue of the New Pin* (1923); *The Dark Eyes of London*, 1924; *Room 13*, 1924; *The Gaunt Stranger* (1925), later issued as *The Ringer*; *The Squeaker* (1927), *The Clue of the Silver Key* (1930); *On the Spot*, 1931; and *When the Gangs Came to London* (1932). The most difficult of all his first editions to find (with the possible exception of his first published work, mentioned above) is undoubtedly *The Tomb of Ts'in*, 1916. It was published by Ward, Lock & Co., in a binding of blue cloth (see illustration, right) but almost the entire first edition was destroyed by a Zeppelin's bombs, while in a London warehouse during World War I. A paperback edition was published later that year.

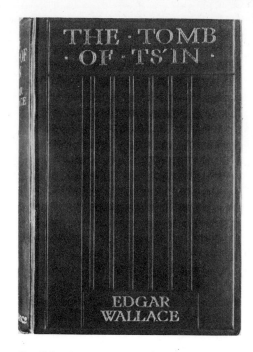

Possibly the rarest of all Edgar Wallace's many titles, this copy of the first edition, dated 1916, was one of the few to survive a World War I bombing of a London warehouse.

Another author whose works overlapped the two Golden Ages of detective fiction was Joseph S. Fletcher (1863–1935), a Yorkshireman whose *The Adventures of Archer Dawe (Sleuth-Hound)*, 1909, is an extremely difficult first edition to track down. So is *The Middle Temple Murder*, 1918, a work which had the good fortune to be openly praised by that avid reader of the genre, President Woodrow Wilson, with the result that this novel, and many of his other stories that followed, enjoyed wide sales in the USA as well as Britain. He had established an early reputation with *When Charles the First was King*, 3 vols. 1892, published at a period when he already had three other novels to his credit. By 1905, the total had risen to 27, and by the 1920s he was turning out new titles at the rate of three or four a year. Fletcher wrote with a gentle facility, conjuring his settings so well that the crimes and techniques of detection often took second place in his books. His detective novels are full of the atmosphere of English scenery and country life, and the backgrounds of many of them remain in the memory long after the stories themselves have been forgotten. He never produced a really memorable detective, with the possible exception of Roger Camberwell, the hero of a series of tales written late in Fletcher's literary career. Amongst the best of his detective stories are *The Ivory God*, 1907; *The Herapath Property*, 1920; *The Million-Dollar Diamond*, 1923; *The Charing Cross Mystery*, 1923; *The Box Hill Murder*, 1929; and *The Yorkshire Moorland Murders*, 1930.

The publication of *The Cask*, 1920, by the Irish writer Freeman Wills Crofts (1879–1957), in which much of the action takes place in Paris, signalled the return of the professional police-detective hero, this time an Inspector Burnley. Before many chapters are behind him he is intent on the methodical breaking down of what at first appears to be a water-tight alibi, a method of approach consistently favoured by the author throughout all his detective works. Crofts' readers had to content themselves with three further mystery stories before he introduced them to the man with whom his name will always be linked, Inspector (later Chief Inspector) Joseph French. The plot revolves around a daring jewel theft from a Hatton Garden firm, coupled with the murder of the chief clerk. Crofts mistakenly titled it *Inspector French's Greatest Case*, 1925, not knowing at that time of the immediate and enduring popularity which awaited his fictional creation. When he wrote the book, the author was still employed as chief engineer of the Belfast and Northern Counties Railway, but in 1929, due to his literary and financial success, he resigned, in order to devote the rest of his career to charting the investigations of Inspector French. *Inspector French and the Cheyne Mystery*, 1926, (published in the USA as *The Cheyne Mystery*); *Inspector French and the Starvel Tragedy*, 1927, (in the USA, *The Starvel Hollow Tragedy*); *The Sea Mystery*, 1928; *Sir John Magill's Last Journey*, 1930; *Mystery in the Channel*, 1931; and *Tragedy in the Hollow*, 1939, are some of his later titles.

During World War I, a correspondent working for the *Daily Telegraph* began writing detective stories to relieve the tedium of periods of inactivity and as a form of escapism from the strains imposed by frequent visits to the front. He chose the framework of the short story in which to present the exploits of his detective hero Reginald Fortune, and his first group of tales were published soon after the end of the war as *Call Mr. Fortune*, 1920. The author, Henry Christopher Bailey (1878–1961), was educated at Corpus Christi, Oxford, where he took first class honours in classics, later joining the staff of the *Daily Telegraph* where he remained in various capacities for the period 1901–46. His series of Reggie Fortune tales, featuring the investigator aptly described by H. Douglas Thomson as 'an infallible intuitionalist', achieved great popularity in the 1920s and '30s under such titles as *Mr. Fortune's Practice*, 1923; *Case for Mr. Fortune*, 1932; *Mr. Fortune Wonders*, 1933; and *Black Land, White Land*, 1937. In 1930, H. C. Bailey created a new style detective in Joshua Clunk, a hypocritical old lawyer who leaves all the routine spade-work to his confidential clerks, who investigate under his none too subtle direction. Typical titles are *Garstons*, 1930; *Clunk's Claimant*, 1937; and *Shrouded Death*, 1950.

Amongst those authors whose reputations have been made in other branches of literature and yet have made significant contributions to detective fiction are A. A. Milne and A. E. W. Mason. Alan Alexander Milne (1882–1956), the creator of Christopher Robin and Winnie the Pooh, gave us *The Red House Mystery*, 1922, dedicating it to his father, John Vine Milne, with the words:

A handful of 'modern' first editions of detective fiction.

My Dear Father,

Like all really nice people, you have a weakness for detective stories, and feel that there are not enough of them. So, after all that you have done for me, the least I can do for you is to write you one. Here it is . . .

And an excellent story it is! Antony Gillingham light-heartedly unravels the mystery, standing at the head of a long, and soon extending queue of humorous sleuths who gave a new and refreshing slant to the business of fictional crime. 'What Fun! Here's a body!' sums up the style; yet this fantasy, with its brilliant dialogue, finely-drawn scenes from the night-life of the 'twenties and credible characters, hold the reader until the final page is turned. The book has never been out of print since the appearance of the first edition quoted above. Milne also wrote *The Fourth Wall*, 1928, a cleverly contrived murder mystery, and *The Perfect Alibi*, 1928, an ingenious detective drama with the audience watching the crime as it is committed, thus knowing the identity of the criminal long before the stage detective.

Alfred Edward Woodley Mason (1865–1948), was educated at Dulwich College, before going up to Trinity College, Oxford, where he won an Exhibition in classics in 1887. For some years he toured the provinces as an actor and actually appeared in the first production of George Bernard Shaw's *Arms and the Man* in 1894 at the Avenue Theatre, London. The fact that he failed to find any further West End work prompted him to try his hand at writing a novel, and *A Romance of Wastdale*, 1895 (Elkin Mathews, London), now the rarest first edition in his whole canon of work, was the result. *The Courtship of Morrice Buckland*, 1896, brought him to the notice of a wider public, who appreciated the merits of 'cloak-and-dagger' story-tellers, and he followed this with *The Philanderers*, 1896, and *Lawrence Clavering*, 1897. But it was with the appearance of *The Four Feathers*, 1902, that the name of A. E. W. Mason became a household word and he was set in the forefront of contemporary novelists. This is still his most famous book, but his contribution to detective fiction, and the creation of one of the genre's most memorable characters, had to wait until the publication of *At the Villa Rose*, 1910, issued in a binding of blue cloth, blocked in gold and black. Later issues of the first edition appeared in a secondary (but more important-looking) binding of red cloth blocked in yellow and white on the front cover, and in yellow and gold on the spine.

At the Villa Rose introduced the first of the Inspector Hanaud series of detective novels, all of which were set in France and all of which achieved success through the medium of subtle but exciting plots and finely-drawn character studies of the protagonists. Hanaud himself, a French Sûreté agent, and his wine-loving Watson, Julius Ricardo, are not forgotten once they have been met in the pages of Mason's small but choice offering of detective stories. Hanaud, heavily-built, and gifted with an exceedingly sharp wit, was described by the author as being 'like a big St Bernard dog', and his love of the mountains, his ruthless efficiency and irrepressible humour, conjure a personality of one of the most endearing of fictional detectives. The second crime novel to feature him, *The House of the Arrow* (1924), considered by many critics to be the best of the series, was not written until fourteen years after his earlier success. It was followed by other Hanaud novels – *The Prisoner in the Opal* (1928); *They Wouldn't be Chessmen*, 1935; and *The House in Lordship Lane*, 1946; all published by Hodder & Stoughton, London, in Mason's usual binding of smooth blue cloth, lettered in black and gold. *Inspector Hanaud Investigates*, 1931, was an omnibus volume containing an interesting apologia by the author, telling how he had planned and written each title in the series.

A series of detective tales derived from the Gaboriau school had been appearing in France during World War I, and were published in English translation as *The Fantômas Detective Novels* under the London imprint of Stanley Paul & Company. Written by Pierre Souvestre and Marcel Allain, their English titles were *Fantômas*, 1916, described by G. K. Chesterton as 'by far the best detective story that I have read for a very long time'; *The Exploits of Juve*, 1916; *Messengers of Evil*, 1917, in which the arch-criminal Fantômas escapes from justice by donning gloves 'made from the skin of a dead man's hands'; and *A Nest of Spies*, 1917. Detective Juve spends volumes pursuing and unmasking Fantômas, only to see him make his escape in the final chapter of every book. In *Messengers of Evil*, when he finally advances with the handcuffs, as Fantô-

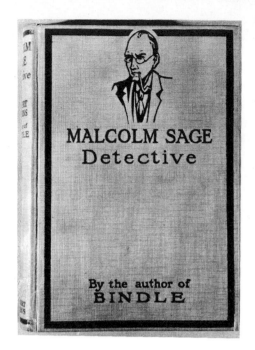

A light-hearted tale of crime and detection by Herbert Jenkins, who combined the roles of both author and publisher. This first edition is dated 1921.

Size of front cover:
19 cm × 12.5 cm.

mas stands surrounded and brought to bay, he is once again thwarted:

> Whilst the detective made a frantic effort to move a step – *he seemed nailed to the floor* – Fantômas, quick as lightning, leaped over the prone body of Monsieur Harvard, gained the door, and banged it to behind him! They heard a triumphant burst of laughter . . . Fantômas was escaping!
>
> 'This is sorcery!' shouted the chief of the detective force, in a voice hoarse with rage.
>
> 'Take your boots off! . . . Take your boots off!' yelled Juve, who, with bare feet was rushing through the house, revolver in hand . . .

So once again Fantômas had won the day, this time by nailing his opponents to the ground 'by the powerful attraction exercised by electro-magnets on the nails in their shoes . . .'

The use of these extra-scientific and obviously unworkable devices was roundly condemned by Monsignor Ronald Knox (1888–1957), whose contribution to detective fiction included critical researches into the techniques that could legitimately be employed by authors who wished to play fair with their readers. Educated at Eton and at Balliol College, Oxford, he maintained a literary output of books as far apart in subject as apologetics, religious controversy, satirical and limerick verse, and detective fiction. Appointed chaplain to the Roman Catholic undergraduates at Oxford, he remained there until the outbreak of World War II, publishing in his last months at the university what was artistically the most successful of his many titles – *Let Dons Delight*, 1939. His first detective novel, *The Viaduct Murder*, 1925 (Methuen), has various memorable scenes and characters, but relies on a railway timetable and the

One of the original paper-wrapped parts of one of the earliest crime and detection novels, the illustrations being by George Cruikshank.

Size of front cover:
18.5 cm × 12.5 cm.

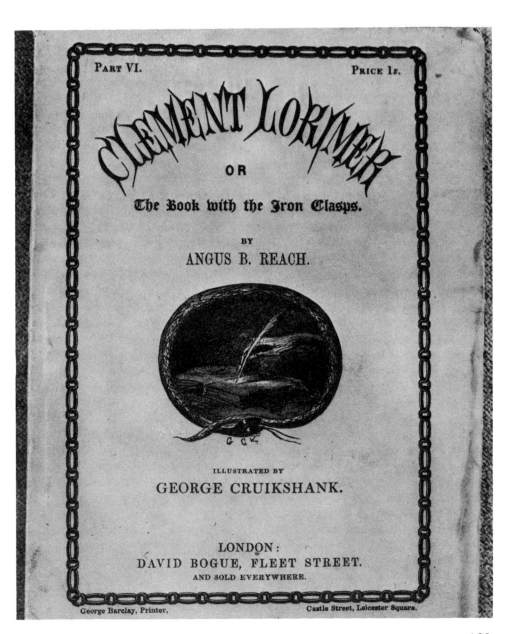

PART VI.   PRICE 1s.

CLEMENT LORIMER

OR

The Book with the Iron Clasps.

BY

ANGUS B. REACH.

ILLUSTRATED BY

GEORGE CRUIKSHANK.

LONDON:
DAVID BOGUE, FLEET STREET.
AND SOLD EVERYWHERE.

George Barclay, Printer,   Castle Street, Leicester Square.

presence of a secret passage for a credible ending. The first in order of production, it lacked the quality of some of his later works in the field, notably *The Three Taps*, 1927 (a detective story without murderer or murder); *The Body in the Silo*, 1933; *Still Dead*, 1934; and *Double-Cross Purposes*, 1937. *The Body in the Silo* was published in the USA by E. P. Dutton & Company as *Settled Out of Court*, 1934. Father Knox's erudite virtuosity was displayed to the full in *Essays in Satire*, 1928, containing his article *Studies in the Literature of Sherlock Holmes*, a work that had first appeared in *The Blue Book* and in *Blackfriars Magazine*. In his introduction to *The Best Detective Stories of 1928*, published by Faber (dated 1929), which he edited in collaboration with H. Harrington, he wrote an introduction which still commands respect from literary historians and knowledgeable critics of the genre alike. In this often-quoted introduction, Knox not only pointed the way to several unexplored avenues that later writers were quick to claim as their own, but he formulated a set of ten rules that authors of detective fiction ought to respect. In essence these were :

1 The criminal must be introduced early, not just brought in at the end.
2 The crime must be solved by logical means, not by supernatural causes.
3 No more than one secret room or passage must be used.
4 No new, undiscovered or undetectable poisons.
5 No foreigners of sinister or malignant aspect (especially Chinamen).
6 The crime must not be solved merely by a lucky accident.
7 The investigator must not have committed the crime himself.
8 He must not wittingly conceal clues or the reasons for his deductions from the reader.
9 If a 'Watson' is introduced, he must not conceal his opinions.
10 Identical twins or 'doubles' are not to be used.

Meanwhile, a husband and wife literary partnership had been formed that worked in the fields of history and economics, and also made a joint approach to the problems of writing successful detective stories. G. D. H. Cole (1890–1959), and Margaret Isabel Cole (née Postgate, *b.* 1893), together wrote more than thirty works of detective fiction (plus a few short stories). The first to appear, *The Brooklyn Murders*, 1923, (which, incidentally, has nothing whatsoever to do with Brooklyn, New York) centres around the last will and testament of Sir Vernon Brooklyn. This controversial document results in a series of three murders, which one Superintendent Wilson has to sort out. This first attempt at a 'whodunit' was G. D. H. Cole's sole responsibility, but his wife joined him as a writer for most of the rest of the series. *Murder at Crome House*, 1927, is considered their masterpiece; but *The Death of a Millionaire*, 1925; *The Blatchington Tangle*, 1926; *Dead Man's Watch*, 1931; *Death in the Quarry*, 1934; and *The Murder at the Munition Works*, 1940; can still be read with a deal of enjoyment. Some of the Coles' works are marred by being overloaded with a repetitive series of painstaking interviews with every suspect in the story; Superintendent Wilson sifting and laboriously assessing the minutiae of evidence through chapter-long dialogues before finally delivering his verdict. The reader occasionally feels tempted to leave the court before the Superintendent at last reaches his conclusions.

Colonel Anthony Gethryn is the military-minded detective hero of Philip Macdonald (*b.* 1896) who also wrote under such pseudonyms as 'Anthony Lawless', 'Oliver Fleming', and 'Martin Porlock'. Gethryn was introduced in the first of Macdonald's stories, *The Rasp*, 1924, a tale extremely popular in its day and often declared to be an epoch-making contribution to the field, by knowledgeable connoisseurs. Reading the story today, it is difficult to perceive why it was ever accorded classical status, for the plot revolves around the conventional body-in-the-study theme and the methods of detection used have an obvious quality. Macdonald's later titles include *The White Crow*, 1928; *The Noose*, 1930, (a tale that shared, with Agatha Christie's *The Murder at the Vicarage*, the distinction of being the first to bear the famous 'Crime Club' label of the London publishing house of Collins); *The Link*, 1930, perhaps the best Gethryn novel; *Murder Gone Mad*, 1931; *The Nursemaid Who Disappeared*, 1938, (published in the USA as *Warrant for X*); and *The List of Adrian Messenger*, 1959. One of the best of his short stories is *The Green and Gold String*, first published in *The Queen's Awards: Third Series*, 1948, edited by Ellery Queen (Little, Brown & Co., Boston, USA).

Anthony Berkeley Cox (1893–1971), wrote some excellent detective stories under the pseudonym of 'Anthony Berkeley', and two masterpieces using the name 'Francis Iles'. What distinguishes these two crime novels is that the reader knows from the start of the book the identity of the murderer and the crime he is planning to commit. Despite what at first sight seems a handicap, tension mounts throughout the story and spine-tingling excitement is maintained to the very last pages.

Strictly speaking, neither of these Francis Iles novels, *Malice Aforethought*, 1931, and *Before the Fact*, 1932, are works of detective fiction. In each, most of the elements of logical deduction and detection have been subordinated to a fascinating study of criminal psychology that takes us step by step closer and closer to the intended victim, with the murder weapon ever ready to hand. The completely new twist which Cox devised is expressed in the first sentences of the opening paragraph of *Malice Aforethought*:

> It was not until several weeks after he had decided to murder his wife that Dr Bickleigh took any active steps in the matter. Murder is a serious business. The slightest slip may be disastrous. Dr Bickleigh had no intention of risking disaster.

The third Iles book, *As For The Woman*, 1939, lacked the freshness of approach achieved by its two predecessors and must be counted inferior to both. As first editions, the earlier works are extremely difficult to find. Both were published as paperbacks at 3s. a copy, under the imprint of Mundanus Ltd., a subsidary of Victor Gollancz, and almost immediately reissued in hardback form in a full-cloth binding. Copies in either format are seldom met with and those that do come on the market command up to £20 ($50). They can be considered key books in any collection of detective fiction compiled with the aim of reflecting important developments in a still evolving form of story-telling, and both had a considerable influence on later work.

Professor Moriarty, the ruthless opponent and arch-enemy of Sherlock Holmes.

"PROFESSOR MORIARTY STOOD BEFORE ME."

A. B. Cox's first book was published anonymously under the title *The Layton Court Mystery*, 1925 (Jenkins). As Anthony Berkeley, he gave us, amongst many other titles, *The Silk Stocking Murders*, 1928; *The Second Shot*, 1930; *Jumping Jenny*, 1933 (published in the USA as *Dead Mrs. Stratton*); *Trial and Error*, 1937; *Not to be Taken*, 1938 (in the USA as *A Puzzle in Poison*); and *Death in the House*, 1939. *The Poisoned Chocolates Case*, 1929, was a notable *tour de force* in which the author's detective, Roger Sheringham, appears at his best. In this, one of his most successful tales, Cox is able to offer no less than six feasible solutions to the mystery of who sent the box of poisoned chocolates to the unsuspecting Joan Bendix. It was a year later, in *The Second Shot*, that he published a preface in which he prophesied that:

> the days of the old crime-puzzle pure and simple, relying entirely upon plot and without any added attractions of character, style, or even humour, are in the hands of the auditor; and that the detective story is in the process of developing into the novel with a detective or crime interest, holding its readers less by mathematical than psychological ties. The puzzle element will no doubt remain, but it will become a puzzle of character rather than a puzzle of time, place, motive, and opportunity.

Later events were to prove this prediction true, and in the 1930s Cox and a handful of other contemporary writers founded the celebrated Detection Club, an institution largely devoted to the evolution of the 'character' detective novel.

In the USA the work of Willard Huntington Wright (1888–1939), did much to revive the flagging public interest in detective fiction. Few of the exciting developments that had been taking place in Britain had occurred in the country, but in 1926 the publication of *The Benson Murder Case*, modelled on the real-life killing of Joseph Elwell, caught the imagination of a wide readership that soon transformed the book into a bestseller. Published under the pseudonym of 'S. S. Van Dine', the book introduced a new type of amateur detective, Philo Vance, an elegant sleuth who had somehow acquired an English accent while developing 'a tremendous flair for the significant under-currents of the so-called *trivia* of life'. Most of the 'S. S. Van Dine' tales are melodramatic in the extreme and crammed with the high-speed violence and blood-letting commonly found in American crime novels of this and later periods. His later titles, such as *The Canary Murder Case*, 1928; *The Greene Murder Case*, 1928; *The Scarab*

Murder Case, 1930; *The Casino Murder Case*, 1934; *The Kidnap Murder Case*, 1936; and *The Winter Murder Case*, 1939, a book left uncompleted at the time of Wright's death; were all first published in book form by Charles Scribner, New York. Wright is also remembered for *The Great Detective Stories*, 1927, published under his own name, a work containing a particularly astute and analytical introduction, and for *The Philo Vance Omnibus*, 1936, with its *Twenty Rules for Writing Detective Stories*.

Vincent Starrett (*b.* 1886), spent many years as a journalist in Chicago, and is an acknowledged, specialist critic of the Sherlock Holmes style books, as well as an established writer of detective fiction. *Murder on "B" Deck*, 1929, in which Walter Ghost acts the part of the detective aboard the *Latakia*; *Dead Man Inside*, 1931; and *The End of Mr. Garment*, 1932; are fair samples of his work. *The Private Life of Sherlock Holmes*, 1933, (Macmillan, New York), has become a classic of its kind, in which Starrett makes known his wish for a chance to spend a few hours with his hero:

> "Granted the opportunity, gentlemen – one might cry, in paraphrase of Dr. Bell – of recovering a single day out of the irrevocable past, how would you choose to spend that sorcerous gift? With Mister Shakespeare in his tiring room? With Villon and his companions of the cockleshell? Riding with Rupert or barging it with Cleopatra up the Nile? Or would you choose to squander it on a chase with Sherlock Holmes after a visit to the rooms in Baker Street? There can be only one possible answer, gentlemen, to the question."

His contemporary, Samuel Dashiell Hammett (1894–1961), had been for some years a member of the Pinkerton Detective Agency, an experience that gave him a factual background for many of his plots. After writing short stories for the magazine *Black Mask*, he published his first novel, *Red Harvest*, 1929, (Knopf, New York), considered by several critics to be his best book. It had originally appeared in serial form as *The Cleansing of Personville*, and has been called the first of the 'rotten town' novels. Writing under the shortened name of Dashiell Hammett (he also occasionally used the pseudonym 'Peter Collinson'), he next produced *The Dain Curse*, 1929; to be followed by his most famous book, *The Maltese Falcon*, 1930. In this classic of the genre, he daringly presented the villain of the piece as a homosexual, made the hero considerably less than bright, and associated the lithe and beautiful heroine with cruelty, treachery and other unladylike qualities. *The Glass Key*, 1931, was a worthy successor; but *The Thin Man*, 1934, was easily the most successful of all Hammett's works.

The name 'Ellery Queen' is one that will always be associated with the history of detective fiction. It is the pen-name used jointly by two cousins, who were both born in Brooklyn, New York, in 1905. Frederic Dannay and Manfred Lee use this same pseudonym for the name of their hero-detective, whose father, Inspector Richard Queen, is the straight-man in the act, serving as foil to his son. With the appearance of *The Roman Hat Mystery*, 1929, a book that has been called 'a landmark rather than a cornerstone', we were given the first of a dozen mystery stories by this joint-authorship; each sub-titled 'A Problem in Deduction'. *The French Powder Mystery*, 1930; *The Dutch Shoe Mystery*, 1931; *The Egyptian Cross Mystery*, 1932; *The Siamese Twin Mystery*, 1933; *The American Gun Mystery*, 1933; etc., all first published in book-form by Frederick A. Stokes, New York; were later to be followed by such titles as *The Spanish Cape Mystery*, 1935 (Lippincott); *Inspector Queen's Own Case*, 1956; *And on the Eighth Day*, 1964; and *The House of Brass*, 1968.

In the autumn of 1941, *The Ellery Queen Mystery Magazine* commenced publication, later becoming a monthly periodical. It continues to appear to the present day, printing and reprinting short stories and novelettes covering the several fields of detection and crime, horror stories, and those dealing with the supernatural. The prefaces and introductory remarks by the editors contain much valuable biographical and bibliographical information in the sphere of detective fiction, and since 1960 the magazine has been issuing annual paperbound anthologies of author's old and new. *Queen's Quorum*, 1948, described in its sub-title as being 'A History of the Detective-Crime Short Story as Revealed by the 106 Most Important Books Published in this Field since 1845', has long since established itself as the definitive work on the subject. It is con-

Doctor Nikola, 1896, by Guy Boothby, as seen by the artist Stanley L. Wood.

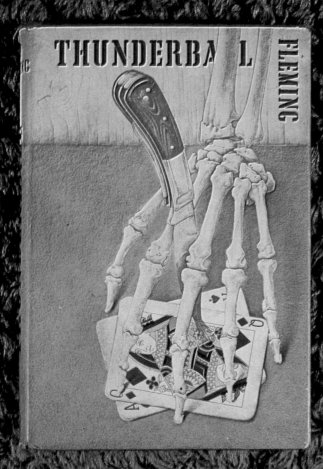

THUNDERBALL · FLEMING

FLEMING

YOU ONLY LIVE TWICE

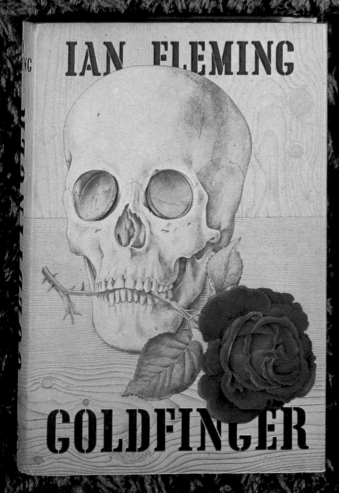

IAN FLEMING

GOLDFINGER

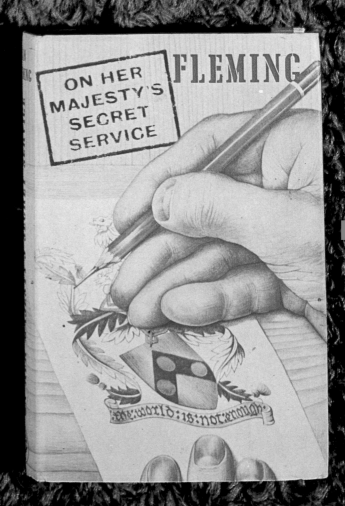

ON HER MAJESTY'S SECRET SERVICE · FLEMING

the·world·is·not·enough

First editions of Ian Fleming's James Bond novels, published by Jonathan Cape, London. The dust-jacket designs are all by Richard Chopping.

stantly quoted in the catalogues of specialist auctioneers and antiquarian booksellers as an authority to be respected.

Amongst other American authors, Earl Derr Biggers (1884–1933), was successful with his first mystery novel, *Seven Keys to Baldpate*, 1913; but is remembered today as the creator of the imperturbable Charlie Chan, the bland Hawaiian detective who has featured in countless films. *The Celebrated Cases of Charlie Chan*, 1936, covers all we need here; while a similar figure is conjured by the name 'Mr. Moto', the Japanese creation of John Phillips Marquand (1893–1960), whose hero's typical *Saturday Evening Post* adventures can be summed up in *Mr. Moto's Three Aces*, 1956.

Following the tough lead given by Dashiell Hammett, Erle Stanley Gardner (1889–1970), a writer who used a variety of pseudonyms, including 'A. A. Fair', 'Charles M. Green', 'Carleton Kendrake', and 'Charles J. Kenny', soon learned to be even quicker on the draw than his onetime mentor. Born in Malden, Massachusetts, and educated at Palo Alto High School, he began his professional career in California as a trial lawyer before becoming a writer in 1933. He has made the name of his legal hawk Perry Mason internationally famous; but has also written other works featuring private detectives Donald Lam and Bertha Cool (mostly written under the pseudonym of 'A. A. Fair'). There remain his 'D.A.' stories in which much police detection is involved, and those early Tong murders centred around the gangster killings of Chinese secret societies. The first of the Perry Mason tales, much sought by collectors, was *The Case of the Velvet Claws*, 1933 (William Morrow & Co., New York); followed amongst many others, by *The Case of the Counterfeit Eye*, 1933; *This is Murder*, 1935; *The Case of the Dangerous Dowager*, 1937; and such 'D.A.' titles as *The D.A. Draws a Circle*, 1939; and *The D.A. Breaks an Egg*, 1949. *The Case of the Crooked Candle*, 1944, has been quoted as being one of the best of the Perry Mason detective stories, and *The Case of the Angry Mourner*, 1951, runs it a close second.

For the rest of the American authors, I have space only to mention a few of the most prominent names of the genre, and this inevitably excludes a great many worthy writers whose works may be sought in specialised bibliographies. Principal amongst those names I have yet to list is Indiana-born Rex Stout (*b.* 1886), who began his writing career in the late 1920s. His earliest novels, such as *How Like A God*, 1929, were more tales of psychological suspense than detective stories; but with the appearance of *Fer-de-Lance*, 1934, we are introduced to a memorable detective in the shape of the elephantine Nero Wolfe, whose two besetting passions are beer and orchids; and an even more memorable Watson in the mercurial Archie Goodwin, a young assistant who so often steals the scene from his boss. Rex Stout has put it on record that his over-riding ambition is to write 'one of the two or three best mystery stories in the world', and in some of his works he has come near to succeeding in this aim. It is difficult to pick the best, but amongst the most readable are *The League of Frightened Men*, 1935; *Too Many Cooks*, 1938; *Some Buried Ceasar*, 1939; *Red Threads*, 1939; *Bad for Business*, 1940; *Plot it Yourself*, 1959; and *Death of a Doxy*, 1966; this last title written when the author was over eighty years of age.

Raymond Chandler (1885–1959), although born in Chicago, was reared and educated in England, where he attended Dulwich College. He returned to the USA after World War I, but it was not until 1939, and the publication of *The Big Sleep*, that he established himself in the front row of contemporary novelists. His books are written with remarkable pace and skill, and to some extent he follows Dashiell Hammett's technique of razor-sharpening violence – summed up in his remark to a literary gathering that when he was in any doubt he always 'brought a man through the door with a gun!' *Farewell, My Lovely*, 1940, judged by the author to be his best book; *The High Window*, 1942; *The Lady in the Lake*, 1943; and *The Little Sister*, 1949; were all first published by Knopf, New York.

Amongst an older generation,' omission of the name of the Irish writer 'Sax Rohmer' (i.e. Arthur Sarsfield Ward, 1886–1959), creator of the sinister figure of Dr Fu Manchu and the exotic thrillers written around that oriental villain, would cause cries of protest. From the time the first of the many titles containing that name of evil omen made its appearance as *The Mystery of Dr. Fu Manchu*, 1913, Rohmer built up an expanding band of devoted followers, eager for each

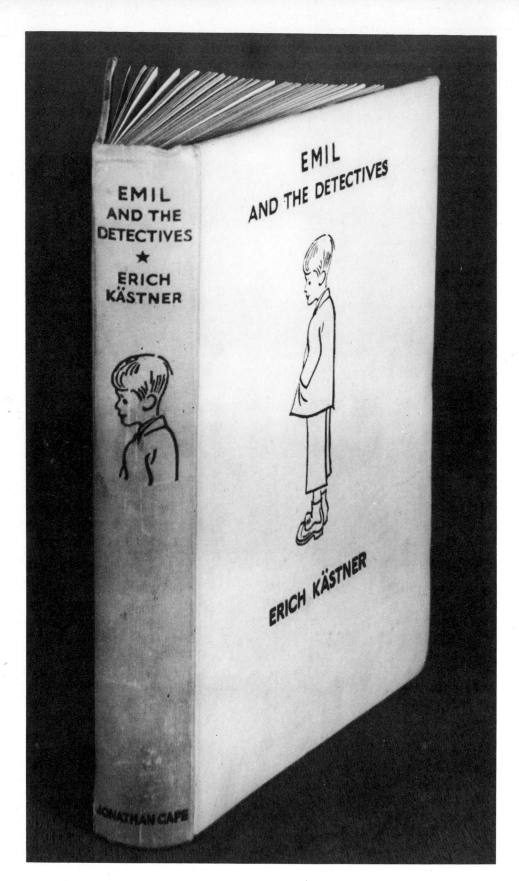

The first English edition, published in 1931, of Kästner's best-seller that was subsequently translated into nearly every European language. The first edition was published in Germany in 1929.

Height of spine: 20 cm.

new duel of wits between the somewhat battered hero, Nayland Smith, and his arch-enemy from the East. The author made sure that the Doctor had the edge over his persistent and seemingly tireless adversary, the detective having to contend with a malign and formidable personality who was not above resorting to 'certain obscure arts and sciences which *no* university of today can teach'. The Doctor was more than a match for any ordinary mortal, endowed as he was with 'the brains of any three men of genius, with a brow like Shakespeare and a face like Satan, a close-shaven skull, and long magnetic eyes . . . imagine that awful being, and you have a mental picture of Dr Fu Manchu, the yellow peril incarnate in one man'. Sax Rohmer's works included *The Hand of Fu Manchu*, 1917; *The Daughter of Fu Manchu*, 1931; and the *Drums of Fu Manchu*, 1939. In addition, many of his other titles are sought by collectors, including *Dope: A Story of Chinatown and the Drug Traffic*, 1919; and *The Dream Detective – Being Some Account of the Methods of Moris Klaw* (1920).

American-born John Dickson Carr (*b.* 1905), who lived for many years in England, has gained a place as one of the foremost modern writers of detective fiction. Born in Uniontown, Pennsylvania, be began writing novels in 1930 and moved to England the following year, where he remained until 1948. His first book, *It Walks by Night*, 1930 (Harper, New York), introduced one of the best-known French detectives in contemporary English fiction, the famous Bercolin. *The Lost Gallows*, 1931; *Castle Skull*, 1931; *Poison in Jest*, 1932; *The Corpse in the Waxworks*, 1932; and *Death Watch*, 1935; (all first published by Harper, New York), were amongst his earliest work. He used the pseudonyms 'Carr Dickson' and 'Carter Dickson', on some of his title pages. *The Case of the Constant Suicides*, 1941, was called 'Carr at his best,' by several critics; but *The Nine Wrong Answers*, 1952, and *The Ghost's High Noon*, 1969, must run it close in popular esteem.

In Europe, the Belgian writer Georges Simenon (*b.* 1903), led the revival of interest in the *romans policiers*. (Simenon's name was originally Georges Sim.) He has been named by various critics as the spiritual heir of nearly every well-known writer in the genre, from Conan Doyle to Edgar Wallace, and is one of the few to rival the latter author in sheer quantity of output. His own potted autobiography is couched in characteristically terse and stacatto terms:

> At sixteen years of age, reporter on the *Liége Gazette*. At seventeen, published my first novel, *Au Pont des Arches*. At twenty, marriage; moved to Paris. From twenty to thirty, published about two hundred novels under sixteen pseudonyms, and travelled, chiefly in a small boat, all over Europe. At thirty, living aboard my yacht *Ostrogot*, then moored in northern Europe; wrote my first detective novels and created the character Maigret. For two years I wrote a novel in this series every month. At thirty-three abandoned mystery novels to devote myself to more personal works. That's all!

Maigret was as realistic a French police officer as his predecessor Lecoq had been theatrical. Up to date, he has figured in about 60 of Simenon's works, translated into English under such titles as *Maigret Travels South* (1940); *In Two Latitudes* (1942); *Lost Moorings* (1946); and *Maigret Afraid* (1961). Possibly the best of the author's 'straight' novels, without Maigret, is *L'homme qui regardait passer les trains*, 1946 (entitled in English, *The Man Who Watched the Trains Go By*). For collectors anxious to obtain the first English editions of his works, all of which were first published in Paris, usually by Presses de la Cité, the earliest translations appeared here during the period 1932–34 and were issued under the Hurst & Blackett imprint.

'Michael Innes' is the pseudonym of John Innes Mackintosh Stewart, (*b.* 1906), one time Professor of English at the University of Adelaide, and later Tutor at Christ Church, Oxford. He began his career as a detective fiction writer in 1936 with the appearance of *Death at the President's Lodging* (Gollancz) published in the USA as *Seven Suspects*; and achieved fame with his next title, *Hamlet, Revenge!*, 1937. His stories often feature his Scotland Yard detective, Inspector John Appleby (later Sir John). His third novel is possibly the best we have yet had from his pen; with *Lament for a Maker*, 1938, he produced a title worthy of a place in any collection of detective fiction. The plot owes something to Wilkie Collins's *The Moonstone*, but the refreshing, new aspect was introduced, described by the author as giving his works 'a somewhat literary flavour' which placed then 'on the frontier between the detective story and the fantasy'. This was supplied by his suave and erudite detective, full of learning and sage quotations and with a knowledge of English Literature extending from Chaucer to Virginia Woolf. *Stop Press*, 1939; *There Came both Mist and Snow*, 1940; *The Weight of the Evidence*, 1943; *The Long Farewell*, 1958; and *Appleby at Allington*, 1968 (published in the USA as *Death by Water*), are among some of the best of his many works.

'Nicholas Blake', pseudonym of the present Poet Laureate Cecil Day-Lewis (*b.* 1904), is another of the post-Sayers generation of literary detective story writers. His first novel, *A Question of Proof*, 1935, drew heavily on his experiences as a master at Summer Fields School, near Oxford, and introduces for the first time his detective, Nigel Strangeways. *Thou Shell of Death*, 1936, was almost immediately successful and brought his name to the attention of a wide public, both in Great Britain and in the USA. *There's Trouble Brewing*, 1937; *The Beast Must Die*, 1938; *Malice in Wonderland*, 1940; *Minute for Murder*, 1947, possibly Blake's masterpiece, with a first-class plot and finely-wrought characterisation; and *A Penknife in My Heart*, 1958, are all well worth reading, and display the author's virtuosity to the full.

Mention the name Leslie Charteris, (the pseudonym of Leslie Charles Bowyer Yin, (*b.* 1907), and one thinks immediately of 'The Saint', the likeable rogue-hero cast in the role of a modern Rocambole, who started his career as long ago as *Enter the Saint*, 1930, and has retained an undiminished popularity ever since. The picaresque Simon Templar plays the ever-extending part, that has long since broken bounds from the early days of the novel to excite viewers on cinema and television screens alike. Born in Singapore, and educated at Rossall School and King's College, Cambridge, Charteris retains the name 'The Saint' in most of his titles, none of which are easily distinguishable as first editions. *The Saint Meets the Tiger*; *Enter the Saint*; *The Saint Steps In*; *The Saint in Miami*, are typical of the continuing saga.

René Raymond (*b.* 1906), is represented in my collection by only a single example of his work, but one with which his name, or, rather, his pseudonym, will always be associated in the minds of his reading public. *No Orchids for Miss Blandish* (1939), published by Jarrolds, London, cannot by any stretch of the imagination be described as a work of detective fiction, but it was the first of a long and continuing line of grimly violent novels by 'James Hadley Chase'. The author also uses the pseudonyms of 'James L. Docherty', 'Raymond Marshall', and 'Ambrose Grant'. This book left its influence on many later titles in which crime and detection figured prominently. The book was dramatised under the same name (with the collaboration of Robert Nesbitt) and opened a long and successful run at the Prince of Wales's Theatre, London, in July, 1942, with Hartley Power playing the exacting rôle of Dave Fenner.

It took me more years than I care to remember to assemble a complete set of the first editions of Dennis Wheatley's 'dossiers', all of which were published for the Crime-Book Society by Hutchinson & Company, London. Dennis Yates Wheatley (*b.* 1897), started his career as a writer with the publication of *The Forbidden Territory*, 1933, a novel that was later made into a film with the same title. Two years later he collaborated with J. G. Links in presenting 'A New Era in Crime Detection', a thick dossier, tied through with red ribbon in the style of a police file, which contained, to quote the author's note, 'cablegrams, original handwritten documents, photographs, police reports, criminal records, and even actual clues in the form of human hair, a piece of blood-stained curtain', all of which were filed in their correct order, 'as received at police headquarters, thereby forming the complete Dossier of a crime'. The author then went on to explain the rules of this new and exciting game, which the reader was expected to play:

> The mystery is presented to the public in exactly the same sequence as that in which it was unravelled by the investigating officer, without any extraneous or misleading matter; photographs of living people taking the place of descriptions of characters which appear in an ordinary detective novel. Clues to the identity of the murderer are scattered liberally through the investigating officer's reports, and are also to be found in the photographs.
>
> On reaching the end of the investigating officer's fifth report all the available evidence is to hand, yet he finds himself unable to solve the mystery. He then receives instructions to arrest the murderer from his superior, who has never seen any of the people concerned, but reaches the correct solution of the mystery solely upon the evidence in Dossier form, exactly as it is presented to you here.
>
> The murderer's confession as to how the crime was committed follows, and the clues which enabled the officer at headquarters to fasten the crime upon him.

The final section was sealed by a wide strip of gummed paper, printed with the words:

DO NOT BREAK THIS STRIP UNTIL YOU HAVE DECIDED, ON THE EVIDENCE

Keep this carefully

It is a First Edition of the first Crime Story ever presented in this way. Should others follow, it is possible that an undamaged copy of "Murder off Miami" may be of considerable interest one day

A prophecy by Dennis Wheatley that has now proved to be true. This is his note, printed on the back-cover of the first (1936) edition of his crime 'dossier', a work published at three shillings and sixpence, but now worth in the region of £10.

Size of printed surface: 12.3 cm × 4 cm.

SUBMITTED, WHO MURDERED BOLITHO BLANE.

The dossiers were sold at 3s. 6d. each and were thought by the public to be excellent value for money. Before long, reprints were demanded and the advertisements announcing new titles boasted of 'British Sales 80,000 copies in 18 months'. The first title, *Murder off Miami* (1936), appeared in the USA as *File on Bolitho Lane*, and was quickly followed by a similar production, *Who Killed Robert Prentice?* (1937), issued in the USA as *File on Robert Prentice*. In all there were four dossiers: *The Mallinsay Massacre* (1938); and *Herewith the Clues!* (1939), completing the quartet. None was dated, but the first editions of each title can be recognised by *not* having the legend '50th Thousand', '80th Thousand', or some such figure, on the front of its printed wrappers. First editions, in pristine state, and with the sealed compartment at the end still unopened, can still be purchased for as little as £10 ($25) each, but I predict with confidence that they will one day be sought avidly at up to ten times that price. Dennis Wheatley and J. G. Links created a new area in the field of detective fiction, and only the outbreak of World War II, with its paper shortage and steeply rising costs, prevented the enterprise continuing, with variations, through a dozen or more titles. The few survivors of this pioneer enterprise deserve an honoured place in any collection, but they will not be easy to find.

One of the most prolific authors of all time, John Creasey (*b.* 1908), can claim credit for having written something over 600 titles, an incredible performance, and one that must make any collector of his works, who wishes to see authors on his shelves in as complete a state as possible, pause and take a deep breath before reserving an entire wall for this choice. *Men, Maids, and Murder*, 1933, published by Andrew Melrose, London, is the earliest book in his daunting list of work that I have been able to track down; which means that, on an average, every year since then, he has produced something in the order of 15 titles, as well as having contributed numerous articles to newspapers and magazines. No mean feat for one who loves to travel and has been elected mayor of his adopted town. His detectives are numerous, but include those well-known names, Inspector West, who appears in (amongst many others) *A Battle for Inspector West*, 1934; *Inspector West Cries Wolf*, 1952, published in the USA as *The Creepers*; and *A Gun for Inspector West*, 1954 (in USA as *Give a Man a Gun*); and also, of course, 'The Toff', whom we have met in *The Toff on the Farm*, 1958; *Follow the Toff*, 1961, and *A Doll for The Toff*, 1963. His other main detective hero is the scientifically-minded Dr Palfrey, who also has a long list of successfully-solved cases to his credit. John Creasey's pseudonyms are almost as legion as his books, but he lists most of these in a candid commentary *John Creasey – Fact or Fiction?*, which he contributed with R. E. Briney to *The Armchair Detective* magazine, October, 1968. He also provides a 17-page bibliography of his works under his many pen-names.

Christopher Bush (*b.* 1885), who occasionally uses the pseudonym 'Michael Home', started well with *The Perfect Murder Case*, 1929; and has made his mark with *The Case of the Dead Shepherd*, 1934, (known in the USA as *The Tea-Tray Murders*); and *The Case of the Platinum Blonde*, 1944; amongst many other titles. Robert Bruce Montgomery (*b.* 1921), is known to his large

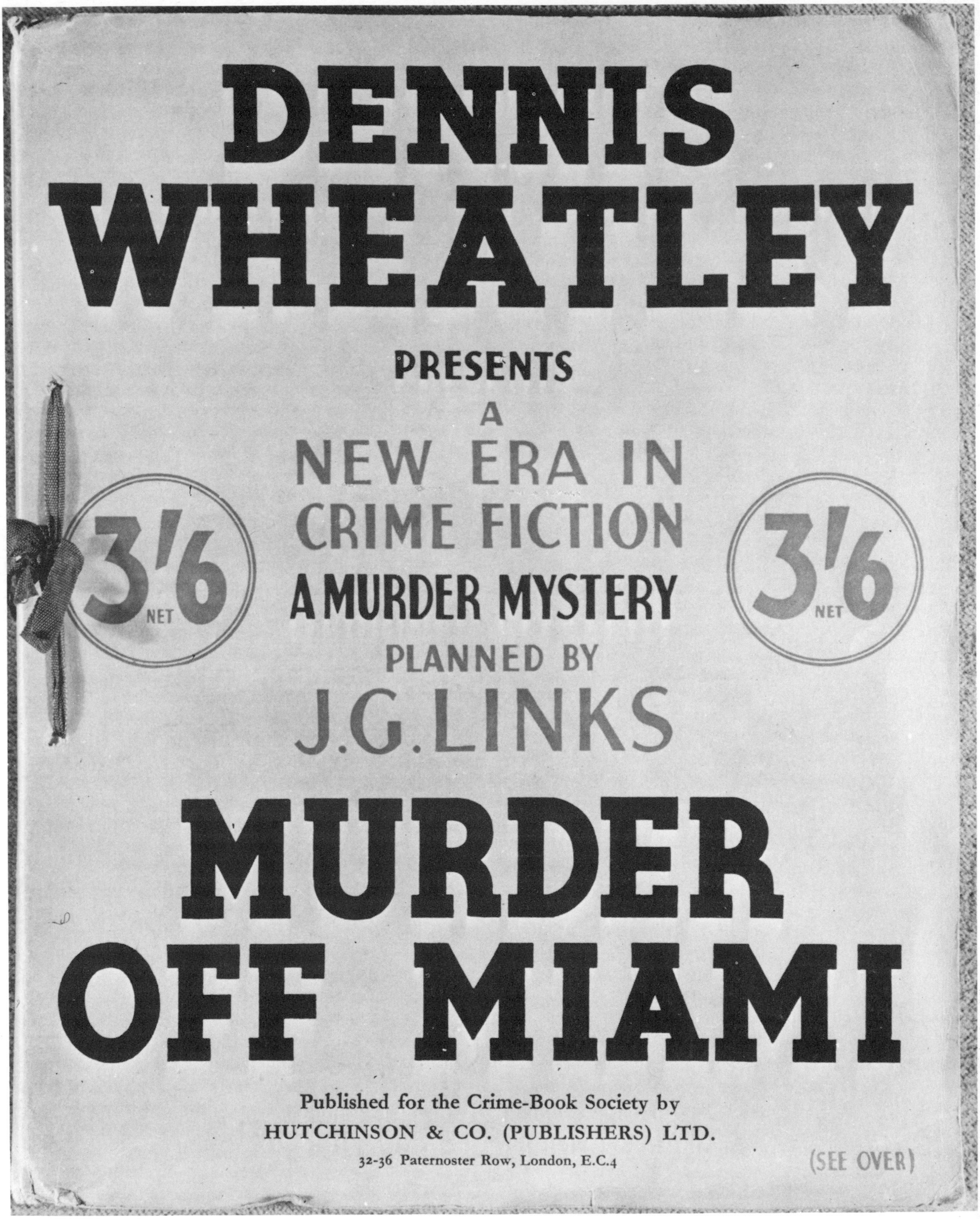

DENNIS WHEATLEY

PRESENTS
A
NEW ERA IN
CRIME FICTION
A MURDER MYSTERY
PLANNED BY
J.G.LINKS

3/6 NET

3/6 NET

MURDER OFF MIAMI

Published for the Crime-Book Society by
HUTCHINSON & CO. (PUBLISHERS) LTD.
32-36 Paternoster Row, London, E.C.4

(SEE OVER)

following of readers as 'Edmund Crispin', and has been one of the acknowledged masters of detective fiction since the mid-1940s. His first novel, *The Case of the Gilded Fly*, 1944, appeared in the USA the following year as *Obsequies at Oxford*, where Crispin had been at St John's College, after attending the Merchant Taylors' School. A man of letters, as well as being a distinguished composer and organist, some of his detective tales feature an Oxford professor

The earliest issue of the first of the Dennis Wheatley crime 'dossiers', published undated in 1936.

Size of front cover:
28.2 cm × 22.2 cm.

118

Police Department

Form RL/2120/C.7.

HAIR FOUND IN MISS FERRI ROCKSAVAGE'S COMB ON THE MORNING OF

9.3.36.

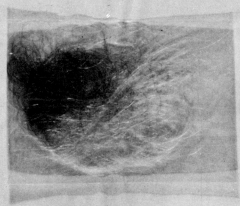

MATCH FOUND IN THE BISHOP OF BUDE'S CABIN ON THE MORNING OF

9.3.36.

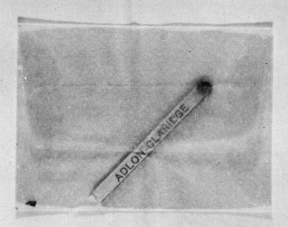

PHOTOGRAPH OF 6´ CIGARETTE ENDS (ALL PLAYER'S) FOUND IN COUNT

POSODINI'S CABIN ON THE MORNING OF 9.3.36.

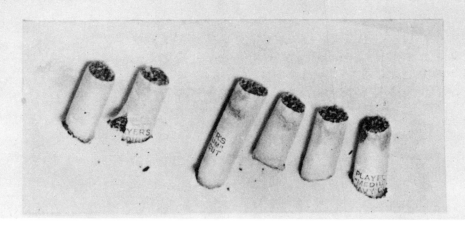

A page of specially manufactured 'clues', one of many similar sets contained in *Murder Off Miami.*

Size of page: 25.2 cm × 20 cm.

of English literature. Dr Gervase Fen. Many of his books are set against unusual backgrounds, and have intriguing titles, such as *Holy Disorders*, 1945; *The Moving Toyshop*, 1946; *Frequent Hearses*, 1950; and *Beware of the Trains*, 1953. All display his talent for original humour as well as a seemingly effortless ability to conjure characters and situations by vividly descriptive phrases. His latest title is *The Glimpses of the Moon*, 1972.

One of the first to introduce pseudo-American tough and stringy detectives to the reading public in Britain was Peter Cheyney (1896–1951), who later turned his attention to spy stories. He used Dashiell Hammett's style of rough and tumble, with quick-fire dialogue and automatic weapons, to achieve bestselling successes with his tales of Lemmy Caution and Slim Callaghan. He believed that *Portrait of a "G" Man* was the best he had written in this style. *Ladies Won't Wait*, 1951, was the last of his titles to appear. Another prolific writer was Major Cecil John Street (1884–1964), better known under his pen-names of 'Miles Burton' or 'John Rhode'. *The Hardway Diamonds Mystery*, 1930; *The Mystery of High Eldersham*, 1930, a classic tale of witchcraft in an English village; *The Menace of the Downs*, 1931; and *Death Takes a Flat*, 1940, published in the USA as *Vacancy with Corpse*, again featuring his detectives Inspector Arnold and Desmond Merrion, are amongst the best of his early works, all first published by Collins, London, under their Crime Club imprint.

One of the best of the modern school of detective story writers is Julian Symons (*b.* 1912), whose reputation also stands high as a historian, literary critic, poet and biographer. Amongst the most readable of his many works of detective fiction are *The Immaterial Murder Case*, 1945; *The Thirty-First of February*, 1950; *The Broken Penny*, 1953; and *The Colour of Murder*, 1957, a title which earned him the special award of the Crime Writers' Association as the best crime novel of the year. His later works include *The Progress of a Crime*, 1960; *The Man Who Killed Himself*, 1967; and *The Players and the Game*, 1972. *Bloody Murder*, 1972, is a critical survey of the history of detective fiction that should go a long way towards establishing itself as a definitive work.

For the rest of the contemporary writers, I have space to mention only a final pair of names, but both are making an important contribution to the continuing saga that started in 1845. H. F. R. Keating (*b.* 1926), was a journalist who published his first detective novel, *Death and the Visiting Firemen*, in 1959. Since then, he has written *Zen there was Murder*, 1960; *A Rush on the Ultimate*, 1961; *Is Skin-Deep, Is Fatal*, 1965; and a series of Inspector Ghote stories. These all feature the Indian detective whose name he has now made famous, starting with *Inspector Ghote's Good Crusade*, 1966; to the latest title, and possibly the best, *Inspector Ghote Goes by Train*, 1972. The other writer I would not like to overlook is F. R. E. Nicolas (*b.* 1927) who writes under the pseudonym of 'Nicholas Freeling'. His first book, *Love in Amsterdam*, 1962, brought him a wide public, and was partly based on his own experience of being unjustly accused of theft, and imprisoned. His Inspector Van der Valk, now Commissaire, is seen again in *Strike Out Where Not Applicable*, 1968, and has appeared in a dozen or more stories, all of which have moved more and more in the direction of the novel of psychological analysis, and consequently towards a more understanding and realistic approach to the whole concept of crime and punishment.

Now the days of the old style Great Detective are over, an era summed up by Ronald Knox when he wrote:

> It is personality that counts. You are not bound to make your public *like* the Great Detective; many readers have found Lord Peter Wimsey too much of a good thing, and I have even heard of people who were unable to appreciate the flavours of Poirot. But he must be real; he must have idiosyncrasies, eccentricities; even if he is a professional policeman, like Hanaud, he must smoke those appalling cigarettes, and get his English idioms wrong.

Yet despite the advent of the press-button crime novel and the sweeping popularity of the modern style of killing by computerised gadgets, epitomised by Ian Fleming (1908–1964), in the series of James Bond novels, it is still necessary for the author to establish a note of familiarity, if not sympathy, between the hero (or anti-hero) and the reader. Fleming endowed James Bond with a number of endearing, or screamingly irritating, little habits, not the least envious of which was his eight-hourly bedding of one or more partly-tamed and startlingly beautiful young women whom he leanly devours before adroitly despatching yet another giant thug. The name 'James Bond' was first used by Agatha Christie for her unwilling sleuth in *The Rajah's Emerald*, one of the stories collected in *The Listerdale Mystery*, 1934, but Fleming's use of the identical name may well have stemmed from another source. His titles are on the shelves of nearly all the collectors I know, yet none would claim that any of the James Bond tales could be classified as detective fiction without bending the rules to an extent that would completely distort the image. Nevertheless, Fleming was the unconscious champion of a new way of literary life that demolished the 'give the underdog a chance' idiom, and substituted a policy of 'shoot first and don't stop to ask questions' for the playing-fields ideal of 'put up your hands I've got you covered'.

The first edition dates of the books that had his readers queueing outside the cinemas as they once queued outside the offices of the *Strand Magazine* are given here, at a time when it is still possible to find copies at a few pounds apiece. The book which first introduced the new James Bond to the world was *Casino Royale*, 1953; still less than twenty years old but already a difficult first edition to find in clean state in its original pictorial dust-jacket. Like many others in the series, it appears to have been literally read to death. It was followed by *Live and Let Die*, 1954; *Moonraker*, 1955; *Diamonds Are Forever*, 1956; *From Russia With Love*, 1957; *Dr. No*, 1958; *Goldfinger*, 1959; *For Your Eyes Only*, 1960; *Thunderball*, 1961; *Spy Who Loved Me*, 1962; *On Her Majesty's Secret Service*, 1963; *You Only Live Twice*, 1964; *The Man With the Golden Gun*, 1965; and *Octopussy and the Living Daylights*, 1966. All were published by Jonathan Cape, London, and the majority were also issued in signed, limited editions, restricted to a few hundred copies, in different vellum-spined bindings. These now fetch up to £100 ($250) each.

As to the future of the detective story, I can only say that the outlook is grave. The crime novel has already replaced it to a degree that threatens the extinction of the species, and the science-fiction thriller has been steadily annexing its territory for several decades. But its acceptance as a dynamic literary form by scholars and historians cannot be much longer delayed. Scholarship in the field of the novel and romance is only a 20th century development, but without doubt the laurels, and the professorial chairs, will be accorded in equal strength to the leading exponents of detective fiction before the 21st century is far advanced. Scholars prefer historical perspectives to be undistorted, but always seem to take an unconscionable time to persuade themselves that what the common man enjoys may be intrinsically worthwhile and intellectually praiseworthy.

Collecting First Editions

Most of the points to look for and pitfalls to avoid have been set out in detail in *The Collector's Book of Books,* in which work I have also included a glossary of terms used in the catalogues of antiquarian booksellers and of specialist auctioneers. Here I will be content in marking out certain guide-lines to aid the novice collector and to afford help to the uninitiated. Experienced bibliophiles can take comfort in my confession that, like them, I have often in the past burnt my fingers. Sometimes the unconsidered trifles I have eagerly snapped up have proved lacking in certain qualities looked for in collector's volumes. Undisclosed deficiences have revealed themselves as they were about to be put on my shelves. Half-titles were reduced to barely discernible stubs, a legacy from a spill-hunting smoker in Victoria's Jubilee Year; advertisement leaves had disappeared; and in at least two instances the words 'second impression' had mysteriously gone the same way. Some were stiff-backed and rheumaticky, having been re-cased and corsetted, while the washed-out look of another series of unjudicious buys betrayed an over-zealous application of cloth-cleaning fluid on the part of a provincial dealer in a West Midland town. He probably needed the money, but I soon parted with his books.

With certain explicable exceptions, I have made a point in limiting my book-collecting to first editions. Collecting only first editions acts as a discipline. It is a formula that restricts the speed with which we can fill our shelves. These books are obviously much more difficult to find than the run-of-the-mill reprints, and often are scarce enough to elude us altogether. The wives of bibliophiles are a long-suffering race, but most of them insist on drawing the line at having book-stacks in the bathroom and in neat little piles on both sides of every stair. Six or seven first edition octavos carried in a brown-paper parcel under one arm in the hope of smuggling them in unseen, do not precipitate the domestic crisis immediately promoted by the unloading of two creaking tea-chests of what appear to be leather-bound quartos from a specially hired van outside one's front door. I cannot immediately call to mind any work of detective fiction issued as a leather-bound quarto, but a full run of *The Strand Magazine*, with or without its original cloth binding, could cause an even more stupendous row.

To allow an absolutely free rein to one's collecting instincts, especially in that most fruitful of all periods for the detective novel – the decades bounded by the start of the Edwardian era and the outbreak of World War II – is to court inevitable disaster. Perhaps not in financial terms, for early reprints of popular titles can still be picked up for less than a pound a time, but in lack of shelf-space and house-room. There were a number of writers in this period of high activity who churned out a hundred – even two hundred – titles, many of which passed through several hard-back editions. But there is a safeguard. By donning a first edition straight-jacket, which has the immediate effect of preventing the collector reaching for too many inconsequential impressions of texts by any author, he not only conserves his precious shelf-space, but helps to ensure a relatively peaceful and well-ordered existence at home.

Most seasoned collectors will at some time have visited houses where the squirrel instinct has obviously overriden every other civilising influence. A consuming desire sometimes grips an otherwise quite rational bibliophile : he starts to hoard every edition of every procurable title in the various fields of literature in which he maintains an avid interest. In one particular sanctum of a rival collector to which I finally obtained admittance this affliction had reached the stage of acute bibliomania. Close-carpeted floors and polished oak-surrounds that must once have been visible to the eye had now almost completely disappeared. His dining-room, lounge, study, several bedrooms, and even the landings, all groaned under the accumulated weight of rising Dutch-walls of books, books, books. On the ground floor, the oak-shelving to ceiling height had long-since disappeared behind double-banked rows of Edgar Wallace, Guy Boothby, S. R. Crockett, E. Phillips Oppenheim, Fergus Hume, Agatha Christie, and William Le Queux, all of whom were jostled by the works of dozens of other writers. What appeared to be complete runs of *Blackwood's Edinburgh Magazine*, *The Quiver*, *The Windsor Magazine*, *Harmsworth's Magazine*, and, of course, *The Strand*, occupied the lower shelves next to about 50 massive folio volumes of *The Illustrated London News*. Even if the mention of an author's name was so slight and ephemeral as to be merely a passing nod in the text of some obscure work or a review in a periodical – my friendly rival added the volume to a corner of the particular room devoted to that writer. He was proud of having made a point of collecting his favourites in as complete a fashion as was humanly possible.

The elderly collector who presided over this empire of cloth-bound volumes clothed in a contrasting rainbow of once bright and resplendent colours, appeared perfectly happy to disregard even the most basic and long-accepted rules of bibliographical practice. Books lay sprawled in undignified positions, in serrated piles on the floor and what remained of the furniture. Some leaned drunkenly at angles of up to forty-five degrees, a form of torture that would result in a permanent limp when they were finally straightened. Others were denied the light of day and remained wrapped and string-tied in dusty-looking unopened parcels, the same parcels in which they had left the second-hand bookseller's premises years before. In most case of bibliomania, displaying similar symptoms, the prognosis is grave. I once knew a Cornish collector who finished by filling his rooms, pushing the final parcels over the tops of the half-open doors, being quite unable to force them fully open due to the weight of books behind. Yet my elderly friend cherished his stacked and scattered volumes, and never reached quite this stage. They brought him much comfort and solace in his declining years, and although he was seldom able to find the book he wanted I am told that he died a happy man.

Collecting only the first editions of detective novels still gives a wide scope for endeavour, although with the earliest writers in the genre we are obviously forced to a defensive position. With the works of Edgar Allan Poe and a few other writers of the period, to seek only 'firsts' would mean that we would never acquire any texts at all. But as a rule to be generally followed, with exceptions made for important illustrated editions, first collected editions (in certain cases), and a few other qualifications, it is an excellent strategy. From the financial standpoint this policy ensures that your library will inevitably appreciate in value with each passing year.

How does one track down the elusive quarry, and having trapped it, how to make sure it is the earliest printing of the text in book-form? To the uninitiated, it will appear little short of miraculous that certain collectors, gifted with the sure eye of experience, can often recognise a first edition at a distance of several feet, and, without actually having handled the book, be proved wrong on surprisingly few occasions. Having made that observation, I have to hedge it about with a number of qualifications, for by no means all categories of books submit to this test of bibliographical skill and expertise. Almost without exception, novels of the 1920s and 1930s would resist an accurate interpretation of their edition, to say nothing of their priority of impression, without a close examination of their title-pages and internal format. Reprints of the same work often appear identical with that of the first edition, with only the words 'Third impression', or 'Second edition', to give the game away.

With those published in an earlier age, a glance at the drab paper-labelled spine of a boarded book, or the gold-blocked magnificence of diagonally-ribbed

"The woodwork snapped, ... and the two men fell over the edge." (Page 313.)
My Strangest Case] [*Frontispiece*

One of the fascinations of collecting detective fiction first editions in the period 1890 to about 1910 is that the inserted illustrations are usually of a quality high in dramatic and pictorial content. This frontispiece to *My Strangest Case*, 1902, by Guy Boothby, is by Harold Piffard.

Size of plate: 19 cm × 12.5 cm.

"He threw me from him" (Page 99.)

An illustration of Dr. Nikola by Stanley L. Wood, which appeared as a frontispiece in the first edition of *The Lust of Hate*, 1898, by Guy Boothby, a half-forgotten novelist listed in the *DNB* but dropped from *The New CBEL*.

Size of plate: 19.2 cm × 12.5 cm.

cloth, or the lustre of straight-grained morocco, each in its own way radiating dates and time-scales, is enough to set a trained bibliophile on the scent. One look at a 19th-century publisher's cloth-binding, and he can date the book to within five years. Not always with certainty, for there are many factors to consider; but as a general rule he will be right in his assessment. A working acquaintance with the binding styles of the period in which you collect, and some knowledge of the social and literary cultures of the age in which the books that attract your interest were written, are both of importance. From the end of the 18th century, the external appearance of a book can reveal a great deal about the probable composition of its interior. This rule applies to some extent to books of any age, but with the appearance of publishers' binding styles it takes on a real significance. By studying the dates of the works illustrated in this present volume, and applying that knowledge to the bindings shown, you will realise how quickly binding styles changed, thus enabling you to become, with experience, a book-collector who can approximately date a title-page without having to open the book. The actual date at which any particular book first appeared can only be learned by bibliographical research, and this means turning to the general and specialised bibliographies. In the case of the vast majority of writers of detective fiction, nearly all of whom have been ignored by bibliographers, one has to do the investigatory work oneself, visiting the larger reference libraries likely to have copies of his or her works, and listing dates and descriptions in a gradually expanding file.

This is a time-consuming task, but intensely interesting, the title-pages and the advertisements all lending clues to the facts you are seeking. Works such as *The New Cambridge Bibliography of English Literature*, Volume 3, covering the period from 1800–1900, an excellent piece of literary scholarship which gives first and other important edition dates, and *The Dictionary of National Biography*, are both invaluable tools if the authors you collect have reached the dignity of inclusion in their pages. The first edition dates which you discover by consulting reference works such as these, plus personal research, will enable you to list a background of facts that will prevent many future mistakes. The British Museum catalogue, and that of the Library of Congress, USA, are two fruitful sources of unexpected facts, as are the university libraries. The advertisements of new and forthcoming books, appearing at or about the time when you suspect your subject first appeared in print, give clues that narrow the field. The writer's published works usually carry advertisements of his previously issued books, and once you have discovered his or her publisher you have a most valuable lead. As I said in *The Collector's Book of Books*, literary research often means hard work and painstaking enquiries, but the satisfaction of having at last established previously unrecorded bibliographical dates and data repays one handsomely for the efforts involved. If you are collecting a previously neglected author, you have a head start in a field unoccupied by the mass of rival book-hunters. This will eventually pay handsome dividends in a number of respects, not the least of which is the financial benefits that will undoubtedly accrue.

If you are satisfied that the title you are examining was first issued in, say, 1905, and the bibliographical references you have consulted confirm that it was so dated, then any other printed date of issue later than 1905 appearing in the volume shows it to be of a later edition than the first. This statement must be qualified by the rider that the volume may be of the first edition in the uncommon (but not unknown) circumstance of a late issue of the same setting of type, appearing with a date subsequent to 1905. Should our supposed book have the date '1917' on the title-page, on the verso thereof, in the colophon at the end, or elsewhere, as an indication of its date of issue, then obviously it cannot be a first edition if the bibliographical evidence that gave you the date of 1905 is correct. This is all very elementary and perhaps self-evident; but the number of times experienced book-collectors and librarians are consulted about books that the hopeful owners believe to be 'firsts' because the words 'second edition' or 'thirteenth edition' do not appear on their title-pages, while a date of some kind does appear, makes me stress the obvious. Always seek the first opportunity to check your references: bibliographies would never need revision if all their stated facts were invariably correct.

The fact that a work was issued in our supposed year of 1905 does not necessarily mean that it will be so dated. If the date in the work of reference consulted is given in parentheses '(1905)', this bibliographical device indicates that it was issued without a date on its title-page (and I have followed this when mentioning titles in this work). Broadly speaking most first editions do bear a date; but it is equally true to say that many do not. Certain publishers have their own house rules, dating the first issue but not re-prints from the same type setting. Others, in the past, did not bother to date even the first issue of a work.

The preliminary leaves are usually the most important factors in deciding to which edition a work belongs. To read the words 'Preface to the First Edition' consigns the volume to a later edition, for in the first edition the word 'Preface' is sufficient. Some publishers and authors, especially in the 19th century, reprinted the prefaces that had originally appeared in as many as four previous editions. Other clues are found on the title-page. The words 'Author's edition',

'First published edition' (revealing that a privately printed edition has already appeared), 'Authorised edition', 'First illustrated edition' (or simply 'Illustrated edition'), and 'First single-volume edition', all strongly indicate that a previous edition, or editions, have already appeared. A foreign imprint on the title-page of a book one would have expected to appear first in England, usually means that the volume is not the first edition : but not always, for one can think of a string of titles where the reverse is true and the foreign (in the case of detective fiction, usually American) imprint in fact denotes the first edition. One has to learn these irregular verbs in schoolboy fashion, and the longer you collect, the greater the store of miscellaneous facts and figures you have to draw on. The longer you collect, the fewer mistakes you are likely to make.

In the USA, a distinguishing mark of a first edition is the date of registration, usually found on the verso of the title-page. If the date on the front of the title-page is, say, 1927, then the legend of entry must carry the same date. In this imagined case it would read in the form of : 'Entered according to Act of Congress, in the year 1927'. If the date given here should be earlier than that on the title-page, then the volume is almost certainly not of the first American edition; and, if the book was first published in the USA this means it cannot be a first edition. Modern practice is simply to give the Library of Congress catalogue card number. Should the book have been first published in England it is usual to give the copyright date, probably followed by the words 'First American edition' with the date of this publication.

In detective novels the tipped-in frontispieces and other plates (if any are called for) assume considerable importance. Should one be missing, then the book's value will often be reduced to as little as a tenth of its full market price. A book normally catalogued at, say, £20, would be worth only £2, while a missing leaf of text in any work produced after 1900 usually condemns it to the dustbin. You may equate the situation described above with that of a cracked or badly chipped item of choice porcelain which in normal circumstances would command a high price at auction. Except in very exceptional circumstances, broken china is worth very little, and the same holds true for any book that is incomplete.

Condition plays an important part in determining the value of any literary work, especially in the comparatively late period in the evolution of publishers' bindings in which most novels of detective fiction first appeared. It may be necessary sometimes to place a book on your shelves that is below the standard of condition you have set yourself. I always view a work in poor or indifferent state as merely holding the fort until a replacement can be obtained. Until I can find a better copy, there it must stay, supplying a text that can be read but acting as a constant bibliophile's irritant. Any collector who wishes to be accorded the respect of his like-minded fellows in the world of books must be able not only to recognise almost immediately, in catalogues and on the shelves, the editions he is seeking for his library (and this pre-supposes a degree of bibliographical know-how), but also to assess their approximate market value. The condition of the book he wishes to add to his collection is an all important factor in arriving at its financial value, both as regards the state of its binding and in its internal make-up. Let me give an example that I have purposely made extreme. A first edition of, say, *The Adventures of Sherlock Holmes*, 1892 re-bound in half-roan about the turn of the century, well-read and marked by generations of readers moistening the pages with their thumbs at the corners, the cheap leather binding cracked at the hinges and scuffed, lacking the final page of text and with the preliminary leaves bady foxed, and, as a crowning eye-sore, a previous owner's name scrawled in ball-point pen across the top of the title-page, would not be a bargain at £2. In fact I would not give such a copy shelf-room if it was presented to me free. In complete contrast, another copy of the first edition of the same title, but this time in clean and unsullied state in its original publisher's binding of light-blue cloth over bevelled boards, blocked pictorially in black and gold, the text unsprung and unfoxed – in fact in much the same state as the copy pictured in the coloured plate – would not be sold for less than £80 ($200). As one of a pair, with a copy of *The Memoirs of Sherlock Holmes*, it would be worth much more. The lesson to remember is that the same issue of the same edition of the same title can command a range of prices so wide as to be unbelievable to those not versed in the art. A glance at *Book Auction Records* will reveal this fact in full measure, and this well known guide to the market price of sought-after books must be interpreted with the bibliographical skill that the bibliophile will gradually acquire and then have at his finger-tips for the rest of his collecting days.

A most valuable asset to a book-collector is his own knowledge of literature, derived from reading the works he wishes to acquire in the form of first and other important editions. Coupled with the use of the bibliographical tools that past and present collectors, or literary historians, have prepared for him, this knowledge enables him to seek out titles that he knows to be worthwhile, rather than to rely on the literary fashions set by others. There are a number of guidelines that I can lay down to assist the novice collector who is hoping to build up a library of first editions of detective fiction, as I did in a wider scope to embrace the whole of English literature in *The Collector's Book of Books*. But the authors collected and the titles selected are a matter of personal choice, and this choice is shaped by the books read and the writers with whom the collector becomes acquainted. I cannot state a set of hard-and-fast rules by which this most absorbing of all hobbies is conducted, much less give a rule of thumb by which a first edition can be recognised with complete certainty. Book-collecting is one of the most satisfying of all leisure occupations; but membership of the club is of necessity confined to students of literature who possess enquiring minds. There is also a lot to learn and many problems to solve, and this can only be done by a critical analysis of the bibliographical facts presented to you.

This first advertisement of the cloth-bound edition of *The Adventures of Sherlock Holmes*, priced at six shillings a copy, appeared in the monthly issue of *The Strand Magazine* for October 1892.

Size of page: 24.7 cm × 16.7 cm.

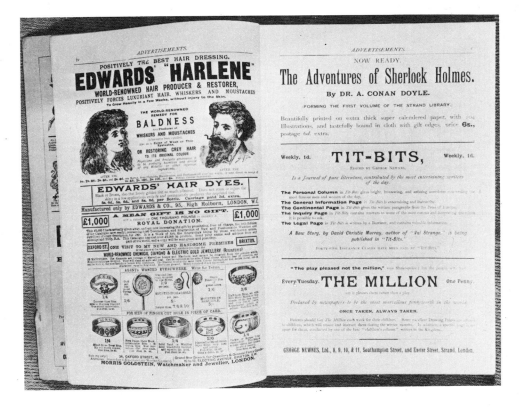

Bibliography

The bibliographical works listed below form a selective reference background that a collector of first editions of detective fiction needs to consult. Some of the best-known writers have their own individual bibliographies which can be bought and consulted separately as your interest dictates, and these are not included in this general list.

Blood in Their Ink, 1953, by Sutherland Scott. Stanley Paul, London.

Bloody Murder, 1972, by Julian Symons. Faber and Faber, London.

Catalogue of Crime (1971), by Jacques Barzun & Wendell Hertig Taylor. Harper & Row, New York.

Collector's Book of Books, 1971, by Eric Quayle. Studio Vista, London.

Crime and Detection, 1926, by E. M. Wrong. Oxford University Press.

Detective Story in Britain, 1969, by Julian Symons. Longmans, Green & Co.

Development of the Detective Novel, 1968, by A. E. Murch. Peter Owen, London.

Histoire et Technique du Roman Policier, 1937, by F. Fosca. Editions de la Nouvelle Revue Critique, Paris.

Masters of Mystery: A Study of the Detective Story, 1931, by H. D. Thomson. Collins, London.

Murder for Pleasure, 1942, by Howard Haycraft. Peter Davies, London.

New Cambridge Bibliography of English Literature, Vol. 3, 1969, edited by George Watson.

New Paths in Book Collecting, 1934, edited by John Carter. Constable, London.

Queen's Quorum, 1953, by Ellery Queen. Gollancz, London.

Victorian Detective Fiction, 1966, edited by Eric Osborne. The Bodley Head, London.

XIX Century Fiction, 2 vols. 1951, by Michael Sadleir. Constable, London.

Index

B

C

133

D

E

M

N

O

P